PRAISE FOR PYRO

"With snakes on the mind, Kohler finds them coming out of the woodwork. The Arizona mountain kingsnake he is after becomes mythic in this conversational and informative deep dive. Searching for a single species, he finds them all."

—CRAIG CHILDS, *The Wild Dark*

"If you've ever wondered about unisexual pseudocopulation, ant orgies, or the kind of person who runs toward snakes rather than away from them, look no further. *Pyro* writhes with energy."

—ELI J. KNAPP, *In the Crosswinds*

"In this captivating blend of field memoir and popular science writing, the narrative is unfailingly driven forward by herpetologist Dallin Kohler's compelling curiosity and genuine enthusiasm. *Pyro* is an entertaining adventure story that helps us to engage deeply with fascinating fellow creatures that too often go unnoticed and unappreciated."

—MICHAEL P. BRANCH, *On the Trail of the Jackalope*

"With an enthusiasm and wonder that can only be described as infectious, this book is a must-read for the snake-obsessed and snake-averse alike. *Pyro* is a joyful addition to the nature writing canon of the American Southwest."

—MOLLY IMBER, Maria's Bookshop

"Kohler is the type of academic that is rare and necessary: accessible, conversational, and genuinely humorous. The deep affection he has for these creatures, as well as his hard-won adventures, makes clear we occupy an enriched planet."

—JONATHAN T. BAILEY, *When I Was Red Clay*

"A must-read for fans of natural history."

—JOHN KNIPMEYER, Octavia Books

"*Pyro* is serpentine storytelling at its best. Kohler's enthusiasm and love for snakes shines through every page. Tagging along on his field trips, you share his joy, his disappointment, his fascination, and his deep respect for the snakes and other wildlife he encounters. *Pyro* is a vivid reminder of how special and unique these limbless reptiles are, of the value of protecting them, and what they give back to us on a spiritual level."

—MARTHA L. CRUMP, editor of *Lost Frogs and Hot Snakes*

"A joyous insight into the ups and downs of being a field biologist that will resonate with anyone fascinated by wildlife."

—TOM MAJOR, *Herpetological Highlights* podcast

"Whether you are already a herpetology enthusiast, full of curiosity, or are absolutely petrified by snakes, I wholeheartedly recommend picking up this book. You will quickly become captivated by Kohler's enthusiasm, knowledge and ability to tell a story. His immersive descriptions of his adventures will pull you into the Southwest landscape, and his conversational style of writing about science and natural history is approachable and informative."

—CORI CUSKER, Bright Side Bookshop

"An artful blending of science and natural history."

—MIKE PINGLETON, *The Field Herping Guide* and *So Much Pingle* herpetology podcast

"Pyro is a wild, unforgettable journey through the quirkiest corners of the natural world."

—ALEXIS POWELL, The King's English Bookshop

Pyro

PYRO

The Quest for a Beautifully Elusive Snake

DALLIN KOHLER

TORREY HOUSE PRESS

Salt Lake City • Torrey

First Torrey House Press Edition, June 2025
Copyright © 2025 by Dallin Kohler

All rights reserved. No part of this book may be reproduced or retransmitted in any form or by any means without the written consent of the publisher.

NO AI TRAINING: Without in any way limiting the author's (and publisher's) exclusive rights under copyright, any use of this publication to "train" generative artificial intelligence (AI) technologies to generate text is expressly prohibited. The author reserves all rights to license uses of this work for generative AI training and development of machine learning language models.

Published by Torrey House Press
Salt Lake City, Utah
www.torreyhouse.org

International Standard Book Number: 979-8-89092-022-5
E-book ISBN: 979-8-89092-023-2
Library of Congress Control Number: 2024944828

Cover design by Joseph Toney
Interior design by Gray Buck-Cockayne
Distributed to the trade by Consortium Book Sales and Distribution

Torrey House Press offices in Salt Lake City sit on the homelands of Ute, Goshute, Shoshone, and Paiute nations. Offices in Torrey are on the homelands of Southern Paiute, Ute, and Navajo nations.

TABLE OF CONTENTS

ONE	1866	1
TWO	A Snake in a Tree and a Whole Lot of Irony	13
THREE	The Sheriff Learns to Sex a Milk Snake	27
FOUR	Kingsnake!	39
FIVE	The Ivory Tower of Academia	57
SIX	Into the Desert	75
SEVEN	Over and Over	89
EIGHT	Color Me Confused	107
NINE	In Too Deep	121
TEN	Fire on the Mountain	133
ELEVEN	Rattlesnake Roulette	147
TWELVE	Roads Less Traveled	161
THIRTEEN	Fall Colors and Rock-Paper-Scissors Lizards	175
FOURTEEN	Everything's Coming up Roses (Except the Boas)	187
FIFTEEN	The Flame Burns On	203
SOURCES		213
ACKNOWLEDGMENTS		231

ONE

1866

If you were asked to name an influential nineteenth-century naturalist that married his cousin, Charles Darwin is probably the first to come to mind. Everyone knows the paradigm-shattering, tortoise-riding Darwin, who is arguably the greatest biologist to have ever lived. But there is another name that belongs on the list of important cousin-marrying naturalists from the 1800s: Edward Drinker Cope. And Cope's choice of a spouse—which admittedly wasn't that strange at the time—was far from the only thing noteworthy about him.

Born in Pennsylvania in 1840, Cope devoted much of his time to studying prehistoric life and is best known for his involvement in the most legendary and cutthroat paleontology rivalry of all time. Known as the "Bone Wars," Cope's decades-long conflict with fellow paleontologist Othniel Charles Marsh ranks right up there with Lakers-Celtics, USA-USSR, Tesla-Edison, and the other great rivalries of history. In addition to Hollywood-worthy fossil espionage, the feud featured a number of vicious ad hominem attacks published in addition to scientific criticisms. For example, Cope once wrote that Marsh would end up in a mental hospital before long. While it is a myth that Marsh named coprolites—fossilized poop—after Cope, that's the level of bad blood the two had. Coincidentally, the Bone Wars also resulted in a flood of newly discovered fossils, as teams of workers employed by Cope and Marsh unearthed countless skeletons.

Cope's other oft-cited historical legacy concerns his death at age fifty-six. It is unclear if Cope and his handlebar mustache were ultimately killed by an unknown illness or by his treatments for said illness, which allegedly included copious amounts of morphine, nightshade, and formalin. Some have said that the mysterious illness was syphilis, and while most historians now dispute this diagnosis they don't deny the numerous extramarital liaisons that could have led to some of his health problems.

Yet none of this is why Edward Cope is relevant to this book. This is a book about snakes, after all. Cope is pertinent because, in addition to being a headstrong paleontologist, he was also a herpetologist.

Herpetology is the study of reptiles (snakes, lizards, turtles, crocodilians, and the tuatara) and amphibians (frogs, salamanders, and caecilians). For context, the Greek root *herpetos* means to creep or crawl and, yes, is the same root as the STI herpes—but no relation to whatever killed Cope. Collectively, reptiles and amphibians are often affectionately referred to as "herps," though in dry academic contexts you might see the more formal "herpetofauna." In casual conversation, the word herp also often gets co-opted into different parts of speech (e.g. herpers go herping).

While reptiles and amphibians aren't close evolutionary relatives, they were initially lumped together in the 1700s by Carl Linnaeus, the father of modern taxonomy, who wasn't fond of either group. The pairing has stuck, partly due to historical inertia and partly because the kind of people interested in one group are usually interested in the other. (Precedent has also kept ornithology—the study of birds—separate, even though all modern biologists accept that birds are descended from, and should thus be considered, reptiles. You could say ornithologists are just hyper-specialized herpetologists, but in my experience the serious birders get offended by this.)

When he wasn't busy digging up fossils or dirt on his nemesis, the enigmatic herpetologist Edward Cope described an impressive total of 385 new extant (living) reptiles. Most importantly, one of those scaly creatures happens to be the maddeningly beautiful species of snake that my life revolved around for several years: the Arizona mountain kingsnake, *Lampropeltis pyromelana*. They are often referred to simply as "pyros" (from their species name, *pyromelana*), and if you ever try to say "Arizona mountain kingsnake" five times fast, you'll realize why the condensed version is preferred. A handful of other common names exist (Sonoran mountain kingsnake, coral kingsnake, and Utah mountain kingsnake), but all of them are a mouthful too.

Pyros are medium-sized snakes, usually measuring two to three feet in length, and are neither particularly chunky nor skinny. They are found in mountainous areas throughout the states of Arizona, Nevada, New Mexico, and Utah. Eschewing the well-camouflaged color schemes of many other reptiles, pyros sport an eye-catching pattern of repeating bands of three colors: midnight black, milky white, and flaming red.

These mesmerizing rings of shiny red, black, and white scales are reflected in their scientific name. Like all scientific names, it is composed of two parts: the genus (*Lampropeltis*) and the species (*pyromelana*). *Lampropeltis* comes from two Greek words: *lampro* meaning "bright" or "clear," and *pelte* meaning "small shield." This aptly-named genus contains the kingsnakes and milk snakes, all of which have reflective, shield-like scales. The species name, *pyromelana*, comes from root words you're likely already familiar with. *Pyro* is in reference to the fiery red of their patterning. The second half, *melana*, like melanin, refers to their black bands, which often spill out onto the red. (Scientific names might look scary, but if you look past the italics and focus on root words, they can be more informative than intimidating.)

Cope's original description of the species was published in 1866 in the *Proceedings of the Academy of Natural Sciences of Philadelphia*. Cope's source material for the publication came from Dr. Elliott Coues, an army surgeon, historian, and ornithologist, who had just completed "a sojourn of sixteen months" in what is today the state of Arizona. A sojourn—sounds exciting. Coues had sent many of the reptiles and amphibians he collected to Cope, including the first specimens of *Lampropeltis pyromelana*. This is why I say Cope "described," not "discovered" species, since he often wasn't the one to collect the specimens and he definitely wasn't the first human to lay eyes on them.

The actual text of Cope's description reads, in part, as follows: "Fifty to fifty-eight black annuli on an ochraceous white ground, on the body; each anteriorly completely, posteriorly more or less incompletely split by a vermillion annulus; all extending with irregularities on the belly."

Apologies if your eyes glazed over there. Cope also included information on the numbers and shapes of various types of scales, but I figured the antiquated description above was already difficult enough to visualize. (At least it wasn't in Latin!)

The name Cope bestowed upon the species in that initial publication was *Ophibolus pyromelanus*, which is different from the currently accepted name, *Lampropeltis pyromelana*. This is routine for scientific names, which rarely stay the same over long periods of time. Some jokingly say that taxonomists continually change names merely to keep themselves employed, though this is a slight exaggeration. The species name underwent minor spelling changes, morphing briefly from the original *pyromelanus* to *pyrrhomelaena* before settling on *pyromelana*. The genus name, *Ophibolus*, which essentially translates to "snake lump" in Latin (a reference to the snake-eating tendencies of many kingsnakes), was eventually replaced by *Lampropeltis*—which had been coined first and thus was given precedent—around the turn of the twentieth century.

Cope's 1866 publication is purely a physical description, making no mention of diet, habitat, or temperament. He hadn't spent any time looking for pyros in the field, otherwise the paper might have included something along the lines of: "despite its resplendently scintillating coloration, locating this variety of serpent appeareth to be an exceedingly arduous task." I say this because I wish I had known that these flamboyantly colored snakes are incredibly difficult to find *before* I pegged my future career prospects to them. Unfortunately for me, I wasn't aware of this paradoxical fact until it was too late.

Fast forward a century and a half later. I was a clueless undergraduate student, halfway through my degree in conservation biology. I'd grown up with a strong interest in reptiles and amphibians, though I had only recently realized that being a herpetologist wasn't a job limited to a handful of charismatic TV hosts. A career in herpetology was almost certainly going to require a graduate degree though, and the best thing I could do at the time to improve my odds of getting into graduate school was to get involved with scientific research. The phrase "publish or perish" is frequently used to describe academia. For a young student, you have to first worry about being published to be born, metaphorically speaking, before worrying about perishing. I wasn't sold on becoming a professor, but I needed to have my name on a scientific paper if I wanted my career to get off the ground.

There were some easy options available; plenty of professors in the biology department involved undergrads in their research projects. I could have signed up to measure dead fish or analyze dirt—both of which sounded absolutely thrilling—if all I wanted was to boost my grad school application. Yet I had a stubborn desire to do research on the group of animals I cared about most. I wasn't interested in doing research just to check a box. I applied to a handful of summer research internships that involved reptiles and amphibians, hoping that a perfect opportunity would materialize, but I got nothing except for rejections.

At the time, I had just started working in the herpetology collection of a museum on campus. Dr. Alison Whiting was the curator of the collection, my boss, and the only herpetologist at my university—my last chance to find the kind of research project I wanted. While her own past research experience included extensive field work with skinks on the biodiverse paradise of Papua New Guinea, I knew Dr. Whiting was only an adjunct faculty member and not actively involved with any research projects with students at that point. I will be forever grateful that she was willing to help a naive, snake-obsessed undergraduate.

Dr. Whiting suggested, almost on a whim, that I study pyros. Despite their legendary status among hobbyists, little scientific research had been published on the species since Cope's 1866 description. To be fair, pyros aren't understudied compared to most species in Africa, Asia, or South America. However, compared to other reptiles and amphibians in the United States, pyros have been neglected; little has been published on their predators, prey, mating, and behavior. This meant that finding something to publish in an academic journal—whether it be just a short note of an interesting field observation or a full experimental study—couldn't be that hard. Right?

Additionally, pyros were a species of conservation concern in the state where I lived (Utah), making any field research on them useful. They also had a decently wide range throughout the state too, so travel wouldn't be a big issue. And to top it all off, pyros just looked gorgeous. Who could say no to those striking colors? I certainly couldn't. We didn't nail down an exact project initially, figuring that it might be better to find one before making any overly ambitious plans for a field study. Dr. Whiting hadn't ever seen a wild pyro either, which in retrospect should have been a red flag.

And so I began looking for pyros on my own the summer before my junior year. Being mountain kingsnakes, after all, pyros are mainly found in the mountains. While many snakes are well-adapted to arid deserts, pyros prefer the cooler temperatures, additional moisture, and extra vegetation found in upland habitats. To be honest though, that was about all I knew about finding pyros at first.

The place I visited the most that first summer was Oak Creek Canyon, just outside the tiny farming town of Oak City, Utah. It was the closest area to where I lived with multiple verified sightings of pyros within the last decade, and I made that ninety-minute drive from my college apartment in Provo enough times to memorize every single turn. "City" is a bit of a misnomer for Oak City, as it is one of those places where the tallest buildings are barns, and you are just as likely to see an ATV driving around town as a regular car.

Oak Creek Canyon is part of the Canyon Mountains, a small, generic-sounding mountain range in central Utah. True to its name, Oak Creek Canyon itself does have plenty of oaks. Unfortunately, much of the area had been burned by wildfires within the last couple years, turning large swaths of hillside into a sea of invasive grasses dotted with charred stumps.

One fateful August morning, I had hiked up a two-track trail along a dry creek bed in Oak Creek Canyon. Much of the dirt path was partially shaded, thankfully, since this was in an unburned portion of the canyon. My hike up the mountain was relatively uneventful. I saw no other people and the only reptiles were a handful of sagebrush lizards (*Sceloporus graciosus*). These common lizards are relatively small, with unassuming brownish colors on their backs, and are found throughout most of the western United States. Sagebrush lizards are indeed fond of sagebrush-dominated landscapes, though they can be found in forests that have enough open spaces.

Much like a teenager who sleeps in until noon, the few sagebrush lizards I saw were slow and lethargic in the cool morning air—they are ectotherms, after all. (Ectotherms are often referred to as "cold-blooded," but this is somewhat misleading as their blood can be very warm when the outside temperature is hot. The important idea is that their body temperature is dependent on the external environment, whereas endotherms, like mammals, produce their own body heat.) I took some pictures of the lizards but wasn't overly preoccupied with them.

On my way up the trail, I also discovered a large Jerusalem cricket. Whoever named them Jerusalem crickets did a terrible job, as they are neither true crickets nor from Jerusalem. Admittedly, at first glance they do look like muscular versions of crickets, though Jerusalem crickets are wingless. The origin of the "Jerusalem" part is unclear, and the number of theories about it exceeds the number of legs these North and Central American insects have.

Jerusalem crickets spend the daytime hiding underground, often under rocks or logs, and the one that I found was probably upset to be suddenly thrust into the bright sunlight when I lifted up its rock. To attract potential mates, these mostly nocturnal insects can produce a remarkably loud drumming sound by rapidly beating their abdomens against the ground, with each of the several dozen species of Jerusalem cricket having a unique drumming frequency.

This individual was the largest Jerusalem cricket I'd ever seen, measuring well over two inches in length. Like most Jerusalem crickets, it had a reddish head and horizontal black bars on its abdomen. I wish I could say which species it was, but invertebrates are largely out of my wheelhouse. I gently put the rock it had been hiding underneath back into place—without squashing my new insect friend—and continued up the mountain.

The trail eventually ended at a ridge near the top. The spot was over eight thousand feet in elevation and afforded a fantastic view of the wide surrounding canyons on both sides. The cloudless blue sky and sweeping valleys looked straight out of a Bob Ross painting, but it wasn't as beautiful as what I would see on my way back down the mountain.

I hadn't gone very far before I saw a gray, vaguely stick-shaped object on the rocky path. The stick—which of course wasn't actually a stick—was intentionally positioned in the center of a thin patch of sunlight perpendicular to the trail. It was a regal ringneck snake (*Diadophis punctatus regalis*), stretched out and blissfully soaking in the morning sun.

I froze. For the next few moments, I simply stared at the motionless serpent before whipping out my phone to take a picture. Ringneck snakes are extremely abundant in other parts of the country—to the point where they are literally the most common snake in some places—but they are one of the rarest snakes to see in Utah. Another notable difference is that the ringnecks in Utah never got the dress code memo; they lack the colorful yellow or orange neck ring that is the namesake of the species.

The snake continued to sit in its warm patch of sunlight, hoping that the lumbering beast it had heard coming down the trail wouldn't notice it. After my initial surprise wore off, I stepped forward and gently reached down to pick up the snake. It was large for a ringneck, though this isn't saying much; it was roughly as thick as my pinky and maybe a foot and a half in length. Lifting the snake off the ground gave me a clear view of its belly, which was a vibrant yellowish orange. It looked like a plain gray snake that had crawled through some brightly colored paint, leaving only its belly colored.

The ringneck didn't attempt to bite, opting to instead curl the last few inches of its body in the air to expose the cherry red underside of its tail. This display is likely an advertisement of their primary defensive tactic: musk. Most snakes can excrete a stinky musk from their cloaca (the all-purpose hole towards the end of the snake used for reproduction and excretion) to deter would-be predators. This particular ringneck did musk a little on my hands, though it wasn't the stinkiest musk I've ever smelled.

These small snakes spend most of their lives rooting around in the dirt and leaf litter, invisible to potential predators. I let the snake crawl under a loose rock on the trail and took some pictures of its adorably small head and round eyes peeking out from underneath.

There's one fascinating thing about ringnecks that I didn't learn until after that wonderful encounter. Ringneck snakes are, in fact, venomous. Now before you think I'm a total idiot for free-handling a venomous snake without knowing it, let me first clarify that ringneck snakes are totally harmless to humans. Some people have reported a mild burning sensation—no worse than a bee sting—from ringneck bites, but ringnecks rarely bite anyway. Their fangs are small and located at the back of their mouth, making landing a solid bite on a large object (e.g. a human hand) difficult in the first place.

Snake venom is primarily an offensive weapon meant to subdue prey, and as such it usually evolves to be most effective on whatever the snake eats. For a species that preys on invertebrates and small reptiles and amphibians, it makes sense that ringneck snake venom has little effect on a large mammal. (Side note: this isn't to say that all snakes that aren't mammal eaters have medically insignificant venom. And if you aren't certain what species a snake is, it is safest to not pick it up.)

It was only in the last couple of decades that ringneck snakes were definitively shown to be venomous. Previously, there was only a smattering of anecdotal evidence, mainly of ringnecks chewing on lizards or small snakes until they died. To prove that it was venom—and not constriction or exhaustion—that was killing the prey, the authors of a 2007 study used syringes to extract the oral secretions of several ringneck snakes and test their potency.

The secretions were mixed together and injected into young

garter snakes, some of whom were lucky enough to only be injected with water as a control. Sure enough, the ringnecks' secretions were lethal, and the water, unsurprisingly, wasn't. The authors estimated that an average ringneck snake had enough venom to subdue at least twelve newborn garter snakes. No tests of the venom's effects on humans were conducted in the study, or at least none were reported. That initial experiment used venom from northwestern ringnecks (*Diadophis punctatus occidentalis*) but subsequent studies on other subspecies have indicated that all ringnecks are venomous.

When I was finally ready to move on from that beautiful regal ringneck snake at Oak Creek Canyon, I extracted it from the rock and released it a few feet away from the trail; I wasn't about to risk it getting run over by an inattentive dirt biker. The snake crawled into the leaf litter and out of sight, probably in search of something to envenomate for lunch. I headed back down the mountain, eyes scanning for another brightly colored serpent. Seeing a rare snake was great, but it was the wrong one.

Yet despite many hours spent at Oak Creek Canyon that weekend and on several previous trips, I never saw a pyro there. I ran into a badger, some tarantulas, lots of deer, and plenty of common reptiles, but not a single kingsnake. That first summer I visited several other picturesque canyons throughout the mountains of Utah too, but no matter how hard I looked I couldn't seem to find any pyros.

Initially, I had thought that the lack of prior research on pyros would be advantageous. But a few months in, the only thing I had discovered was why no one else was studying them. These eye-catching snakes had turned out to be impossible to find, though I wasn't about to throw in the towel. That first lackluster summer was just the beginning of my pursuit of pyros, and things would only get more exciting.

TWO

A Snake in a Tree
and a Whole Lot of Irony

For an animal that doesn't have hands, feet, or even limbs, snakes are pretty good climbers. Thanks to their flexible torsos and abs of steel, it isn't hard for most snakes to nimbly—pardon the pun—scale a tree. But I didn't fully comprehend the awesome climbing ability of snakes until a month after my ringneck snake encounter, when I witnessed a particularly impressive display of it on an autumn day in a forested, red-rock canyon in central Utah.

I had heard a rustle in some fallen leaves and saw a dark blur shoot into the underbrush on the tree-covered hillside adjacent to the trail. The snake had noticed me first and wasn't about to hold still and wait to be spotted. I immediately yelled to alert my friend, coworker, and fellow snake enthusiast, Taylor Probst. Taylor grew up in Texas but his flowing blond hair looks like it belongs on a California surfer. He's an adept rock climber and boulderer, with the toned muscles and calloused hands to prove it.

Even Taylor couldn't out-climb this snake though. In a matter of seconds, it had slithered from the ground to the top of a skinny maple tree that was at least twenty feet in the air. The long, lanky snake stopped at the apex, perched gracefully on the thin branches, practically teasing us. The tree was much too thin to support a person, no matter their climbing skills, but the chase wasn't over yet.

I began to work my way up the hill, pushing through the plants, trying to get into a better position. At the bottom, Taylor gave the young maple tree a good shake, sending the snake scrambling into another, shorter tree on the hillside. It moved gracefully from branch to branch as I continued to climb the hill. Soon I was at eye level with the snake, though it remained stubbornly out of reach.

If there had been any other people hiking up the canyon at the time, they would have been totally baffled by the scene. Two young guys in the woods shouting like total maniacs, one of them trying to poke *something* in the trees with a stick and the other one desperately clambering through the densely vegetated hillside. I'm sure it was a comical sight, but we were dead serious about apprehending our target.

Taylor continued to shake branches and shepherd the wily snake in my direction. Eventually, it made the mistake of choosing a limb that I could reach, and I quickly extended my arm and wrapped my fingers around the middle of its slender body. The snake tensed up, anchoring itself against the branches, but I was able to unwind a few inches of snake at a time until it was completely free from the tree.

But I wasn't out of the woods yet, literally and metaphorically. My initial feeling of triumph faded as I looked around, realizing I was halfway up a steep hillside, completely surrounded by thorny bushes and tree trunks, with no clear path back down. I had barely noticed all the underbrush on the way up thanks to the adrenaline, but now I had to get back down without losing a very wiggly snake. Thankfully, after a few seconds of panic I remembered that I had a fabric bag in my day pack for this very purpose. I was able to finagle the snake into the black bag, tie it tightly, and slowly work my way back down the hill to where Taylor was waiting.

A SNAKE IN A TREE AND A WHOLE LOT OF IRONY

Back at the trail, we untied the cloth bag and pulled out the snake to admire it. No, unfortunately it wasn't my long-awaited pyro. It was a striped whipsnake (*Masticophis taeniatus*), a much more common species. Whipsnakes are slender and can grow six feet in length, thus resembling a whip. At the front of the skinny body is an equally thin head with large eyes. With their long bodies and lengthy tails, whipsnakes are especially good climbers, as Taylor and I had just witnessed. This individual was well over four feet long, and only about as thick as my index finger. As the name suggests, striped whipsnakes have a pair of white stripes that run from head to tail, one on each side of the snake. The rest of the back is a dull brown or black, but the belly is whitish yellow, which gradually shifts to a pink (yes, pink!) color underneath the tail.

While striped whipsnakes look nothing like pyros, they are both part of the same family, Colubridae. This doesn't tell you much though, as more than half of the over four thousand snake species are currently considered colubrids (pronounced like "kuh-loo-brid"). I say "currently" because having two thousand species in a single family is a tad excessive; for comparison, there are fewer than four hundred species of viper (family Viperidae) and less than seventy kinds of boas (family Boidae). Colubridae consists of many subfamilies, each of which will probably be raised to full-family status when the snake taxonomists run out of other changes to make. I'm kidding of course, but only about the taxonomists' motivations; it makes more sense to have a few hundred species in a family instead of a few thousand. (Some people already treat the separate Colubridae subfamilies as full families, but this adoption isn't universal yet.)

Most colubrids are harmless to humans, though a few exceptions exist. One notable example is the boomslang (*Dispholidus typus*), a large, green snake found in Sub-Saharan Africa that is responsible for arguably the most ironic herpetologist death of all time—a story that deserves a brief historical tangent. In 1957, Dr. Karl Schmidt of the Chicago Natural History Museum was bitten by a captive juvenile boomslang. Wanting to document the effects of what he thought was a non-lethal venom, Schmidt refused medical attention and took detailed notes of his symptoms. He vomited a lot at first and slept poorly that night.

The next morning, Schmidt felt much better though, as he recorded his breakfast ("cereal & poached egg on toast & applesauce & coffee") and telephoned his coworkers to say he'd be coming in for work the next day. Unfortunately, around noon things took a turn for the worse, and by 3 p.m. Schmidt was taken to the local hospital and pronounced dead shortly thereafter. This is why you shouldn't assume that a snake that doesn't usually eat mammals can't kill one. The next year, one of Schmidt's colleagues published his notes and a synopsis of the event in an academic journal. For science, right?

Though boomslangs and whipsnakes are even part of the same subfamily (Colubrinae), striped whipsnakes are perfectly harmless. The one Taylor and I caught that day wasn't even inclined to bite, though it kept squirming in our hands. Photographing a snake that won't stay still is a frustrating task, so Taylor and I let it climb into a small tree, where it would feel more comfortable. It immediately relaxed and slowed its pace, meandering among the leafy branches. An important note: I may have used the word "photographing" above, but please don't imagine me with a thousand-dollar camera and a light box snapping professional pictures. I'm just a guy using auto mode on his budget smartphone, trying to get some half decent shots. The best way to enjoy a snake is with your eyes anyway.

While we were taking pictures of the whipsnake, we heard a familiar rustle in the leaves; the sound of something without legs smoothly sliding through the underbrush. Oddly enough, the noise was moving towards us for once. The source turned out to be a yellow-bellied racer (*Coluber constrictor mormon*), a snake named for the actual color of their underside and not for any lack of bravery. Racers are extremely fast—you usually only have a second or two to apprehend one before it, ahem, races away—and if caught will defend themselves vigorously. This racer somehow hadn't noticed the two humans it was moving towards until it was too late, and Taylor quickly reached down and snagged it. With my eyes still fixed on the whipsnake in the tree, I absentmindedly reached my hand to take the flailing racer from Taylor. The unhappy snake flung its head towards my outstretched hand and landed a solid bite, its small teeth quickly sinking into my finger. This evoked a yelp of pain from me and a good laugh from Taylor. We'd caught—and been chomped by—two other feisty yellow-bellied racers already that day, so we opted to quickly release the bite-happy snake and return our full attention to the well-behaved whipsnake, which was still elegantly posed in the tree.

Our September trip was off to a good start, though the primary objective was still to see a pyro. With my junior year starting, I was in sore need of demonstrable evidence that I had research and field experience if I was going to get into grad school. In the summer, I had already come to grips with the fact that a true field study involving pyros was going to be impossible. Finding enough to have meaningful, statistically significant data seemed about as likely as seeing an alligator in the Arctic. I was still clinging to the hope that I might get lucky and witness something unusual—mating behavior, predation, or an individual in a previously undocumented mountain range—that would be worthy of a brief note in a scientific journal, given the dearth of published information on the species. But by this point I also needed to find a pyro for the sake of my pride. Thanks to eight hundred pieces of paper that had fallen into my lap, I had a different path to publication on pyros—more on this later. But for me to write a scientific paper about a species I had never seen? That might be more ironic than a herpetologist dying of snakebite.

And thus, with the weather starting to cool down, Taylor and I had embarked on one last weekend trip in search of an elusive red, white, and black banded snake. Our first stop—where we saw the whipsnake and racers—was in an offshoot of Kanosh Canyon, located near the sprawling metropolis of Kanosh, Utah (population: 474). Named after a Ute Native American leader, Kanosh is nestled between the highway and the western edge of the Pahvant Mountains, which are named for the band he led. It's one of those wonderful towns with more gas stations (1) than traffic lights (0). Kanosh's idyllic orange sandstone canyon was the site of many past pyro sightings, though we didn't see any during the afternoon we spent there.

Our other main stop that weekend was Monroe Canyon, adjacent to the small town of Monroe in central Utah. Massive formations of dark igneous rock in portions of the canyon resemble the walls of an imposing medieval castle, a dramatic contrast from the gentler slopes of Kanosh. Monroe Canyon also has many large sections of talus—piles of loose, fallen stones. These rocky slopes provide plenty of crevices for pyros to hide in, as well as ideal habitat for their main prey item, lizards.

Our hike up the canyon along Monroe Creek was relatively uneventful. The mix of evergreen and deciduous trees made for plenty of shade, even on a relatively sunny day. We did manage to spot some fragments of shed snakeskin near a fallen log. It was far from a complete skin, but it was enough to deduce what kind of snake it had come from. The biggest clue was that the scales were strongly keeled, meaning each had a distinct ridge in the middle running parallel to the snake's body. The large size of the pieces and the faintly discernible pattern also indicated that the likely owner of the skin was a Great Basin rattlesnake (*Crotalus lutosus*), the only rattlesnake species in the area. Taylor and I poked around the rocks and leaves in the vicinity of the skin—carefully—but the snake that had left the shed was long gone.

On our way back down the canyon, we encountered some different snakes with keeled scales: garter snakes. The garters that Taylor and I saw were western terrestrial garter snakes (*Thamnophis elegans*), and the sightings came in rapid succession.

A SNAKE IN A TREE AND A WHOLE LOT OF IRONY

The first snake was slithering in between some rocks and was quickly apprehended by Taylor. A few minutes later, we caught a brief glimpse of another, but it fled into a thorny bush, and we lost track of it. Shortly thereafter, I heard rustling in the dry grass next to the trail. I dove after the sound and was rewarded with yet another garter snake. All of the individuals were under two feet in length; typical size for the species. Like most western terrestrial garter snakes, they each had three indistinct yellow stripes, one on top and one on each side, with black blotches interspersed on an otherwise grayish-brownish back.

I'd be willing to bet that if you live in North America, you've seen a garter snake; these water-loving snakes are diurnal, abundant, and found in many urban areas. I'm also confident that if you've ever caught a garter snake, you've been musked on. The stinky sludge they expel from their back end is meant to make a real predator think twice about eating the snake; I can vouch that after being musked on I have never had the desire to try garter snake steak. Musking isn't unique to garter snakes, but in my experience they are the most eager to do it. One of the few papers to quantify how frequently snakes will musk was a 2014 study conducted in Denver, Colorado, on two species of garter: the plains garter snake (*Thamnophis radix*) and the western terrestrial garter snake (*Thamnophis elegans*), the same kind Taylor and I found up Monroe Canyon.

The paper dresses up the methods in scientific jargon, but basically the scientists grabbed any garter snake they saw at their four study sites and wrote down if it musked. For each snake, they also recorded a host of other variables (length, weight, sex, previous injuries, etc.) to look for correlations. The results were surprising, at least to me. Only 60 percent of the western terrestrial garter snakes musked when handled, while 92 percent of the plains garter snakes did. In my experience with western terrestrial garters, the number has been much closer to 100 percent. The only plains garter snake I've ever seen musked on me too, if that counts for anything. I don't doubt the veracity of the paper—they specify in the methods section how the scientists "cleaned [their] hands with moist towelettes and hand sanitizer after each encounter," so I firmly believe they conducted the experiment—but perhaps there is variation between populations. I should at least be grateful that garter snakes aren't capable of spraying their musk several feet in the air, skunk-style, like some large-bodied snakes can.

Taylor and I were glad to at least see some garter snakes up Monroe Canyon, even if our hands smelled bad afterwards. The rest of the hike had been devoid of interesting finds, and our stop in between Kanosh and Monroe was even less exciting.

With the weekend ending, I knew that my first year of looking for pyros was over. The weather would soon turn too cold—September is the tail end of the snake season in Utah—and I would be busy with school anyway. This left me with no choice but to confront the irony: I was going to be writing a paper about a species I had never seen.

Apparently, there were some advantages to picking a species that was criminally under-studied, as it wasn't clear exactly *where* pyros were found. Cope's 1866 description didn't contain any locality information beyond its existence in Arizona. The first range map for the species was published in 1921, and it basically consisted of a big oval around a few western states. In 1953 and 1983 there were slightly more detailed maps courtesy of the herpetologist Wilmer W. Tanner. There was a much better map that had been published in 2004 by notable field herper Brian Hubbs in his book on mountain kingsnakes, but it was in need of updating, and wasn't available online to begin with.

There were two main issues to resolve. First, pyros had been documented in several remote mountain ranges in western Utah and eastern Nevada in the past couple of decades, findings that weren't depicted on contemporary range maps. But more intriguingly, there was a major problem with their range in the northern half of Utah. On the basis of historical records, maps typically depicted the northernmost extent of the range of pyros to be near Salt Lake City. According to the range maps, there were supposed to be pyros in the mountains that were just minutes from my college apartment in Provo. Yet there was a curious absence of sightings in recent years in this portion of the state, a mystery in need of investigation. It was unknown if pyros were still found in the area, or if the old records had been incorrect and there were never pyros in this portion of Utah to begin with.

My key source of information was a series of surveys that had been organized by the Utah Devision of Wildlife Resources (UDWR). Past state regulations prohibited people from handling, let alone collecting, pyros and western milk snakes (*Lampropeltis gentilis*). The hobbyist reptile enthusiasts of the state were, needless to say, unhappy with these ultra-strict rules, arguing that these snakes were more secretive than rare. From 2002 to 2006, the two sides worked together in a coordinated effort to document the distribution of pyros and western milk snakes across Utah. Over eight hundred surveys were conducted and state regulations were loosened based on the results. In Utah today, the limited collection of both species is allowed with the proper permit, which can be acquired by passing a brief online course and paying a small fee. No paperwork or fees are required if you simply gently handle the snake and release it in peace.

But although UDWR changed their regulations and the herpers of the state felt validated, no one had paid much attention to the lack of pyro sightings in the northern half of Utah. Those hundreds of pieces of paper, each representing hours of searching, had been put into three-ring binders and left to accumulate dust. This data was especially informative because it showed that many areas where pyros were supposed to be found had been searched by people who knew what they were doing, yet none had turned up.

There also weren't any observations of pyros from this area posted to iNaturalist, an online citizen science platform. iNaturalist (or iNat for short) takes advantage of the fact that smartphones are now ubiquitous and every phone has a camera—or two, or five—on the back. All it takes is a quick photo or two and an observation of any living thing can be recorded. Your phone automatically saves the location, day, and time—even if you're out of cell service. iNat's community of users will suggest an identification to uploaded observations, even if you don't know what it is (though please don't be that person that expects someone to identify their horribly blurry photos). The platform already has over a million observations of snakes, but not one of these is a pyro in the northern half of Utah.

As part of my research, I also obtained data from HerpMapper.org, another citizen science initiative. HerpMapper is dedicated specifically to herpetofauna, and is much more secretive—unlike iNat, its data is only available upon request by someone with a legitimate need-to-know. Many snake enthusiasts are notoriously tight-lipped, and prefer privacy over iNaturalist's relative openness, though both platforms have their pros and cons.

The last source of location data I examined was from museum collections. Scientists have been preserving specimens for hundreds of years, and these collections serve as vast repositories of biodiversity knowledge. At the time, I worked in the herpetology collection of the Bean Life Science Museum (named after its benefactor; no relation to legumes unfortunately). The collection is housed in the basement of the museum, in a chilly, dimly lit room full of rows of white, movable shelves. Clear jars, each with one or more dead specimens suspended in ethanol, fill the metal shelves. With proper care, specimens last almost indefinitely, with little change save for the fading of bright colors. The Bean Museum's collection is home to over forty thousand reptile and amphibian specimens, and millions more are preserved in similar collections across the globe.

Museum records are typically seen as the gold standard for

biological data, largely because there is a physical specimen associated with the record, which can also be measured and even dissected later. But for old specimens especially, there is a small potential for error; place names change, records can get lost, and paper records may be digitized incorrectly.

In total, there were eight museum records of pyros in the northern half of Utah, all of which were from at least eighty years ago (or had no date at all). Given how similar pyros look to their cousins, the western milk snakes (*Lampropeltis gentilis*), it was entirely possible that these specimens had been misidentified. To investigate, Dr. Whiting contacted the curators at the various museums that held these specimens to request photographs. After examining the pictures and counting hundreds of scales—the two species have distinctly different amounts of ventral (belly) scales—I was able to determine that three of the eight specimens were mis-identified milk snakes masquerading as pyros. There was also one specimen that had been lost and couldn't be verified. However, the remaining four specimens were undoubtedly pyros. Barring some sort of bizarre locality mix-up with all of these specimens—all from different museums—it seems most likely that pyros were found in parts of the northern half of Utah at some point in time.

In a way, this left the mystery unsolved. There was evidence of the presence of pyros from decades ago, but no recent sightings, which—in my opinion—indicated that they had likely been extirpated (gone extinct in a certain area) from much or all of this portion of Utah. This is where most of the state's population growth and urbanization have occurred in the last century, which perhaps pushed already-dwindling populations past the brink. But the lack of recent sightings, even with a plausible explanation, is not indisputable proof. These areas were searched thoroughly during the UDWR surveys, but I can attest that pyros are hard to find even in areas where they are well known. It is entirely possible that they are still hiding somewhere in this area, but until there is contemporary evidence for it I will remain skeptical. (And if you strongly disagree, then please prove me wrong by finding one! I would genuinely love to be disproven on this.)

Conversely, the other main finding of my research was that pyros are found in quite a few places not previously depicted on range maps. Most of these are isolated mountain ranges in eastern Nevada and western Utah, places rarely visited by people. It is likely that in the coming years, these elusive snakes will be documented by citizen scientists in even more remote areas.

Though the conclusion on the status of pyros in the northern portion of Utah was still somewhat hazy, the information that I had found—combined with the citizen science success story—was worthy of publication in a scientific journal. After digitally recording all of the eight hundred UDWR surveys, I combined the location data with the other citizen science observations and museum records and drew an updated distribution map for *Lampropeltis pyromelana*.

That winter, Dr. Whiting and I submitted the research paper for peer review. A fundamental part of science, peer review is the process where a paper is sent to anonymous reviewers who are experts in the subject matter before it is published. Like the authors, reviewers aren't paid by scientific journals either. The reviewers suggest changes and decide if the publication should be accepted as is, ought to be revised, or if it should be rejected outright. The middle outcome (asking for revisions) is the most common one. The peer review process has its flaws and is painfully slow at times, but it (usually) stops bad science from being published and ensures a higher quality of publications.

Submitting that paper lifted a big weight from my shoulders. Being listed as the first author on a paper would dramatically increase my odds of getting into graduate school, and I was glad to be able to contribute something, no matter how small, to science. But the irony was killing me. I had just written a paper about where pyros were found *despite the fact that I had never found one*. I felt like a scientific hypocrite.

The irony and shame also made me extremely hesitant to talk to other people about my research. I'd typically deflect questions, dreading having to admit that I had never seen the species I was supposedly studying. Sure, I'd seen the captive pyro that lived at the local aquarium, trapped behind a wall of plexiglass. And I'd seen faded, lifeless specimens in the Bean Museum herpetology collection, in addition to countless photos. But none of those counted.

To be clear, my paper didn't claim that *I* had ever found a pyro. It wouldn't have made much of a difference either; the data and my paper represented the collective experiences of hundreds of people. But it just felt wrong. Once the weather warmed up again, I was going to have to find one. Or die trying.

THREE

The Sheriff Learns to Sex a Milk Snake

Every year, usually in the late fall, the Bean Life Science Museum's herpetology collection hosts a pickle party. The pickle party involves neither cucumbers nor cake, but rather dead reptiles and toxic chemicals. Not the kind of party to hire a DJ for.

The purpose of the event is to connect snake enthusiasts in the area with the resources to preserve the roadkill reptiles they've collected over the past year as scientific specimens. One of the best ways to find snakes is to drive slowly along low-trafficked roads in hopes of spotting a snake crossing the pavement or basking on it. On warm summer nights, snakes are often found soaking up the leftover warmth on the asphalt many hours after sundown. But one of the realities of "road cruising" (as those in the hobby call it) is that you'll also find a lot of reptiles that were run over by less attentive drivers. Depositing a DOR (short for "dead-on-road") specimen into a museum collection takes away a sliver of the sadness of seeing your intended quarry smashed flat on the pavement—though if the animal's insides are now its outsides, it is best left for scavengers.

Before the dead snake can be repurposed for science, it has to be "pickled" with formalin, a nasty-smelling solution of formaldehyde and water (and one of the substances a delirious Edward Cope prescribed himself). Herp enthusiasts come to the museum's pickle party to swap stories and inject their DORs, and the museum ends up with a bunch of free specimens. It's a win-win situation.

At my first pickle party, I felt very out of place. Most of the other participants already knew each other and had brought lots of roadkill. I knew nobody except for Dr. Whiting, and I hadn't even brought any specimens to pickle. The others were busy sharing stories about finding caecilians on tropical adventures, the kind of stuff I could only dream of. I was just an awkward college kid who was invited because his professor was in charge of the event. Even worse, I am incredibly squeamish around needles, not a good thing when the most important part of pickling is injecting the dead animal with formalin.

Despite feeling out of place, I knew this was my chance to talk to people, like Hunter Meakin and Bryan Hamilton, who were bona fide experts on the species that had eluded me the previous summer. I needed to make sure that the upcoming year wasn't a repeat of the first. Despite my obvious naivety, several of the experienced snake enthusiasts were more than happy to talk. Many heavyweight herpers are protective of their favorite spots—largely out of paranoia that someone with ill intentions will collect all the snakes there or ruin the habitat—but I've never met one that wouldn't at least offer general advice. The most forthcoming pyro expert was Mark Hazel, who has been looking for pyros for longer than I've been able to tie my shoes.

Technically, I had met Mark prior to the pickle party, albeit in paper form; he was one of the original volunteers that helped with the UDWR kingsnake surveys in the early 2000s. He was gracious enough to chat with me about finding pyros while he carefully injected his specimens. Mark has a normal full-time job in a university's gastroenterology research lab and his PhD is in human genetics, but he has as much field knowledge as any professional herpetologist I've ever met.

I briefly detailed my futile attempts from the previous season, trying my best to avoid looking at any of the needles. Mark was friendly enough to offer some tips and share a few of his experiences. Most importantly, he offered to let me tag along on future expeditions, an offer I gladly accepted.

Fast forward a few months later, and the icy grip of winter had finally relaxed enough to go looking for reptiles again. It was the last weekend of April when Mark picked me up in his 2005 Subaru Outback—the kind of car you see parked at backcountry trailheads everywhere—and we headed south and west towards the East Tintic Mountains. On the drive there, Mark told me a bit about his background. He had grown up in Ohio and gone to college in New Jersey (at Princeton, no less), and came out West to Utah as a graduate student. An avid outdoorsman, Mark fell in love with the Great Basin, the arid region of the western US that has the distinction of being the largest area of land in the country with no rivers flowing out of it. He also confessed to me that his flip phone of eleven years had finally kicked the can and he had recently acquired his first smartphone.

I had driven past the Tintics before but had never stopped to explore this relatively uninspiring range. With its tallest peak barely reaching eight thousand feet, the Tintics hardly seem like real mountains in comparison to the towering peaks found in other areas of Utah. The name "Tintic" is derived from a legendary Native American leader whose small band had claimed the surrounding area at one point, though today the inhabitants of the Tintics and nearby areas are few. "Nondescript" is a fitting description for the place, but even if the mountains themselves aren't noteworthy, that doesn't preclude the presence of worthwhile reptiles.

Our target species for the weekend was the western milk snake (*Lampropeltis gentilis*, or *Lampropeltis triangulum taylori* as some prefer to still call it). Pyros would have to wait for another time. Given the weather, season, and amount of free time we had, Mark wanted to try for a milk snake closer to home instead of driving further in hopes of finding a pyro. I was fine with that; I still had lots more questions to ask and knew there'd be many more weeks in the year to find my pyro. In the meantime, it was off to find a milk snake.

Despite the name, milk snakes neither produce nor drink milk. Supposedly back in the day, farmers found milk snakes in their barns and assumed that they were coming to drink milk from the livestock. Imagining a snake dangling from the udder of a cow is comical. Picturing one coiled around a cow's udder attempting to squeeze milk into a bucket is even more ridiculous. It is much more likely that any milk snake that visits a barn is attracted to the resident rodents, but I guess the name "rat snake" was already taken.

In many ways, western milk snakes are not that different from pyros. First off, both are part of the kingsnake genus, *Lampropeltis*. (Don't ask me why "kingsnake" is usually written as one word and "milk snake" as two. That's just how it is.) The genus currently encompasses twenty-six species found in North America, Central America, and the northwestern portion of South America. The term "kingsnake" comes from their ophiophagous (*ophio* meaning "snake" and *phagous* meaning "to eat") tendencies. When your body is a long skinny tube and your mouth can't actually chew food, it makes a lot of sense to eat other long skinny tubes—even if it sounds like cannibalism. Several of the larger kingsnake species, like the California kingsnake (*Lampropeltis californiae*) or the eastern kingsnake (*Lampropeltis getula*), are well-known predators of rattlesnakes, giving even those that are snake-haters a good reason to appreciate kingsnakes. Kingsnakes aren't obligate snake predators though, and will feast on lizards, mammals, and birds too.

The second similarity shared by pyros and milks is their color scheme. Both are tricolor snakes, nicknamed for the repeating

THE SHERIFF LEARNS TO SEX A MILK SNAKE

bands of three colors (red, black, and white, though other tricolors have yellow in lieu of white) on their back. The patterning of harmless tricolor snakes loosely resembles coral snakes, which use bright colors to advertise their deadly venom to potential predators. Their mimicry isn't perfect though. As a kid, I memorized the rhyme "red touches black, friend of Jack; red touches yellow, kill a fellow." Unfortunately, in my experience the number of people who merely remember the existence of a rhyme far outnumbers those who can recite it accurately; the best I've heard was, "red next to black, you're dead, Jack." The rhyme, even if you don't have it backwards, doesn't hold up in Central or South America though; just avoid picking up any brightly colored danger noodles unless you know what you're doing. Mimicry in snakes is incredibly fascinating and honestly deserves its own chapter (so I gave it one; see chapter eight).

Despite the commonalities, pyros and western milk snakes have some important lifestyle differences. Milk snakes are generally stockier than pyros, an adaptation to their more fossorial lifestyle. Although they are occasionally active on the surface, the best way to find these subterranean dwellers is by checking under rocks, wooden boards, and any other object a milk snake could be hiding under. This strategy is usually referred to as "flipping," though any object that gets flipped should be returned to its original position as neatly as possible so as to limit habitat disturbance. (If you hear someone say a snake was "flipped," it means they found it by flipping, not that they flipped the snake on its back or something weird like that.) Snake enthusiasts will often seek out old plywood boards or sheets of metal (referred to as "tin" regardless of the actual kind of metal), or put some out themselves, as this kind of shelter is both conducive to herps and easy to check under. Rocks and logs are fine too if artificial objects aren't around; any large cover object offers significant protection and the added benefit of second-hand heat transferred from the sun.

At our first stop, a grassy hillside not far from the highway,

Mark offered me an extra pair of gardening gloves he'd brought. I declined his first offer, thinking my hands would be fine; this wasn't the first time I'd flipped rocks. But in retrospect, my poor fingers weren't quite prepared for just how many they'd be turning that weekend.

It didn't take long for us to find our first and second snakes of the day. Mark found two yellow-bellied racers (*Coluber constrictor mormon*) under rocks within about ten minutes of each other. Many racers, like the one Taylor had caught back in September, are more than eager to bite, but both of those Mark found that morning were still warming up and were calm—a welcome change. Racers are diurnal and active predators, with large eyeballs that intently watch your every move. The larger of the two was around two feet long, the other a few inches smaller, both with olive-colored backs and the characteristic yellow belly. After snapping a few photographs, we allowed both to slither off.

If you're an observant reader, you've noticed that I list a subspecies here and elsewhere, but not in all instances. (In this case, *Coluber* is the genus, *constrictor* is the species, and *mormon* is the subspecies. A species is basically a distinct kind of organism, and a subspecies is essentially a kind of a kind of organism.) In recent years there has been a trend in herpetology of moving away from subspecies, with subspecies that are evolutionarily distinct being elevated to their own species and those that aren't distinct being disregarded. For species with wide geographic ranges and many recognized subspecies, it is highly likely that future taxonomic research will elevate some of these subspecies, so in these cases I've listed a subspecies name. Yellow-bellied racers (*Coluber constrictor mormon*) were once treated as a full species (*Coluber mormon*) and I imagine it won't be long before they are recognized as a species again. For the animals that I don't list subspecies for, either there are no recognized subspecies, or I anticipate it is more likely for the subspecies to be disregarded than elevated. Apologies for the taxonomy tangent.

THE SHERIFF LEARNS TO SEX A MILK SNAKE

Mark has mastered the art of using the satellite view on Google Maps to scout potential flipping sites, and we visited several other preselected rocky areas around the Tintics. Besides the two racers, we didn't find much initially beyond common lizards; a few sagebrush lizards (*Sceloporus graciosus*) and some side-blotched lizards (*Uta stansburiana*). We kept turning rocks, and I eventually humbled myself and accepted Mark's offer to use one of his pairs of gloves. My fingers were rubbed raw, to the point that my phone stopped recognizing my fingerprint—and wouldn't until several days after the trip was over.

With enough persistence, we eventually found a more interesting kind of lizard that first day: western skinks (*Plestiodon skiltonianus*). While the skink family (Scincidae) is one of the most species-rich lizard families at roughly 1,500 members, western skinks are the only species of skink found throughout most of Utah. And though they have a wide range across the state, these fossorial lizards are infrequently encountered by us aboveground-ers. Skinks are covered in very smooth scales, and many species have elongated bodies and reduced limbs—with some having no limbs at all. Western skinks, like the handful Mark and I saw that day, have dinky little limbs that can barely hold their bodies off the ground. Having small limbs and smooth bodies makes it easier for them to crawl under objects and dig through the ground, and they move with undulations that look remarkably snake-like.

Color-wise, western skinks are brown with light stripes, and the young have an endearingly bright blue tail, which is intended as a *Hey you! Bite here!* signal to predators. Skinks as a family have gone all in on the strategy of caudal autotomy. (Caudal means tail, and autotomy basically means self-amputation.) Like many other lizards, skinks can easily detach part of their tail when grabbed. Their tail vertebrae have specially adapted breakage points that make "dropping" the tail quick and painless. The surrounding muscles contract and stop blood flow almost immediately, and the lizard will eventually regrow the tail segment with a cartilage rod in the middle. The amputated segment will continue to twitch, and the bright wriggling tail is usually enough to distract a predator while the rest of the lucky lizard escapes.

While effective, caudal autotomy is mainly a last resort tactic. It takes time and energy to regrow the tail, and losing a part of your body sure doesn't sound pleasant. The lizards would much prefer to not be caught in the first place. Western skinks rarely venture out into the open, and the handful of individuals that Mark and I found that day were all hiding under rocks or logs.

The other notable find of the first day was a juvenile Great Basin rattlesnake (*Crotalus lutosus*). Mark had called me over to the spot of hillside he was investigating, saying he had seen a skink but it had gotten away. I walked around the hillside, overturning a few rocks opportunistically in hopes of spotting the same (or a different) skink. While scanning the ground, I spotted the small rattlesnake curled at the base of a cube-shaped rock. Funny enough, the rock was slightly askew, indicating that Mark had flipped it previously. The clump of tall grass next to the snake hid it from easy viewing but didn't block the light from the setting sun from reaching its pint-sized body; a perfect basking spot.

The sunbathing rattler, which was less than a foot long and not even a year old, sat there perfectly coiled. Its light brown body, with darker brown blotches evenly spaced along the length of its spine, blended perfectly in with the dirt, sticks, and rocks surrounding it. The tiny serpent felt no need to rattle or flee, let alone strike. Rattlesnakes are often unfairly villainized because of their potential for harm. True, they are venomous. A bite from a rattlesnake is a medical emergency that *could* be deadly. But rattlesnake bites in the US are almost never fatal—they cause only one or two deaths every year on average—because of the effectiveness and availability of antivenom. Car keys and a traveling companion are pretty much the only snakebite kit you need in the US, thankfully. Furthermore, rattlesnakes also have zero interest in biting humans. Venom evolved as an adaptation to hunt prey and is only used secondarily as a defense. If it can't eat you, it isn't interested in biting you. Rattlesnakes even have a built-in warning system—their trademark rattle—so if you get bit, it was probably your own fault.

I managed to get a few photos of the neatly coiled snake as it sat there, chill as a popsicle. After a few minutes, it decided that the giant apes weren't going away and casually meandered its way underneath the rock. There was no sense of urgency and still no rattling. It just wanted some more personal space.

Throughout the trip, I was impressed with Mark's extensive knowledge of the natural world. He knew his herps, which I expected, but he also could give the common and scientific names for most plants we encountered—and knew which ones were invasive. The first day, he didn't mention any birds though, so foolishly I thought I might have him beat in that category. I had just taken a semester-long ornithology class and had learned to identify almost all of the birds of Utah (which are much more numerous than the state's non-avian reptiles). As Mark was eating breakfast at the beginning of the second day, I took a quick walk with my binoculars to observe the songbirds' morning chorus. Upon returning to our primitive campsite, I casually mentioned that I had heard and seen some blue-gray gnatcatchers—which are adorable small passerine birds with an equally adorable call—but hadn't gotten any good pictures. I hoped that Mark would be impressed that I could identify the birds by sound—a skill that wowed my roommates—but alas. Turns out he had heard the distinctive chirp of the blue-gray gnatcatcher enough times to recognize it too. At least he wasn't disappointed in my bird expertise though, like he was with my nonexistent plant identification skills.

While seeing some of my favorite birds might seem like a good start for the day, the weather was far less promising. Temperatures were in the low fifties, and the cloud cover and imminent rain were less than ideal. But Mark said there was still a chance we could get lucky, so we headed to a place where he had found a milk snake previously. Even if it was too cold for a snake to be active above the surface, finding one buried a few inches underground beneath a rock was still possible.

Cautiously optimistic, we headed to the quasi-ghost town of Eureka (pronounced by locals as "your-ik-uh"), Utah. Unlike the friendly small-town vibes of many rural Utah towns, the main street of Eureka, which has a population of less than a thousand people, is less welcoming and has more storefronts that are boarded up than open. "Eureka" is Greek for "I have found it," a fitting name for the place given its start as a gold mining town back in 1869. The settlers may have named the town for the precious metals they found, but Mark and I were headed here to look for a different underground treasure.

Our prospects looked good. The hillside itself was strewn with rocks, many of which were a wonderful Goldilocks size: big enough to provide deep shelter to entice a milk snake to hang out underneath, but not so big that the stone would be impossible to overturn. After parking, Mark and I donned our gloves and crossed our fingers.

It only took a few minutes of flipping for Mark to strike gold. "Milk snake!" he called out. I hurried over, eager to see our quarry. (Sorry, too many mining puns.) The snake was underneath a large chunk of quartzite, the bottom of which was several inches into the ground. It was sluggish from the cold, but the sun that glinted through the clouds beautifully illuminated its shiny red, white, and black scales. Mark was surprisingly calm about the find, and the cold snake's attitude was similarly chill.

The snake was maybe a couple of feet long, and on the skinnier side for a milk snake. What it lacked in size it more than made up for with its stunning colors. It was my first tricolor snake, and the combination of red, white, and black bands was mesmerizing. The contrast of colors in person was far more vivid than any photograph, but I was happy to have Mark take a picture of me holding it anyway.

There were plenty more rocks to flip in the area, so after

admiring the snake for a bit I wandered off while Mark took some additional photos and measurements. After turning rocks for a few minutes, I glanced back and saw another person who had parked a large white truck near our vehicle walking towards Mark. Deciding it would appear weird if I continued to turn rocks like someone looking for buried treasure, I casually took my gloves off and headed over to say hi like a normal human being. As I got closer, I realized that the man was wearing a uniform and the truck had the words COUNTY SHERIFF printed on the side. Apparently two people flipping rocks on a hill in full view of the highway looks slightly strange.

I have no idea what the sheriff was expecting to find, but I am glad that we had already found our milk snake; I'm not sure how quickly he would have believed that we were looking for a red, white, and black snake he'd likely never seen before. With a smile on his face that made me wonder if he'd had similar encounters before, Mark explained what we were doing and showed the sheriff the milk snake. The sheriff maintained that he was "not a snake person," but was curious about the colorful snake and accepted our strange explanation.

Seeing the sheriff's curiosity, Mark even went so far as to show him how to sex a snake. The procedure is simple: you hold the snake near the cloaca (the multi-purpose orifice towards the back end) and apply pressure from the tail towards the cloaca. If the hemipenes (the paired male intromittent organs) pop out, it's a boy. If not, it's a girl. Or you're doing it wrong. This milk snake was male and didn't seem to mind the sexing procedure too much. I'm not sure how the sheriff felt about this particular detail, but he was impressed with the overall beauty of the snake and was surprised that it lived in the area. He even asked sheepishly if he could take a picture of it, probably to supplement his latest "you'll never guess what happened at work today" story for his kids.

Eventually, the sheriff returned to his patrol and Mark and I were left to turn more rocks in hopes of finding a second milk snake. Unfortunately, the rest of the rocks in the vicinity yielded only dirt and invertebrates. We stopped briefly at another couple spots, but the looming clouds and cold temperatures convinced us to call it a weekend. One milk snake was plenty for me, anyway. In retrospect, our timing was excellent; we were in the car when the real downpour of rain came soon after.

Over the course of those two days, we had flipped a *lot* of rocks. Far more than I had ever flipped on a herping trip before. Although my muscles were sore and my fingers felt like they had been sanded, I was satisfied with the trip. I was excited to add another species to my life list, but I felt a tinge of frustration at the fact that this was now the sixth species of snake that I'd seen for the first time since I'd started looking for pyros. I would have traded any of those six new snakes for a pyro, and I couldn't help but wonder how many other species I would encounter for the first time before I finally found one.

At the very least, I learned a lot from Mark that weekend; I'd certainly pestered him with enough questions. I learned that pyros liked temperatures slightly cooler than I thought, and that recent rain is a good indicator that pyros in the area will be active. Though pyros can be found by road cruising and flipping, Mark's preferred search technique was to simply hike, especially on warm nights. Understanding microhabitat was important too; during the day a pyro would be more likely to be hiding at the base of a large bush or tucked in a rock crevice than out in the open. But I also learned that I hadn't necessarily done anything wrong the previous year. Pyros were hard to find, even for experts. It was only a matter of time.

FOUR

Kingsnake!

In retrospect, my failure to find a pyro in my first year of searching shouldn't have been too unexpected. As it turns out, finding snakes has been a difficulty confronted by herpetologists for as long as there have been herpetologists. There are even entire papers dedicated solely to the vexing subject. The title of a 2015 review paper sums up the problem neatly: "A Snake in the Hand is Worth 10,000 in the Bush." The generally secretive lifestyle of snakes makes researching them a pain, as any study hinges on having a large enough sample size to produce statistically significant results.

One study that perfectly illustrates the difficulties of finding snakes took place on the Pacific island of Guam and concerns one of the most notorious invasive species of all time: the brown tree snake (*Boiga irregularis*). Native to Australia, Indonesia, and Papua New Guinea, these long, arboreal snakes are brown and come in a variety of patterns (hence the species name *irregularis*). The exact date of their invasion of Guam is unknown, but reports started turning up in the 1940s, which is when the island became a hubbub of traffic due to World War II. Given its geographic isolation

—the island lies over a thousand miles from the nearest major land masses—snakes never made it to Guam by natural means. The fauna of the island evolved in a snake-free bliss until humans came along. Snakes could only make the long oceanic journey once boats and planes were invented (by people, not snakes).

The brown tree snakes quickly took over their newfound tropical paradise, chowing down on the many vertebrates that hadn't evolved to deal with snake predators. In total, the voracious tree snakes ate enough mammals, birds, and lizards on Guam to cause the extirpation of at least fifteen native vertebrate species and decimate the populations of countless others. Brown tree snakes also frequently cause local power outages by climbing into electrical boxes and onto power lines. Given the threat of further ecological and economic damage, a huge amount of resources have been poured into controlling this invasive population, making them one of the best-researched snakes in the world. If there was ever a snake that regular people cared about finding, it'd probably be the one that was eating all the pretty birds and knocking out the power.

The researchers implanted radio transmitters in twenty brown tree snakes enclosed within a fifty-five hectare area (for reference, one hectare is about the size of a football field). This density of about 0.36 snakes per hectare (think about one snake for every three football fields) in the controlled area was significantly lower than estimates for peak densities in Guam, which are thought to have been as high as a whopping fifty snakes per hectare shortly after the initial invasion.

The authors of this 2020 study conducted several experiments with this set of radio-tracked snakes, but the most interesting one was simply regarding their detectability. The researchers were split into two teams, one that was locating snakes using the radio tracking equipment and one that was searching without any technological assistance. The surveys were conducted at night, when brown tree snakes are most active, along marked transects within the enclosed area. Since the radio tracking team was able to easily find the snakes (thanks to the transmitters), it allowed the scientists to keep track of whenever the regular visual survey team *could* have seen a snake. These possible encounters, determined by whenever the visual team passed within a certain radius of a snake that had been detected by the telemetry team, could then be compared to how many snakes they actually spotted.

The results of this part of their study are simply staggering. The visual survey team could have encountered eighty-seven brown tree snakes. They did not see eighty-seven. They saw one. One! *They walked past the other eighty-six!* That's a shockingly low rate, and it speaks volumes about how difficult it can be to find snakes of any species.

Obviously, there are some major differences between brown tree snakes and pyros; this isn't an apples-to-apples comparison. Being brown (duh), brown tree snakes blend in with branches and dirt. They are much more cryptic than the flamboyant coloration of pyros. Additionally, brown tree snakes are arboreal—tree is literally in the name—and spotting a snake up a tree is more difficult than one on the ground. Conversely, the radio-tracked brown tree snakes were below ground only 9 percent of the time, whereas pyros and most terrestrial snakes likely hide underground—totally out of sight—significantly more. Brown tree snakes also can grow to be twice the size of pyros. With all these differences, it wouldn't make sense to extrapolate these exact detection rates from brown tree snakes to pyros or to any other species. Regardless, these findings clearly demonstrate the low detectability of snakes in general. I'd still like to think that I didn't walk past eighty-six pyros in my first year without seeing a single one, but I must have walked past at least a few.

Despite the long odds, I knew at some point I would eventually get lucky, and with the weather warming up it was time to try again. My first pyro hunting trip of the year came in the first full weekend of May, a week after the milk snake expedition with Mark. May is generally regarded as the best time of year for finding pyros. The logic is simple: in May, the weather is warm enough that all the snakes have awoken from hibernation and will be out and about looking for both their first meal of the year and a mate. Additionally, temperatures during the month of May are warm enough for long periods of activity but not so hot that the pyros simply hunker down for the vast majority of the day, as can happen in the warmest summer months.

A couple of days before leaving, I received an email from a crestfallen Mark, who told me that he couldn't make it that weekend. He wouldn't be there to help me search in person, but I still felt more prepared than the previous year thanks to all of his sage advice. And even if Mark couldn't come, I had recruited another pair of eyes to tag along.

The extra pair of eyes belonged to Jacob Searcy, a fellow herpetology enthusiast who was a couple of years older than me. I had met Jacob, who had already graduated with a biology degree, when he had started volunteering in the Bean Museum herpetology collection. I had dropped by the collection workroom to grab another binder of survey data from the old Utah kingsnake surveys and saw Jacob with an arm elbow-deep in a jar full of preserved rattlesnakes. I put two and two together and assumed that we had a common interest, and within a few minutes we'd planned a Saturday expedition to look for snakes in the nearby area. That outing was unsuccessful, but it was just the first of many herping trips Jacob and I would undertake together. At the time I met him, Jacob kept several pet snakes in his closet (both literally and metaphorically, as his apartment didn't allow pets of any kind). He even went several months without his roommate knowing he kept snakes—yes, the guy literally living in the same room as him. The other important thing you should know about Jacob is that he is much more fond of bugs than I am, and almost all of my meager invertebrate knowledge can be traced to him.

Our destination for the weekend was Kanosh Canyon, within the Pahvant Mountains, which was where Taylor and I had chased a whipsnake up a tree the previous September. The beautiful sandstone canyon, with its oak and maple trees, was only two hours from where Jacob and I lived. Most importantly, it was supposed to be great pyro habitat. In fact, this was probably the only upside about not having Mark along for the weekend. Mark has been finding pyros in Utah for so many years that his goal is to find them in previously undocumented mountain ranges. By comparison, the Pahvants are one of the easiest places to find a pyro. So although Jacob and I didn't have a pyro expert by our sides that weekend, we were at least going to be in territory that was too easy for Mark.

One of the most pyro-friendly features of Kanosh Canyon is its water. Unlike many places where the canyon and stream share the same name, the main body of water here is called Corn Creek—named after the corn that the native Ute people had planted along it when the first white settlers arrived. Well over a century later, the corn is gone but the creek is still going strong. The presence of water year-round is good for pyros for two reasons, as it supports additional vegetation—meaning more cover for the snakes—and offers a source of drinking water. Heading to the creek for a sip is one of the few good reasons a pyro would have to be moving across a trail, and that's precisely what Jacob and I were hoping for.

I picked Jacob up early in the morning and we headed south from Provo to Kanosh. We arrived at the canyon itself without a hitch and were eager to hit the trail while the temperatures were still cool. We first hiked the north fork of Corn Creek, which only runs above ground intermittently. The sandstone canyon that makes up the north fork of Corn Creek is much narrower than the main fork, though not narrow enough to qualify as a slot canyon by any means. The single-track trail is flanked by trees on both sides, providing shade and an excellent blanket of fallen leaves for pyros to hide under. There were lots of other plants that I'm sure Mark could have identified, but I was happy enough to recognize that some of the trees were oaks.

PYRO

It only took a few minutes of hiking to spot the first snake of the weekend, a yellow-bellied racer (*Coluber constrictor mormon*). Unlike the racers I saw with Mark the week before, this one was true to form and scrambled (or, dare I say, raced) up the hillside in a flash. "Snake!" I yelled, and Jacob quickly abandoned the rocks he was overturning to join the pursuit. The beast had slithered into the leaf litter under some large bushes on the hillside and frozen in place, hoping to remain unseen. I pulled my phone out of my pocket and took a couple pictures to later upload to iNaturalist. The snake continued to hold still, its round pupils intently watching my every action. After experiencing the usefulness of data from iNat in my own research, I had become dedicated to documenting my findings on the platform and helping others identify theirs.

Satisfied that the olive-colored snake would be visible in at least one of the pictures, I pocketed my phone. I crept closer, trying to move branches out of the way with as little disturbance as possible. Before I could get within striking distance, the snake decided it had had enough and bolted. Neither Jacob nor I were able to follow its escape route, as it disappeared down some unknown hole or into another stand of leaves. We contemplated doing a more thorough sweep of the area in hopes of rediscovering the snake but opted to take it as a good sign and continue on. It was only a racer, and we had other reptiles to find.

The canyon was crawling with small lizards of two species: sagebrush lizards (*Sceloporus graciosus*) and plateau fence lizards (*Sceloporus tristichus*). Both of these species are mostly a dull brown on top, with plateau fence lizards being slightly larger and slightly spikier. They are both part of the genus *Sceloporus*, a group of spiny lizards found all across North America. These lizards are often called "blue-bellies" because of the bright colors that are found underneath. Normally hidden from view, these blue belly patches are only visible when the lizards suck the sides of their body in while they display to other lizards. Or when you catch one and turn it over. There were enough lizards in the canyon that Jacob and I could have chased lizards all day, but we were more interested in the legless reptiles.

We did catch a brief glimpse of yet another yellow-bellied racer (*Coluber constrictor mormon*). This one wasn't even nice enough to let me get a picture though, making itself scarce immediately after being discovered. Silly survival instincts. After returning to the car, we drove further up the main dirt road to scout out our campsite for the night. The primitive camping area—which was really just some clearings with a few makeshift fire pits—was unoccupied except for some western tanagers, happily calling in the trees.

After a late lunch, we set off for our second hike of the day feeling refreshed and energized. This one was up the larger, main fork of Corn Creek, which Taylor and I hadn't explored the previous year. The geology and surrounding plant life of this canyon were similar to the smaller north fork, though both the canyon and trail were a bit wider. However, the animal life of this canyon would prove far superior on that day, as we would quickly discover. We hadn't walked more than ten minutes up the trail when the moment I had been waiting for over a year finally happened.

Jacob was on my right, the side of the two-track trail closest to the creek. To my left, the ground beneath the thin stand of oaks was covered in fallen leaves, bathed by the afternoon sun. I don't know if I just happened to scan the right spot, or if the flash of brilliant vermillion drew my eyes. There it was, a few inches of red, white, and black banding peeking through the sunlit leaves. Though the majority of the snake was hidden from view, I knew instantly that I had finally found my quarry.

I immediately lunged towards the spot in the leaves where the serpent lay concealed. "KINGSNAKE! KINGSNAKE!" I yelled with unbridled excitement. I grabbed at the part of the snake that was visible, but it had already disappeared into the leaves. I furiously brushed away the surrounding debris and was rewarded with another flash of red amongst the dull colors of the leaf litter. This time, my hand was fast enough, and I was not about to let go. I felt the snake's teeth momentarily sink into my hand, but adrenaline blocked out the pain (which, to be fair, would have been minimal anyway). I lifted the beautiful banded serpent into the air and "emerged triumphantly from the leaves" (Jacob's words), clutching my first pyro.

The rush of joy in that moment was incomparable. The months of frustration melted away and were replaced by ecstasy. Red, black, and white scaly ecstasy. In my hand, at last, was a pyro in all its glory. Jacob and I were elated. I'm sure I said, "Oh my goodness!" at least a thousand times.

Not only was the snake drop-dead gorgeous, but she was also in excellent physical condition. She was at least three feet long and rather chunky, even for a full-grown adult, a sign of good health. Well, I say "she" but to be honest I was not totally confident in my snake sexing skills at the time. I had witnessed Mark's demonstration to the sheriff the week prior, but I hadn't given it a go myself until that point.

The snake was rather well behaved. The initial bite was the pyro's only attempt at dissuading me with her teeth. The snake did excrete a little bit of musk—the stinky, foul-tasting substance meant to deter predators—but it wasn't much. One of the most remarkable things about snakes is that they will oftentimes realize that you aren't a predator. The level of aggression and flighty-ness varies, but with many species it only takes a few seconds of gentle handling for the snake to comprehend that its life isn't in immediate danger, after which it becomes quite relaxed. (Note: free handling venomous snakes is another story.)

A lengthy photoshoot ensued, with Jacob and I posing our new friend on several different backgrounds. She was still somewhat antsy, naturally, but still cooperated. The pyro's red, white, and black bands were striking, regardless of what background we posed her on. She looked good on the rocks. And in the grass. Even on the plain old dirt, this snake was a stunner. I was in awe.

We were getting ready to release her when I had a brilliant idea: pose the snake in a tree. I had learned from past experience that snakes were quite photogenic in trees. The nearby oaks weren't tall enough to allow the snake to escape, so I held her close to some branches at eye-level and let her meander onto them.

It was at this point that we heard the rumble of an engine coming up the trail, and Jacob and I turned around to see a middle-aged man on a four-wheeler with two young boys seated behind him. Still overcome with shock and awe—and standing in between the trail and the incredibly conspicuous snake in the tree—we just smiled awkwardly and waved as they rumbled past. After they had passed us, we heard the dad say "Did you see that snake in the tree?" to his kids. At that point, my normal social skills kicked back in and I yelled to ask if they wanted to come check it out. Curiosity piqued, the man threw the four-wheeler into reverse and drove back to get a better look.

My social skills were still impaired from the snake-induced high, so I'm sure the ensuing interaction was at least slightly awkward. We explained that the brightly-colored snake was totally harmless, and made sure to inform them that none of the red snakes in Utah were venomous and should never ever be killed for any reason whatsoever. The older of the two boys was the only one brave enough to take up our offer to touch the snake, though he was still somewhat apprehensive. Jacob and I probably seemed at least slightly crazy as we explained that we had come to this spot with the sole intent to find this species of snake. We were too excited to care. After the dad and his kids had had their fill, they continued on their way, allowing Jacob and me to say our final goodbyes to the beautiful pyro.

Jacob did jokingly attempt to convince me to keep the snake; he did have the permit to legally collect it, after all. I responded that I wasn't ready to be a dad. I generally frown on the collection of wild snakes as pets; captive-bred snakes simply make better pets, as parasites and eating problems are common issues with wild-caught individuals. I also didn't have any sort of enclosure ready to house the snake—and I'm confident my human roommate would have been mortified if I had brought home a new legless roommate.

I also appreciate the feeling of releasing snakes. Catching a snake is always a rush, but letting it go has a different set of emotions. An appreciation for nature. The feeling of hope that the beautiful animal will survive and make more beautiful babies just like it. Even if the impact of collecting is small, it isn't zero. Why should I have the right to take it out of its home?

Apparently I haven't been the only one to notice the pleasing feeling that accompanies releasing a wild animal, because it's also an old Buddhist practice. Buddhists do it for good karma, and typically with animals that are destined for the dinner plate, though the tradition has come under fire because of the ecological consequences of releasing non-native animals. But I think that the root of the practice is the same feeling I felt watching those shiny scales slide into the leaves and out of sight.

It had taken far longer than I thought it would, but I had finally found a pyro. A burden had been lifted from my shoulders. All the blood, sweat, and tears were finally worth it. I also felt like much less of a scientific hypocrite. I may have already submitted my paper, but it was still in peer review, so I no longer had to bear the irony of publishing a paper on a species I'd never seen.

Still giddy with excitement, Jacob and I continued up the trail, the broad two-track later giving way to a narrow path. We eventually turned around several miles up at a pristine sandstone pool of crystal-clear water. The creek had hollowed out a large pond, home to several good-sized fish. A trio of small waterfalls poured out of the edge of the pool, the soaked rocks green with algae. At some parts, the water's edge looked like one of those "infinity pools" you might see on social media, except this one was all natural. Even a regular hiker that had walked past the pyro hiding in the leaves would have left awestruck by natural beauty on this hike.

We also found a small western terrestrial garter snake (*Thamnophis elegans*) near the water. The drab colors of the garter snake—gray accented with black and very faded yellow stripes—paled in comparison to the vivid colors of the pyro we had just seen, but Jacob has a soft spot for these common snakes. Garter snakes are almost always found near water, and these small- to medium-sized snakes are rather fond of eating fish. Their swimming ability isn't unique—all snakes can swim—but few other North American snakes have fish as a significant portion of their diet.

Jacob happily snapped a few pictures of the young garter snake and we let it on its way. It had been a couple hours since we'd found the pyro but the euphoria still hadn't worn off. We didn't see any other snakes on our hike back to our campsite, but I didn't care. I had finally found a pyro. I wasn't a failure. My hours of searching were no longer for naught.

I also could barely believe that even with only a small portion of the pyro's body poking through the sun-dappled leaves, I immediately recognized that it was a snake. Interestingly, some scientists would argue that spotting even the most well-camouflaged snake isn't a fluke but rather something that has been hard-wired into our primate brains. And advocates of what is referred to as the "Snake Detection Hypothesis" have an intriguing case—and one that's worth a bit of a lengthy tangent.

The story is simple if we rewind the evolutionary clock. Picture the earth sixty million years ago. An asteroid blast had just knocked the dinosaurs off their perch as the ruling group of organisms, and a shake-up was in order. Mammals had already been around for millions of years prior, but it wasn't until this time that they really started to diversify. When you think of mammals, you probably think of big, charismatic ones like tigers or gorillas. But the vast majority of mammals at the time were small, nocturnal creatures with relatively poor vision—though more than half of the mammal species today are rodents or bats, so don't think too much has changed.

PYRO

Imagine that you are an early primate, a small fluffball that looks like a cross between a shrew and a lemur. You've spent the whole day tucked away in a tree cavity. At night, you gingerly crawl out and your hyper-sensitive nose detects a hint of ripe fruit a few trees away. Something smells a little out of the ordinary, but you neither see nor hear any potential predators. You carefully clamber from branch to branch, nearing your sweet, sweet target. And then, in a flash, BANG! Rows of sharp teeth sink into your flesh, and your furry body is rapidly crushed on all sides by scaly skin. Within a few seconds of constriction, your heart gives out, absolutely annihilated by the pressure. A few minutes later, your body has been swallowed whole and begins to be digested. You didn't even see what hit you.

The predator, of course, was a snake. All snakes are carnivores, and they would have been more than happy to chow down on the furry mammals that started to proliferate after the extinction of the dinosaurs. At the time of our hypothetical scenario, the largest snake that probably ever lived—the forty-two foot Titanoboa—was slithering around along with thousands of smaller relatives.

Supporters of the Snake Detection Hypothesis, a theory first proposed by Lynne Isabell, argue that snakes were such significant predators of mammals that there was a strong pressure to evolve visual systems capable of spotting them before it was too late. Obviously this isn't the only possible strategy; other mammalian groups became breeding machines to overcome losses with sheer numbers (e.g. rabbits), or evolved resistance to snake venoms (e.g. mongooses), or evolved ninja jumping skills (e.g. kangaroo rats, and this one deserves a search on YouTube if you've never watched high-speed footage of kangaroo rats dodging rattlesnakes mid-strike). The primates, so the theory goes, evolved to deal with the threat of snakes by simply watching out for them better. Those with good vision avoided snakes better and were thus more likely to survive, reproduce, and pass on their good vision genes than those with poor eyesight.

It is clear that primates have good vision, especially compared to other mammals. All primates have front-facing eyes better suited to watching the area immediately in front, as opposed to animals with eyes on the sides of their head that are better suited to spotting a predator that is sneaking up. Most mammals are partially colorblind, but not primates—an adaptation that would make spotting snakes, especially brightly colored ones, much easier. And to go along with this, the parts of the brain that process vision are more advanced in primates than the rest of the mammals.

Yet good vision has a multitude of possible benefits, so why are some convinced that snakes are connected to the advances in primate vision? Isbell's initial argument, published in 2006, largely centered around the relationship between brain structure and the presence of venomous snakes. Essentially, primates that never coevolved with venomous snakes (lemurs) have less developed visual processing systems than primates that had an "interrupted co-existence with venomous snakes" (the New World monkeys), which in turn are less developed than the primates that always evolved with venomous snakes (the Old World monkeys, including the apes). This line of thinking is logical, though it overlooks predation pressures from nonvenomous snakes—and the majority of large snakes (i.e. those capable of eating a medium- to large-sized primate) today are nonvenomous.

The fear of snakes is another possible line of evidence for the Snake Detection Hypothesis. Several studies have shown that in humans and other primates, seeing pictures of snakes elicits an unconscious mental response to the perceived threat. The primate fear response is hypothesized to be innate, as some studies have shown that captive macaques and mouse lemurs that had never seen snakes before were still scared of them. However, studies on rhesus monkeys showed juveniles to gain an "intense and persistent fear" of snakes only after watching the responses of adult monkeys. In my personal experience doing educational programs with live animals, the same is true for *Homo sapiens*; most young human children are not afraid of snakes at all, indicating that the ophidiophobia many adults experience is acquired, not innate. In my opinion, fear is another lukewarm piece of evidence.

That being said, studies that have focused on the crux of the Snake Detection Hypothesis—the human ability to spot snakes—have shown more convincing results. For example, a 2016 paper showed that people are significantly better at recognizing pictures of snakes than other, non-threatening animals. Participants in the experiment were shown images, with varying degrees of added blurriness, depicting snakes and other objects. At resolutions where other animals were usually unrecognizable, people could still consistently identify the snakes. Previous studies have had similar results, indicating that both adults and kids are faster at detecting images of snakes than other objects.

Admittedly, I am neither a psychologist nor a neuroscientist, and the Snake Detection Hypothesis is more complicated than the simplified case I've presented here—and I'm sure that ten years from now there will be even more information on the subject. Given the current evidence, I think it is plausible that there is some link between snakes and primate vision. However, I wouldn't go so far as to say that snakes have been the primary driver in the evolution of our vision. And I wonder what Lynne Isbell would say about the eighty-six brown tree snakes that the researchers on Guam walked past. Anyway, whether or not my eyes were specifically adapted for the task, I couldn't have been happier to have spotted that beautiful pyro that day in Kanosh.

The next morning, Jacob and I packed up camp, had a makeshift breakfast, and hopped in the car to head to a new destination. We stopped outside the sole gas station in Kanosh to pull up directions. Craving the comforts of modern life after twenty-four hours of deprivation, Jacob went into the gas station to forage for a Dr. Pepper. He returned shortly thereafter, fuming about how much he hated Kanosh. I was shocked; at this point Kanosh might have been my favorite place in the whole world. Apparently the small convenience store wasn't open quite yet, despite the neon "OPEN" sign in the window, and the grumpy old man behind the counter refused to sell Jacob a Dr. Pepper. I guess that's where Jacob draws the line. If you get between him and Dr. Pepper, it's over.

After the fiasco at the gas station, we headed north towards the town of Fillmore. Fillmore was once the capital of Utah, back before it was even a state, chosen because of its central location and equal distance from the main population centers in the north (Salt Lake) and south (St. George). With a population of around 2,400, it's about six times the size of Kanosh but still looks like a town whose glory days were last century—or the one before. Fillmore is big enough to have a couple restaurant chains, though these are dependent on traffic from highway travelers. It also has a gas station where Jacob was finally able to satisfy his unquenchable thirst for Dr. Pepper.

It didn't take long for the road out of Fillmore to turn to dirt and for me and Jacob to arrive at a suitable parking spot in the mountains. Our original plan for the second day was to hike along Chalk Creek, but after seeing several signs referring to the "Chalk Creek Hieroglyphs" we decided to take a quick detour first.

The hieroglyphs here have an interesting history, and an internet search quickly leads down a rabbit hole of treasure-filled conspiracy theories. Discovered in the 1930s, they consist of several rows of symbols etched into rocks near a small, mysterious cave. Some of the symbols are easily recognizable as hands and faces, though some are just unusual pictograms. There is also a stone with two additional symbols (one of which appears to be a yin-yang symbol, oddly) that has been transported into the town of Fillmore. After their discovery, it was naturally assumed that the hieroglyphs meant there was gold hidden nearby, though several adventurous treasure hunters have come up empty-handed over the years. Despite the lack of evidence, the hieroglyphs remain shrouded in mystery and superstition even today.

I jokingly said to Jacob that the treasure hunters had found nothing because the real treasure of these mountains were the snakes, which are beautiful, hard to find, and hang out underground a lot (sounds like buried treasure to me!). While said in jest, my statement quickly turned prophetic. As we were exploring the sparsely vegetated hillside just past the hieroglyphs, I spotted the head of a striped whipsnake (*Masticophis taeniatus*) poking up through the rocks. Whipsnakes have excellent eyes and are active hunters, and they'll often raise their head a foot or more off of the ground to get a good look at the surrounding area. This whipsnake spotted me at the same time I spotted it, and we sprang into action simultaneously. The snake desperately tried to find shelter among the fallen rocks, but I ran over fast enough and was able to secure it.

The snake, like most whipsnakes, was wiggly and adamantly refused to hold still, making photographing it a pain. It was an adult and in excellent physical condition, with beautiful white stripes running from head to tail. Hoping to get it to hold still, we let him crawl into a large bush on the hillside. The snake happily slid into the bush and did its best impression of a branch, hoping we would go away.

We continued to take pictures until we heard a noise coming from the other side of the bush. It almost sounded like the rustle of a lizard, but not quite. Curious, we moved around to the other side of the big bush and were greeted by the source of the sound: a cantankerous rattlesnake. It was a hefty adult Great Basin rattlesnake (*Crotalus lutosus*), yellowish-brown with large darker splotches, and we had interrupted its morning routine. Judging by the crawl marks on the loose dirt of the hillside, the snake had been moving down the hill and had gotten almost all the way to the bush that the whipsnake was in. Upon noticing us, it started to work its way back up the hill, possibly muttering to itself that it should have slept in another hour.

Forgetting all about the whipsnake in the bush (which was exactly what it wanted), we turned our attention and phone cameras to the rattling brown beast on the hillside. The rattlesnake slowly crawled upwards, occasionally rattling its disapproval. Eventually it retreated into a hollow underneath the roots of a tree, and coiled up, staring at us with its cold eyes. The rattler was only a tad shorter than the whipsnake but it was many times heavier, its chunky body as thick as my wrist. Its scales had a golden marshmallow hue to them, though it wasn't projecting any warm campfire vibes.

Eventually, we complied with the rattlesnake's wishes and left it in peace. Jacob and I headed away from the area with the bizarre hieroglyphs and to the trail along Chalk Creek we originally planned on hiking. It wasn't very far along that rocky path that we encountered yet another striped whipsnake (*Masticophis taeniatus*). This one was practically a baby, only a foot long and thinner than a pencil, a perfect miniature version of the whipsnake we had encountered earlier. It was likely born towards the end of the previous summer and was out looking for its first meal after awakening from hibernation. Thankfully for the young snake, the two giant creatures that it encountered weren't actual predators. After admiring the tiny snake, we let it go to find its own lizard lunch. Survival rates for young snakes are low—no natural predator is as merciful as Jacob and I—but with some luck this one would grow up to be as big as the one we found earlier and have baby whipsnakes of its own.

I remarked to Jacob that since we had found a young whipsnake after the adult one, we were bound to see a baby rattlesnake next. Funny enough, it only took a few minutes for my words to come true. We heard the familiar rattle before we saw the snake, and we doubted our luck for half a second. But then there it was, a small rattlesnake (same species, and the only one found in the area, *Crotalus lutosus*), moving erratically along the rocky trail. Like many Great Basin rattlesnakes, it was a light brown color, with dark brown blotches regularly spaced down its back. The pint-sized snake wasn't happy to see us and at first it absolutely refused to hold still for pictures, repeatedly skirting back and forth around the rocky path. Eventually it settled down next to a larger stone and stared at us with all the grumpiness it could muster—though to be fair, the lack of facial muscles means that any expression on a snake's face is simply a projection of human emotions.

As though the snake gods weren't done blessing us, we even ran into another adult Great Basin rattlesnake, this one a lighter brown in coloration, on the way back to the car later. The snake was in the middle of lazily crossing the dirt road, but it quickened its pace as we approached. Once on the other side, the snake coiled itself nicely under the overhanging roots of a tree, occasionally buzzing its rattle as we looked on.

Hopefully by this point you've caught onto the familiar theme with rattlesnakes: all they want is to be left alone. That's it. Give them space and they'll be happy. Some people think that killing a rattlesnake is the best way to ensure it doesn't hurt anyone. This is complete idiocy. Attempting to kill a rattlesnake instead of just leaving it alone increases your chances of being bit by roughly 5000%. Okay, I made that number up, but you get the point. If you've already noticed the rattlesnake and it hasn't bitten you yet, it won't—unless you do something stupid. Both harmless and venomous snakes can strike in the blink of an eye—or technically two to four times faster than a blink—so don't think you have any realistic hope of dodging it. Just calmly back away from the snake and both parties will be fine.

That last adult rattlesnake was the final live serpent we encountered on the two-day trip, bringing our total to nine snakes, all encountered while hiking. Eight of those nine were wonderful snakes, but the pyro was truly sublime. I had been waiting over a year—what felt like an eternity—to spot those beautiful scarlet scales. I felt incredibly relieved I was no longer a scientific hypocrite claiming to research a species I had never seen. But I was also especially glad I had found a pyro that weekend because seeing any on my next trip was going to be bittersweet.

FIVE

The Ivory Tower of Academia

On a cold May morning in the Coconino National Forest in Arizona, I woke up to a strange feeling: I was missing a toe. On my right foot, I had four freezing toes and then a total absence of feeling where my pinky toe was supposed to be. What was supposed to be the greatest trip of my life, a nineteen-day research and collecting adventure in the Southwest, had gotten started off on the wrong foot.

My traveling companion was Taylor Probst, the fellow undergrad and herpetology enthusiast whom you met in chapter two. We had spent the entire day driving south from Utah to Arizona and arrived in Flagstaff in the dark. After finding a camping spot in the national forest, it was time to get some rest. We both threw out our tarps, hastily inflated our sleeping pads, and crawled into our insulated sleeping bags. Taylor slept fine in his zero-degree bag, but mine wasn't quite so warm. My decision to put on three pairs of socks for warmth may have hindered my circulation. When I awoke in the morning, I literally could not feel my little toe. I peeled off my socks and used my hands to start to warm up my ice-cold feet, paranoid thoughts racing through my mind.

Where do you even go to have a toe amputated? Herpetologists were supposed to lose digits to snakebites, not the cold.

Thankfully, after I stood up and started to walk around our rudimentary campsite, feeling slowly returned to my poor toe. It was a rough start to the day—which just so happened to be Friday the Thirteenth—and to the trip in general. Leaving our campsite among the pine trees, Taylor and I drove further south towards Sedona to start the day's adventure. The atmosphere of Sedona (and nearby Flagstaff) is very trendy and contemporary. Culturally it is a world away from Kanosh, but Sedona has pyros too, so Taylor and I took some time to stop before continuing our journey further south.

All thoughts of frozen toes and bad omens had melted away by midday when we came across the first snake of the trip, a beautiful black-tailed rattlesnake (*Crotalus molossus*), on our late morning hike. The snake was meandering across the trail when we came upon it, its scales glistening in the fragmented rays of sunlight that filtered through the trees. It hurried the rest of the way across the trail. The snake rattled a bit and briefly assumed a defensive posture—body coiled, neck cocked in an S-shape—to let us know we were taking too many pictures.

As the name suggests, the last few inches of a black-tailed rattlesnake (before the rattle) are completely black. The rest of the body is patterned with dark, diamond-shaped blotches separated by yellow and brown scales. Like other rattlesnakes, their scales are keeled—meaning each scale has a raised ridge in the middle—giving the whole snake a distinctly rough appearance. The species name, *molossus*, supposedly comes from a breed of watchdog known as the Molossus, though the comparison to a vicious hound seems a little excessive. No rattlesnake will bite you unprovoked. This particular black-tailed rattlesnake eventually got tired of staring at us and casually crawled away into the dry leaves further away from the trail.

Black-tailed rattlesnakes, which are only found in the southwestern US and Mexico, were one of the many species I was hoping to see for the first time on this trip, but it wasn't the main species Taylor and I were after. Surprise surprise, we were looking for pyros.

In all, our two-and-a-half week trip to Arizona and New Mexico had three purposes. The first was to visit the herpetology collections at the University of Arizona in Tucson and the University of New Mexico in Albuquerque to photograph specimens for a study we were conducting. Purpose number two was to collect some specimens for the Bean Life Science Museum herpetology collection, especially in an area of taxonomic uncertainty for pyros. And the third and final purpose? To have the selfish enjoyment of finding a slew of snakes I'd never had the chance to lay eyes on, like the black-tailed rattlesnake. It would have had a fourth purpose too—to find the first pyro of my life—but that had finally been accomplished the week before.

The trip was funded mainly through a $3,500 grant that I had applied for from *Western North American Naturalist*, a scientific journal linked to my college, Brigham Young University (BYU). I also had been awarded another, smaller grant directly through BYU for undergraduate research. The main grant proposal itself, which I wrote and Dr. Whiting edited, was only two pages of actual text. $1,750 per page of writing sounds like what you'd hand a best-selling author, not an undergraduate student. The proposal outlined the methods to be used in our study, which were based on previous studies on other coral snake mimics. In line with the guidelines of this specific grant, the proposal also explained how the project would utilize and add to museum collections.

This meant that this wasn't a pure "catch and release" trip; Taylor and I would also be preserving a small number of specimens. Museum collections have immense scientific value, but I knew I would struggle to stomach euthanizing. I was especially glad that my first pyro was able to be released alive, because any pyros we saw on this trip would be destined for a jar filled with ethanol.

PYRO

Our special scientific research permit from the state of Arizona had an allotment of sixteen mountain kingsnakes, as opposed to the five that would be allowed under a standard state hunting license. (Yes, a regular hunting license is required for the legal collection of herps in Arizona. Most states have some sort of permit system; always be aware of local laws.) Collecting was a main reason this whole trip had been funded, though I was worried that euthanizing even just one pyro was going to extinguish a part of my soul.

Taylor and I left in the middle of May, the best month for finding pyros. Unfortunately, the day that we left was unseasonably cold—the mountains around Provo even received a dusting of snow—so rather than stop at any Utah localities, we drove several hundred miles all the way to Flagstaff. Turns out Flagstaff wasn't much warmer, as my cold toes that morning could attest, and we continued working our way south. Outside of the black-tailed rattlesnake though, the first two days of the trip were relatively uneventful in terms of reptile sightings.

On the third day, we finally ran into another snake on my wish list: a patchnose snake (either *Salvadora hexalepis* or *Salvadora grahamiae*; I'm not sure which, for reasons that will be clear momentarily). In my mind, I had always thought that patchnose snakes were nocturnal and easygoing. I'm not sure where I got this ridiculous idea from, because it turns out that patchnoses are diurnal and lightning fast. This patchnose snake was sprawled out on a side road in the middle of the afternoon. Taylor slammed on the brakes, and I immediately jumped out to apprehend it.

Oftentimes when you drive up on a snake, it will kind of just chill on the road as you approach. But sometimes, the snake decides it wants nothing to do with the hulking metal object careening towards it and will immediately make a beeline for safety. This patchnose snake chose the second option. I dove out of the passenger seat as fast as possible, but the snake was already headed off the pavement. Lunging forward, I grabbed it and immediately felt a searing, stabbing sensation in my hand. The sharp jolt of pain loosened my grip and the snake careened away into the bushes. The small drops of blood now coming out of my fingers hadn't come from the teeth of the snake though. I'd been impaled by a thorny vine on the side of the road the snake had been crawling over.

Looking for safety, the patchnose snake immediately shot up into a large tree. Much like that striped whipsnake Taylor and I caught the previous September, it knew it would be safer off the ground. But although this tree was tall, it had a thick trunk and easily climbable branches, at least for an expert climber like Taylor. By this point, he had pulled the truck to the edge of the little-traveled road and hopped out to join the chase. After I pointed out where the snake was, Taylor glanced at the sturdy trunk and said, "I bet I can get it." I'd already seen Taylor climb sheer rock faces, so I didn't doubt his ability to get up the tree. But I wasn't sure if he could out-climb the snake.

As Taylor started up the tree, I tried to position myself directly beneath the snake. There were several large, prickly bushes surrounding the tree that would make things tricky if the snake decided to bail. Initially frozen in place among the branches, the snake began moving again as Taylor clambered up. After outmaneuvering him for several minutes, it eventually decided that it had had enough and dropped out of the tree. Despite my best efforts to position myself, the patchnose deliberately dropped into a bush that was well out of my reach and immediately slithered out of sight into the safety of the underbrush. While slightly disappointed, Taylor and I were happy to see any snake—this was only the second one of the trip so far.

Taking the patchnose sighting as a good sign, we spent the rest of the day and several hours into the night exploring the surrounding area. We were near Superior, which rivals the towns of Surprise, Carefree, and Why for most interesting city names in Arizona. Oak Flat campground was relatively primitive as far as campgrounds go, and there were plenty of rocky hillsides to explore in the area. There were also some good bouldering spots Taylor was eager to try out. Biologists use the term "saxicolous" to describe organisms that live on or around rocks; I think Taylor might qualify.

The patchnose snake was our only notable daytime encounter, but at night a closer inspection of the nearby pond revealed some endearing amphibians. In the darkness, the muddy edge was alive with red-spotted toads (*Anaxyrus punctatus*). These small toads grow a few inches long at most and rely on toxins instead of speed to deal with predators. True to the name, their gray or brown bodies are covered in red, wart-like spots. The red-spotted toads weren't the only nocturnal animals around the pond; quite a few bats were skimming across the water, both to drink and to catch airborne insects.

The other amphibians we found in the dark were barred tiger salamanders (*Ambystoma mavortium*). As adults, these chunky black and yellow striped salamanders are (usually) fully terrestrial, averaging six to eight inches in size. Some adults have enlarged teeth and are prone to cannibalism, which clashes with the permanent silly grin on their faces.

Taylor and I saw no adults, but the pond was full of larval salamanders. They had feathery external gills, large tails, and limbs that were little more than nubs. We didn't have any nets with us, which made trying to catch the swimming salamanders an adventure. Standing at the edge of the muddy shore, Taylor would gently slide his hands into the water underneath the unsuspecting amphibian, then slowly lift up. It took a few tries, but the technique eventually worked. We caught a couple larval salamanders and admired them briefly before returning them back to the water.

We also spent some time that night road cruising on the paved road near the campsite. The stretch of pavement wasn't very long though, and driving back and forth over and over soon became monotonous. After seeing the glint of the same beer can off to the side of the road for the umpteenth time, we called it a night. At least we had seen some new herps that day.

Besides, we hadn't yet reached the area where we needed to find a mountain kingsnake. Of course I would have loved to see one in the first few days of the trip, but finding one at our next destination was far more important. Now, for this to make sense, I'm going to have to open the can of worms that I have procrastinated mentioning. There's a bit of taxonomic controversy regarding pyros, and Taylor and I were hoping to shed some light on the debate. Buckle up.

To start with some context, let's rewind the clock back to 1940 (and I apologize in advance for the oncoming deluge of scientific names; remember, don't be intimidated just because they are in italics). This year, the famous American herpetologist Edward H. Taylor described a new species of mountain kingsnake, *Lampropeltis knoblochi*, based on two specimens from Chihuahua, Mexico, collected by his friend Irving Knobloch. Edward Taylor's paper notes the similarity of this species to *Lampropeltis pyromelana* (our wonderful pyros), though the new species had unique "zig-zag lateral white line[s]" running along each side. The paper even includes a black-and-white photograph of the holotype specimen, a nice touch for such an old publication.

Thirteen years later, Wilmer W. Tanner, a herpetologist who did his PhD under the direction of Edward Taylor, published a paper on the phylogeny of *Lampropeltis pyromelana*. Describing subspecies was very much in vogue at the time, and Tanner himself published many such descriptions. Back then, the best way to determine the evolutionary relatedness of reptiles was by counting scales; the number of scales, especially those around the head, are mostly consistent between members of the same species but vary between different species. If you think tallying hundreds of small scales on a preserved snake sounds tedious, you'd be right. But that didn't deter herpetologists like Tanner from counting lots and lots of them, something that was only possible thanks to the many specimens collected and preserved in museums. It was based on scale counts that Tanner described two new subspecies of *Lampropeltis pyromelana*: *woodini* and *infralabialis*.

In that 1953 paper, Tanner also recommended that *Lampropeltis knoblochi* be treated as a subspecies of *Lampropeltis pyromelana*, arguing that the two weren't different enough to be considered separate species. Tanner had examined the two specimens of *Lampropeltis knoblochi* that Edward Taylor had used as well as additional specimens from Mexico, some of which he felt had intermediate characteristics between *knoblochi* and the new *woodini* subspecies of *pyromelana*—indicating that the two weren't distinct species. This left one species (*Lampropeltis pyromelana*) with four subspecies (*knoblochi*, *woodini*, *infralabialis*, and the nominate subspecies, *pyromelana*).

Pyro taxonomy stayed stable for several decades, sticking to Tanner's recommendations of one species with four subspecies, until the twenty-first century. This was when molecular data burst onto the scene and, for better or for worse, began to revolutionize biology. Sequences of DNA—the wonderful molecule that is the code of life—can be much better at showing phylogenetic relationships than scale counts alone (though in the first few years, sequencing was outrageously expensive and not advanced, which meant that some of the earliest snake genetic studies were based on insufficient data). With the increasing prevalence of molecular data nowadays, herpetology has generally moved away from using subspecies. The overarching idea behind the shift is that the species should represent the fundamental unit of evolution, and if a subspecies is a distinct evolutionary lineage it should be elevated to full species status—and eliminated if not.

In 2011, the modern taxonomists came for the pyros. Armed with their newfangled DNA sequencing machines, they were hellbent on sowing chaos throughout the world of herpetology to advance their own careers. These lab coat hotshots had never counted a scale in their life, let alone caught a wild snake, yet they thought they had all the expertise necessary to say which subspecies names would be immortalized and which would be sent to their graves.

Well, at least that's how some herp hobbyists have portrayed the split that happened to *Lampropeltis pyromelana* (and many others). The 2011 paper is titled "Speciation at the Mogollon Rim in the Arizona Mountain Kingsnake (*Lampropeltis pyromelana*)," written by Frank Burbrink and five other authors. After sequencing three genes (two nuclear and one mitochondrial) from forty-one specimens, the authors determined that the species *Lampropeltis pyromelana* contained two distinct evolutionary lineages that had diverged a long time ago. They recommended splitting the species into two along the geographic divide between the lineages, with the northern lineage retaining the original name, *Lampropeltis pyromelana*, and the southern lineage being dubbed *Lampropeltis knoblochi*.

But there was a problem that upset countless herpers. Previously, the *knoblochi* subspecies, with its chain-like side pattern, was visually distinct from the other three (though some questionable "intergrades" exist), so much so that some had called for it to be considered a separate species like it was originally. But the Burbrink paper had lumped in all the *woodini* and some of the *pyromelana* subspecies along with *knoblochi* and called it all one species. With no morphological characteristics to distinguish between what was now considered *L. pyromelana* and *L. knoblochi*, all that was left was an invisible geographic boundary plucked out of thin air by some scientists in a lab.

One poignant comment by iNaturalist user "@bobbyfingers" (who has since been banned from the platform) on an observation he felt should be *L. pyromelana* accurately summarizes the distaste many field herpers feel towards DNA-based splits. He wrote: "The more folks that come to realize that every shoddily-researched, poorly field-sampled piece of scrap paper that blows outta some dumpster behind some nameless 'Ivory Tower of Academia' isn't necessarily herpetological 'Holy Writ' - the better." Harsh, man.

Taxon slander isn't unique to this species, though this is one of the thornier splits I'm aware of. Part of what has driven a wedge between academic herpetologists and hobbyist enthusiasts is the increasing prevalence of molecular work. Scale counts and physical descriptions are a lot easier to grasp than the advanced computer techniques that turn strings of A's, T's, C's, and G's (the four nucleotides that make up DNA) into evolutionary trees. For those whose knowledge is based entirely on field experience, it can be hard to trust results from a herpetologist who spends more time in a lab coat or in front of a computer than in the wilderness.

The "Ivory Tower of Academia" also communicates in a language and fashion that is not only hard to understand, but often trapped behind paywalls. For those not affiliated with an academic institution that pays exorbitant access fees to many scientific journals, it can be difficult to read articles for free (though there are ways around this). More journals are publishing open -articles, but this still isn't the norm and it often means that the scientists themselves are paying extra fees to get their work published. It shouldn't be surprising that the gap between the two sides is growing if there isn't effective communication going on. Most of the attacks posted on iNaturalist or on various forums regarding the *pyromelana* split are personal rather than scientific criticisms. It's not hard to tell that many commenters haven't actually read the paper they are criticizing.

I personally am inclined to trust the results of the Burbrink paper and acknowledge the split. Before any of you die-hard field herpers throw this book in the trash can and light it on fire, please hear me out.

While the authors did not mention scale counts or any sort of physical characteristics, they did have multiple lines of evidence. First, they looked at multiple genes; one mitochondrial locus and two nuclear ones. Some of the early papers that used molecular data to split species used only one mitochondrial gene, which is now known to be insufficient, true. But using three genes—like in the Burbrink paper—increases the accuracy of the analysis and should, generally, be trusted (though with sequencing costs decreasing every year, studies today typically use more than just three). Secondly, in addition to their genetic work, the authors also used climatic data to model the ecological niches of the two species, showing *L. pyromelana* to occupy a slightly cooler, wetter, and more seasonal environment than *L. knoblochi*.

Additionally, the proposed boundary between the two lineages—the southern edge of the Colorado Plateau—has been shown to be a dividing line in several other unrelated groups as well, lending more support to their conclusions. The boundary may have been unexpected given the previous subspecies arrangements, but it still followed a reasonable geographic pattern. Lastly, it is important to remember that the authors of this and other taxonomic papers want the same thing as casual field herpers—to better understand these beautiful creatures. Just because some of that process of understanding takes place in a lab doesn't invalidate it. I will admit that I am not a genetics expert, but if it is a split accepted by the taxonomic experts at the Society for the Study of Amphibians and Reptiles (SSAR, the largest herpetological organization), they're not just blowing smoke.

But although I may side with the "Ivory Tower of Academia" on this taxonomic controversy, there is one legitimate complaint that Taylor and I hoped to address on our trip. The Burbrink study that had split *L. pyromelana* and *L. knoblochi* calculated that the two lineages had diverged prior to the Pleistocene about 2.5 million years ago and that there had been little to no gene flow since, meaning that there was no migration and thus no interbreeding of individuals of the two species. However, there was a hundred-mile gap in between the southernmost *L. pyromelana* and the northernmost *L. knoblochi* they sampled—and in reality there are some populations of mountain kingsnake in between that weren't included. If there was recent gene flow between the two proposed species, it was going to be in these unsampled populations—meaning there was a chance the divergence between the two lineages wasn't as deep as originally found.

Thus, one of our trip objectives was to find a mountain kingsnake within this gap area. If successful, Taylor and I could take a tissue sample and sequence the same three genes from the Burbrink study back in the lab, allowing it to be compared with samples north and south of it and hopefully put (some of) the debate to rest. If the mountain kingsnakes in this area were closely related to those further south—which makes the most sense biogeographically—it would strongly support the split of the Burbrink paper. But if they were closely related to the kingsnakes further north, or equally related to both, changes might be in order.

After a few days of camping, driving, and herping in the northern half of Arizona, Taylor and I finally arrived at the wonderful Madrean Sky Islands, one of the most biodiverse areas of North America. Sometimes referred to as the Madrean Archipelago, this area is a collection of fifty-five isolated mountains that rise out of the surrounding desert in Arizona, New Mexico, and Mexico. They're referred to as sky islands because, from a biological perspective, many of the organisms on them are isolated, unable to cross the harsh desert that lies between them—just like how the ocean isolates terrestrial organisms found on regular islands. The controversial Burbrink study had samples from the sky islands at the southern border of Arizona, but not any of the sky islands further north. These northern sky islands are the gap area, and our main targets were Mount Lemmon and Mount Graham.

I've seen a lot of mountains in my life, and I used to think that calling a mountain a sky island was a quaint, poetic exaggeration. But having now seen them in person, I say they deserve the title, even if it sounds overly romanticized. Surrounded by miles of flat, parched desert, these massive mountains erupt thousands of feet into the sky. And the biological communities of these sky islands really reinforce their distinctiveness. Rather than coral, cacti dot the dry landscape. As you move up in elevation, the plant life of the sky island shifts gradually. The hardy desert plants give way to oaks and chaparral. Go further up and you'll find pines, and eventually, fir trees. You can get lost in a green forest and completely forget you're technically surrounded by desert on all sides if you just go a few miles out.

When the earth was cooler—the planet has undergone many climatic fluctuations in the past—species once restricted to the mountains could intermingle in the cooler lowland areas. But when global temperatures warmed again, the area in between the "islands" was transformed back into desert, constricting the ranges of the less heat-tolerant species to the mountains. These fluctuations, combined with the variety of habitats available and the difficulty for most species to move between them, make sky islands hotspots for endemic species—those that are found in one place and that place only.

The first sky island Taylor and I visited was Mount Graham, one of the northeasternmost islands of the Madrean Archipelago. Though it was in the sampling gap, I consider it valid to classify the mountain kingsnakes in this area and anywhere south to be *Lampropeltis knoblochi*, not *pyromelana* (until proven otherwise), so I won't refer to them as pyros. Since "knob" doesn't roll off the tongue as naturally as pyro, I'll stick with the more general term of "mountain kingsnake."

In addition to mountain kingsnakes, I was also hoping to spot a twin-spotted rattlesnake (*Crotalus pricei*), which I consider the cutest of the over fifty species of rattlesnake. Rattlesnakes are iconic serpents, but "cute" isn't how I'd describe most species. Twin-spotted rattlesnakes though? Absolutely adorable. These miniature rattlers barely get two feet long, tipped with a tiny rattle. These light brown or bluish gray snakes have pairs of dark spots—hence the name—running down their backs. Twin-spotted rattlesnakes even have an endearing dark stripe on their face that goes through their eyes, almost like evolution got carried away with the eye shadow.

PYRO

It was a blazing hot Arizona afternoon on the valley floor as Taylor and I approached Mount Graham. The road up the mountain is paved, and we climbed rapidly in elevation. By the time we got out of the car, we were roughly eight thousand feet in the air and the temperature was perfect. Mount Graham is more than ten thousand feet at its peak, but that is a little too chilly.

Aside from the incredibly stunning view of the sea of desert from off Mount Graham, this stop was a total bust. We didn't see any snakes, which wasn't too surprising given our luck on the trip so far. But the only vertebrates we could find any trace of were birds. There were no lizards, even though everywhere else in Arizona was crawling with them. There were no fish or frogs to be found in the creeks either. I don't even think we saw a squirrel the whole afternoon.

In retrospect, we should have stopped a couple thousand feet lower—the areas we explored were all between seven thousand and eight thousand feet, the upper limit of suitable mountain kingsnake territory—but we were drawn to the breathtaking view near the top. We might have gotten lucky if we had simply stayed longer, but after a few hours of absolutely nothing we decided it was time to move on.

After a week of camping, Taylor and I were in need of a warm shower and a night in a real bed. And we were in luck, because we were finally close to Tucson, where my aunt Emily and uncle Brandon lived. They were generous enough to allow us to stay with them and their two wonderful kids while we were in the area. This meant we could look presentable before our scheduled visit to the herpetology collection at the University of Arizona. Their house also served as our base camp for our time in Tucson, as the city is situated at the base of Mount Lemmon, our main target area for the gap between *L. pyromelana* and *L. knoblochi*.

Our photographing at the University of Arizona herpetology collection went smoothly, but unfortunately the same can't be said for our snake finding on Mount Lemmon. We spent many long hours on that mountain, hoping to catch a glimpse of a red, black, and white kingsnake.

Unlike Mount Graham, Mount Lemmon had plenty of lizards, though catching them was another story. For some species, like tree lizards (*Urosaurus ornatus*), catching them is accomplished easily enough by hand. These small, grayish lizards will usually let you approach within an arm's length, at which point a quick swoop of the hand is enough to pin them. A look at the underside reveals bright colors on a seemingly drab lizard: a blue belly along with green, orange, or blue on the neck. When they display to other lizards, especially when defending territory, they can suck in the sides of their body to show the colors underneath.

While tree lizards are easily apprehended, it was nigh impossible to get close to some other lizards Taylor and I saw on Mount Lemmon. The worst offenders were the whiptails (genus *Aspidoscelis*). Named for their long, whip-like tail, there are over forty species of these slender lizards found throughout North America. Whiptails are impossible to sneak up on, remaining warily out of reach at all times and rarely holding still for even a second. These lizards don't have the endurance to run a hundred-yard dash—lacking a diaphragm, they can't breathe and run at the same time—but I can guarantee you'd lose a five-yard race to a whiptail.

I had caught a plateau striped whiptail (*Aspidoscelis velox*) a few days earlier near Sedona. Taylor and I chased it back and forth multiple times before the lizard finally ran out of steam. Usually though, it's hard to get close enough to even take a decent picture of a whiptail. This makes identifying the different species an absolute nightmare. There are only two native species of whiptail in Utah but there are ten in Arizona, many of which look very similar. (By the end of the trip, I practically gave up trying to differentiate them; who let the lizards that were the hardest to identify also be the hardest to catch?) But that didn't stop Taylor and me from attempting to apprehend one every so often.

PYRO

Our best whiptail encounter on Mount Lemmon came on a hike relatively low in elevation, a rocky area with more cacti than trees. Taylor and I started early in the morning, hoping to beat the heat. An hour or so into the hike, we were chasing a good-sized whiptail close to the dry trail. The lizard was on the adjacent slope above us, the ideal position. Trust me, catching a lizard that is at eye level is much easier than bending down to grab one. Despite a couple of near misses, the whiptail remained stubbornly out of reach as we chased it around a rocky outcropping. After another unsuccessful lunge, the lizard ran down the hillside, over the trail, and near some bushes on the other side. Hoping that it was almost tired out, we scrambled down after it.

As my eyes were scanning the hillside, trying to relocate the whiptail, I noticed something far more interesting. Coiled at the base of a tall bush was a large, dark snake. "Taylor! Snake!" I yelled, forgetting all about the lizard. The snake hadn't moved at first, but quickly tried to shoot up into the bush. I was able to grab the long snake before it got too tangled, though I quickly realized that this variety of whipsnake was much feistier than the ones I was used to.

It was a Sonoran whipsnake (*Masticophis bilineatus*), and it meant business. I had the tail of the lanky snake in my left hand, but any attempt to move my right hand near the upper body resulted in an open-mouth lunge towards it. While they lack giant fangs, nonvenomous snakes like whipsnakes have dozens of razor-sharp teeth, and the bigger the snake, the more it can shred your flesh. Thankfully I had my trusty snake hook, which looks like a golf club but with a blue metal "U" at the end instead of a club. Usually my snake hook just gets used to prod lizards that have hidden in a bush, or occasionally shepherd a venomous snake off the road. With most harmless snakes using a hook is unnecessary, but it came in handy with this whipsnake. I was able to rest the upper third of the snake's body on the metal hook while grasping the tail in my other hand. It was an impressive physical specimen, measuring over four feet long with a diameter twice as thick as the striped whipsnakes (which belong to the same genus) I was used to catching in Utah.

Sonoran whipsnakes might have been named striped whipsnakes if the name wasn't already taken. Their species name, *bilineatus*, refers to the two white lines that run on either side of the snake's body. These diurnal snakes are blue-gray or olive-green on top with a yellow underbelly. Like other whipsnakes, they are just as comfortable in the limbs of trees as they are on the ground. This individual wouldn't hold still for pictures in our hands, so Taylor and I let it clamber into the tall bush it had initially been coiled at the base of. It nimbly climbed inside, camouflaging quite well with the surrounding branches. After a few good pictures, Taylor and I moved on, allowing the snake to go about its day. I'm sure it would have better odds of catching whiptail lizards than we would.

Taylor and I went on a multitude of other hikes on Mount Lemmon over the next several days. Mountain kingsnakes have been found at lower elevations than where we found the whipsnake, but we figured our chances would be better in more forested habitats higher up. Yet despite days of repeated searches at varying locations and at different times, Mount Lemmon refused to reveal a mountain kingsnake, leaving us no closer to resolving the ugly taxonomic controversy.

Our first objective of the trip—to visit the herpetology collections at the University of Arizona and University of New Mexico—was going smoothly; one down, one to go. The second objective though—to get a tissue sample from a mountain kingsnake in the sampling gap between *L. pyromelana* and *L. knoblochi*—was not going well. Rather than get frustrated though, Taylor and I decided to temporarily turn our attention to the third, less scientifically meaningful objective: to see as many amazing new snakes as possible. As pretty as the scenery was, it was time for a quick break from the mountains.

SIX

Into the Desert

Surrounding the sky islands of southern Arizona and northern Mexico is the iconic Sonoran Desert. The landscape is bone dry for most of the year aside from the torrential summer monsoons, and the plant life tends to be sparse and prickly. Yet despite the stereotypes often associated with deserts, the Sonoran is anything but desolate—especially when it comes to reptiles. Taylor and I were disappointed at the meager number of snakes we had seen so far and were eager to try some new habitat, even if it was unsuitable for mountain kingsnakes. It was time to swap the pine trees of Mount Lemmon for the towering saguaro cacti of the Sonoran to see what we could find during a night in the desert.

We arrived at Saguaro National Park—a place home to an incredible number of these green desert giants—in the late afternoon. Many of the diurnal desert lizard species were out and about, enjoying the rays of warm sunshine still streaming down from the Arizona sky. Taylor was hoping to find a desert iguana (*Dipsosaurus dorsalis*), a species of large, whitish lizard that is primarily a vegetarian. He saw a brief glimpse, not much more than a flash, of one darting down a burrow, but that was it.

PYRO

As we wandered across the dry landscape, another fast but much more common lizard species we saw was the greater earless lizard (*Cophosaurus texanus*). These agile lizards follow the same general color scheme of many desert lizards—drab on top, flashy on bottom. The blue and black stripes on their flanks and underside are often accented with yellow or orange, creating a kaleidoscope of colors.

Greater earless lizards have a peculiar method of communicating to potential predators just how fast they are: their tail. In this species and a couple others, the underside of the tail has alternating bars of black and white. When they see a predator, greater earless lizards will flick their tail in the air, exposing the stripes, signaling *Hey you! I see you. Don't even think about trying to catch me!* It's quite an endearing display in my opinion, though it sure feels like you're getting teased.

Scientists have even shown that the patterning on the tail corresponds to the speed of individual lizards (in biology, this is referred to as an "honest signal"). Lizards with higher sprint speeds have more black on the underside of their tails. Females will even prefer males with more black—they want those fast genes for their offspring. It is unclear if predators notice the amount of black and use it to decide if chasing the lizard is worth it—I'd bet most don't—but predators certainly notice the tail-flicking display itself. It's a situation that happened countless times while Taylor and I were in Arizona. You get close to an earless lizard, but before you come within reach, it jets away. The lizard stops after a little ways, turns around to look at you, and then casually flicks its tail in the air. *Yeah, that's what I thought. Can't catch me, slowpoke!*

As the sun was starting to set, we headed to a nature area northwest of Tucson. Close to a subdivision and with a large artificial pond nearby, it wasn't the wildest place I've looked for snakes. And yet it was here that we found perhaps the most interesting snake of the entire trip. The pond itself was swarming with mosquitoes, so we followed the dirt path away from the water.

As Taylor walked along the wide path, he spotted a pink, limbless creature wiggling on the ground. It wasn't very graceful in its movements, and Taylor stared at it for a few seconds before he realized its true identity. The small, elongated animal superficially resembled a worm, but this was no worm. It was a blind snake.

Blind snakes are a group of several families that are only distantly related to the rest of their snake relatives. One of their key defining features is their vision, or rather lack thereof—bet you didn't see that coming. Their eyes are covered with opaque scales, meaning that they basically can only differentiate light and dark. Turns out that working eyes are an unnecessary luxury when you live underground; all you need to know is when you have accidentally stumbled into the horrors of broad daylight. The poor snake probably had a heart attack when it was suddenly illuminated by Taylor's flashlight beam.

This individual was a western blind snake (*Rena humilis*), which is found in the deserts of the southwestern US and Mexico. Blind snakes are also sometimes referred to as thread snakes, as their bodies aren't much thicker than a string. Imagine a spaghetti noodle covered in pink scales and you've got a pretty accurate picture of what Taylor saw wriggling in the dirt. These small subterranean specialists mainly eat ants, termites, and any other invertebrates they encounter underground. The smooth, scaly bodies of blind snakes slide easily through the tunnels they dig with their reinforced skulls. I have no clue why they are pink.

Their skulls are a key difference between blind snakes and most other snakes. The vast majority of snakes have super-flexible skulls, an adaptation that makes them swallowing machines. Blind snakes have a thick, rigid skull that is perfect for burrowing, but as a consequence have a much more limited gape.

Neither Taylor nor I had ever seen a blind snake before, and we were thoroughly mesmerized by the find. As it squirmed in our hands, we noticed a strange sensation. The snake was oddly wet. It is a misconception that snakes are slimy—but this one was.

The source of the moisture was the inordinate amount of musk that the blind snake was excreting onto our hands. Thankfully, the blind snake's musk was significantly less pungent than most snakes, though I was impressed that an animal that weighed only a few grams could make both of my hands wet—and I wasn't even the first person to handle it.

As a group, blind snakes are extremely understudied. Finding regular snakes is hard enough, but finding ones that spend almost all their time underground is even harder. Yet there is one species of blind snake that scientists do know a fair amount about since it insists on popping up everywhere: the Brahminy blind snake (*Indotyphlops braminus*). Brahminy blind snakes are similar in size and shape to the western blind snake Taylor and I found, though the two are in separate families and are not close evolutionary relatives. Native to Southeast Asia, these snakes have colonized warm areas from Hawaii to Florida to Africa. They are greatly assisted by their ability to reproduce asexually (without mating), meaning it only takes one to start a new population, but that's a tangent for another time.

Brahminy blind snakes are also one of only a few species of snake that don't always eat their prey whole; most of the other four thousand or so species swallow their prey in one go. As a 2015 study conducted by Japanese scientists showed, Brahminy blind snakes will actually decapitate termites and eat only the body. The paper has some hilarious photos of a snake grasping a termite in its tiny mouth and dragging it against the ground to tear the termite's head off. The snakes only tore off the heads about half the time, but since the head and mandibles were usually pooped out undigested, the scientists concluded that they decapitate the termites just to remove an indigestible part.

While termite decapitation hasn't been documented in the western blind snake (yet), it has been documented in one of their close relatives, the Texas blind snake (*Rena dulcis*). Given how poorly studied blind snakes as a group are, I'm sure there are many more interesting things to discover about them.

Knowing that the herpetology collection back at the Bean Museum had very few blind snakes, we stashed it in a small black bag to euthanize later. Part of the reason the trip had been funded was to bring back specimens, even if Taylor and I both were reluctant to do so. We understood the value of scientific collections—we not only were conducting a research project that utilized museum specimens, but we also literally worked in a museum collection—but it just seemed both unfair to the snake and arrogant of us humans. Taylor and I felt better knowing that blind snakes aren't truly rare; they are simply rarely seen because they don't often come to the surface.

We made it back to the truck well after dark. Rather than drive directly back to my relative's house, we opted for some desert road cruising for the next couple of hours and were not disappointed. Night had just fallen, and the evening air was still warm. The black pavement was even warmer and would retain the heat from the day's sun for many hours. This heat is a wonderful temptation to snakes, who can warm up easily on its surface—assuming they don't get squished by a moving car. Taylor and I just had to hope that the first vehicle to reach any snake on the road was ours.

It wasn't long before we saw the outline of a snake stretched out on the road. Taylor jumped out, ready to apprehend the snake. I pulled the truck over to the dirt shoulder of the rural road, eager to find out what we had happened across. Turns out, neither of us recognized the small, brown serpent in his hands. It was only about a foot long, with alternating light and dark brown patches on its back. The distinct upturned snout of the snake seemed familiar, but the snake wasn't a patchnose; I had made sure to look up all the patchnose snakes in my field guide in case we ran into one again. Part of me thought it was a spotted leafnose snake (*Phyllorhynchus decurtatus*), which I could recall seeing in the Bean

Museum herpetology collection, but I knew that wasn't quite right. I'd been puzzled by lizards—especially all those whiptails—a lot recently, but it had been a long, long time since I'd been stumped by a snake.

The mysterious brown snake was a little jittery in our hands but overall was rather ambivalent about being snatched off the warm road. We sexed the snake—male—and took some photographs. After later consulting my field guide, I realized it was a saddled leafnose snake (*Phyllorhynchus browni*). I had the right genus, but the wrong species. This genus contains only two species, and the saddled leafnose is the much rarer of the two—which is probably why I could only remember the spotted variety.

Leafnose snakes, as the name suggests, are named for their endearingly upturned noses. Their genus name, *Phyllorhynchus*, even translates to "leaf nose" in Greek. Technically it's not their nose—their nostrils are elsewhere—but rather the extra-wide scale at the front of their face that is vaguely leaf-shaped. This enlarged rostral scale is an adaptation for burrowing, not unlike the iconic snout of the more well-known hognose snakes (genus *Heterodon*).

Saddled leafnose snakes are secretive, nocturnal snakes. These desert dwellers are thought to mainly eat lizards and their eggs, though not much is known about them. In retrospect, it was the rarest snake we encountered on the entire trip, at least based on total numbers of sightings posted to iNaturalist. Whoops. That probably would have been a good one to bring back for the collection. In my defense, its leafnose face was too adorable to euthanize anyway. We released it a safe distance from the dangerous pavement and continued on.

It wasn't too long after the leafnose snake that we saw our next serpent, though unfortunately we weren't the first car to come across it. The hefty snake, which was immediately recognizable as a rattlesnake, was still twitching as Taylor gingerly pulled it off the road with his metal snake tongs. We stared dejectedly at the poor western diamondback rattlesnake (*Crotalus atrox*) as it took its last few breaths. After it had ceased moving entirely, we put the unlucky snake in an empty five-gallon bucket to pickle later. While I felt uneasy about sacrificing a perfectly healthy snake for the sake of science, I had no such qualms about collecting one that was already dead.

Thankfully, we soon encountered a western diamondback that was still alive and kicking. Errr, slithering? Snakes can't kick whether they're dead or alive. I pulled the truck off to the side of the road, trying to avoid driving over any cacti, while Taylor moved the snake off of the pavement with the long aluminum tongs. It coiled itself near the base of a prickly pear cactus, rattling angrily. Although they are named for the diamond-like pattern on their back, the white and black zebra-esque stripes just below the rattle are a more distinctive feature to identify these snakes. Western diamondbacks are extremely common in their range, but as someone who had never been inside their range, I was thrilled to see one.

The diamondback was less thrilled to see me, continuing to voice its displeasure through its trademark warning system. Rattlesnakes can't talk, but you could roughly translate the sound of a rattle to *Alright buddy, back off and no one has to get hurt*. Ten times out of ten the snake would rather be left alone than bite a person. The rattle itself is not living tissue, but rather is made of loosely interlocking layers of scales that produce a loud noise when the tail is vibrated.

Each time a rattler sheds its skin, it adds an additional segment to the rattle, though segments break off occasionally. Though the rattle is unique to rattlesnakes and is a trait that only evolved once, tail shaking is actually a remarkably common defensive behavior in snakes. Many snakes will vibrate their tails when threatened, including the majority of colubrids (the largest family of snakes) and almost all vipers, the family that includes rattlesnakes. The rattlesnakes just took things to the next level.

It's not just the rattle that has made rattlesnakes one of the most successful groups of snakes in North America. Western diamondbacks and all other pit vipers (subfamily Crotalinae) are heat-seeking missiles of destruction for warm-blooded creatures. Their vision is supplemented by the heat-sensitive pits at the front of their face. Located on either side of the upper jaw, these pin-head-sized pits face forward and are able to detect minute temperature differences thanks to a thin membrane that is sensitive to infrared heat. It's basically like having a thermal imaging camera built into your face. Studies have shown that they not only use the pits to detect their warm-blooded prey, but that they also use them when selecting basking sites. I imagine that the whole road must glow in their heat-vision, so it makes sense that rattlesnakes are some of the most frequently seen snakes while road cruising.

Taylor and I drove back and forth for a few miles on the stretch of road where we had found the live western diamondback. Cars were few and far between, and both sides of the road were flanked by desert vegetation. Perhaps we'd get to see a desert kingsnake (*Lampropeltis splendida*), a lowland-dwelling relative of the mountain kingsnakes we couldn't seem to find. Desert kings are a splendid black and yellow, a color scheme not unlike the road we were on. Or maybe we'd find a Sonoran lyre snake (*Trimorphodon lambda*), a skinny, brown, nocturnal, and mildly venomous snake I would have loved to see.

We stopped for several false alarms. Sticks, bits of tire rubber, odd smudges on the pavement—anything can resemble a snake when you're driving at night with snakes on the mind. Anyone who has been road cruising before knows the feeling of slamming on the brakes, not sure if that was a piece of trash at the edge of the road or—fingers crossed—a snake. My least favorites are rope snakes, which can perfectly resemble an actual snake when viewed from a moving vehicle.

After a few passes, we decided to head back for the night. Staying out too late would make getting up early enough the next morning difficult, and looking for snakes in the heat of an Arizona afternoon is neither enjoyable nor particularly productive. But on our way back, the desert had one last treat in store for us.

As we were coming down a hill, a large, dark object on the road came into view. I braked hard, and we squinted through the headlights, attempting to recognize what was in front of us.

"Snake?" Taylor said uncertainly.

"Uhhh, alligator lizard?" I said, still unsure at what the creature—which definitely had legs—was. Then something in both of our minds clicked simultaneously. We hadn't been expecting to find one, but it should have been immediately obvious.

"GILA!" we shouted in unison. Throwing caution to the wind, we both flew out of the truck and headed towards the oversized lizard crossing the road. Without space to fully pull off—there was no shoulder, only a steep hillside—I threw on the hazard flashers and hoped no one would be flying down the road too fast behind us.

The orange and black behemoth of a lizard was casually strolling in the other lane, forked tongue flicking in and out, as we ran up. It ignored us as we shined our flashlights at it, clearly not viewing us as a threat. And why would it? Gila monsters (*Heloderma suspectum*) are the largest native lizards in the United States, closer in size to a small dog than they are to other local lizards. They also have the distinction of being the only venomous lizard in the country, and one of only a few in the world. When the Gila monster was described by Edward Cope—the same fossil-feuding, formalin-drinking scientist who described pyros—in 1869, he gave it the species name *suspectum* because he suspected that the lizard was venomous, given its teeth and what he assumed were large venom glands.

The venom, while not lethal to an adult human, is said to be incredibly painful. Unlike the rattlesnakes we'd seen earlier, Gila monsters don't have hollow, needle-like fangs to deliver their venom. Instead, their sharp teeth are simply grooved. As the lizard gnaws on the prey or predator, the venom oozes from glands in the lower jaw into the wound. Maybe not as efficient as fangs, but more badass for sure. Their imposing orange and black armor, big claws, and dragon-esque face further complement the monster image, though I refer to them as monsters in the most affectionate way possible.

Gila monsters are also excellent at conserving energy, which is a nice way of saying they are lazy lizards. A two-year study published in 2014 collected some fascinating data on wild monsters in southern Nevada that illustrated this. The researchers captured a total of nine adult Gila monsters and anesthetized them in a lab to implant radio transmitters. The transmitters were used to locate the lizards multiple times a day in the active season and a few times per week the rest of the year. Usually the scientists would give the monsters a wide berth and just record the location, behavior, and temperature. But periodically they also would recapture them to measure their mass and take blood samples in order to measure the metabolism and water use of the lizards.

The results showed that the tracked Gila monsters spent the vast majority of their time underground, which was unsurprising. What was more surprising was that they only used about half of the energy expected of a desert lizard of their size. Based on the researcher's estimations, the monsters in the study on average used only 775 milliliters of water and 3,766 kilojoules of energy—which works out to roughly 900 calories—annually. Imagine: If you could live for a whole year on one bottle of water and a dozen chocolate chip cookies, you'd basically be a Gila monster without the venom.

The individual Taylor and I found that night was a full-grown adult, measuring well over a foot long. Like all Gila monsters, its orange and black skin is covered in bumps, almost like a bunch of BBs embedded in the skin. These bumps are osteoderms, knobs of bone that literally translates to "bone skin." If any animal's skin looks absolutely bulletproof, it's the Gila monster's. (And, not to leave anyone out, the other species of beaded lizards in the family Helodermatidae have equally tough skin.) I didn't touch this

Gila—I wasn't about to break the law just to personally find out how painful their venom is—but having held a captive Gila monster, I can say their skin feels otherworldly. Given their impressive defensive and offensive capabilities, it's no wonder that the Gila monster that night paid us little heed. It kept walking leisurely, unaware that its defenses would be no match for a car tire.

Thankfully, the Gila monster made it off the road before any cars came. I say thankfully because I probably would have stood defiantly in between it and any moving vehicle. Gila monsters are a protected species in every state they occur in, but not all drivers are paying attention to a small, dark creature crossing the road at night. We waited, gawking in sheer awe, until the monster was safely off the road and clambering down the hillside. It meandered off into the night, probably looking for a nest to raid.

Exhausted after a long day, Taylor and I eventually arrived back at my aunt and uncle's place. Before we could go to bed, there were some specimens to take care of. We set up our makeshift workstation on the tailgate of the truck. Since the rattlesnake was already dead, all we had to do was extract a tissue sample and inject the specimen with formalin. Livers are, for some reason, especially good for extracting high quality DNA for later, and are thus the preferred tissue to sample. I had made an incision, found the liver, and snipped a piece, after which Taylor went to work injecting the rattlesnake with formalin.

Wanting to show the blind snake to my young cousins the next morning, we opted to not euthanize it that night. Snakes are notorious escape artists, so I made sure to double knot the cloth snake bag and put it at the bottom of a drawstring bag. Unfortunately, I underestimated my opponent, as we awoke the next morning to discover that the sneaky blind snake had escaped. It had likely wiggled its way to freedom through a hole in one bag and through the knot in the other. We were initially worried it would be stuck inside the house, but we searched the whole room unsuccessfully and figured if it could escape the bags it could make it out of the house. I am a terrible nephew—in exchange for free housing, food, and showers, I let loose a snake (albeit a totally innocuous one physically incapable of harming a human) in their house. I didn't even know how to bring it up, and figuring that we'd hear about it if it turned up in the next couple of days, I didn't. I guess the cat is out of the bag now.

The next day, Taylor and I left the Tucson area and headed east. We were scheduled to visit the herpetology collection at the Museum of Southwestern Biology in Albuquerque, New Mexico, so it was time to say goodbye to Arizona and Mount Lemmon for now. We hadn't found our mountain kingsnake there yet, but we would be back after a brief stint in New Mexico.

We eventually arrived at the Museum of Southwestern Biology, located on the campus of the University of New Mexico. Our contact person here was Tom Giermakowski, a herpetologist involved with a wide variety of amphibian and reptile research. Like our stop at the University of Arizona's herpetology collection, Taylor and I were here to photograph a bunch of kingsnakes and coral snakes to investigate an evolutionary puzzle regarding mimicry (more details on this in chapter eight).

Compared to the University of Arizona, the University of New Mexico was crawling with herpetologists. Tucson is a mecca for retired reptile enthusiasts, yet the University of Arizona didn't have a single herpetologist on staff at the time. It was the mammalogist, who was in charge of the mammal, bird, and herp collections, that showed us around. Things at the University of New Mexico were very different. Tom, who was one of several herpetologists on staff, gave us a nice campus tour and introduced us to several graduate students and an undergrad involved with herpetological research. Although I wasn't interested in moving to Albuquerque for graduate school, I was impressed by the welcoming atmosphere at the University of New Mexico. Their herpetology collection was comfortably familiar too—rows of movable shelves filled with jars of specimens in a poorly lit basement.

Our photographing didn't take long, and by the afternoon we were headed out of Albuquerque and back towards Arizona. But before leaving New Mexico, there was one snake I wanted to try to find: the Trans-Pecos rat snake. These big colubrids are often called "subocs," a name that derives from their scientific name—*Bogertophis subocularis*. Subocs have adorably large eyes that bulge slightly out of their head and are famous for having a gentle disposition. These long, large snakes are generally tan in coloration, with black stripes extending beyond the head which morph into a series of "H" shaped markings along the back.

Given their nocturnal lifestyle, road cruising is by far the best way to find subocs. Hoping to get lucky, Taylor and I drove along lonely roads for several hours near Las Cruces, the northwesternmost portion of the species' range. The country roads were sparsely traveled, and the darkness of the night obscured the flat New Mexico landscape. We might have tried road cruising for pyros in the mountains in the southwestern portion of the state, if the forest there wasn't literally on fire at the time.

At one point, we saw the unmistakable form of a sizable tan snake sprawled out on the black asphalt. When road cruising, anything that vaguely resembles a snake can trick your eyes. But when it's a snake, especially a big one, you know for certain. Taylor braked hard and I hopped out, hopes sky high. A large tan snake with dark markings on the back was a description that not many other snakes fit. But unfortunately it wasn't my suboc. It was a gopher snake (*Pituophis catenifer*), a much more common species. Even worse, it had been hit by a car. Disappointed, we continued on, eyes straining in the darkness for the silhouette of a different large snake.

The rest of the night was unfulfilling, and we made camp in the flat New Mexico wilderness without having glimpsed any live herps. Road cruising can be very productive at times, but sometimes—especially when the weather has been dry for weeks—it just isn't. I usually have rotten luck when I road cruise and I don't enjoy being reminded of how many snakes get flattened by cars every night, so my preference is usually to search on foot.

As much as I would have loved to try again for a suboc the next night, there were places to be in Arizona. We were still hoping to put the taxonomic squabble regarding pyros to rest, and the mountain kingsnakes weren't going to find themselves.

SEVEN

Over and Over

After the brief stint in New Mexico, I was excited to reach our next destination back across the Arizona border: Chiricahua (pronounced like "cheer-ah-cow-uh"). This large sky island is located in the southeastern corner of Arizona. The place is interesting purely from a geological perspective, boasting an impressive array of rhyolite hoodoos—bizarrely shaped columns of volcanic rock carved by years of wind and ice. But it was this mountain's wide array of reptiles that brought Taylor and I there. Chiricahua and the surrounding area has a whopping thirty-seven species of snake. For context, the entire state of Utah has only twenty-six.

Chiricahua owes its incredible biodiversity to two factors. First: elevation. Like other sky islands, Chiricahua is home to an array of different habitats at different elevations, from deserts at the base to pine forests up top, creating a large variety of ecological niches for species to fill. Second: location, location, location. Chiricahua is located on the eastern edge of the Sonoran Desert and the western edge of the Chihuahuan Desert, meaning that it has the advantage of inheriting species from two ecoregions instead of one.

PYRO

Now that Taylor and I had visited both of the herpetology collections we needed to, our lone remaining scientific objective was to get a tissue sample from a mountain kingsnake in the sampling gap between *L. knoblochi* and *L. pyromelana*. Admittedly, Chiricahua had been sampled in the controversial Burbrink paper and declared to be *Lampropeltis knoblochi*. This meant that Taylor and I didn't technically *need* to visit Chiricahua for research purposes. But we were also looking to accomplish our less serious objective—to see as many new snakes as possible—and since it was on the way back towards Tucson we couldn't help but take a quick detour for what we hoped would be snake paradise.

Unfortunately, Chiricahua didn't just refuse to give us any snakes in the day and a half we spent there—it even went so far as to mock us. Our first hike was along a pristine montane creek. The green forest scenery was beautiful and the habitat seemingly perfect, but we had seen nothing besides a few lizards. Afterwards, Taylor was in the outhouse and I was halfway through chugging a bottle of Gatorade when an older couple, probably in their sixties, drove into the parking lot on a four-wheeler. Seeing my blue snake hook leaning against the truck, the man commented, "That's a nice snake stick you got there." I grinned and nodded, feeling slightly too tired to engage in conversation—and sheepish that we hadn't seen any snakes that morning. My attitude changed when he followed his initial statement up with, "We saw a snake earlier today! It was a coral snake." That got my attention.

"Really? That's cool. Did you get any pictures?" I asked, feeling immensely jealous.

"Oh yeah." he replied, explaining how they had driven up on the snake as it was crossing the dirt road. The man said he wished he had a fancy snake stick like mine instead of the wood sticks he improvised with in order to avoid being bitten by the lethal serpent. I smiled and nodded, surprised he had elected to risk his life to save the snake. I'm stereotyping here, but I imagine that most people who drive off-road vehicles would be excited to smash a snake under the wheels of their lumbering driving machines, especially if it was venomous. I was also a little amused that he felt the urge to move the snake, rather than simply waiting for it to cross the road.

It took the old man a few seconds to navigate to the pictures on his cell phone as his wife described more of the incident to me. Eventually he pulled up a very blurry picture of a snake, with two sticks held behind its head like oversized chopsticks. It did superficially resemble a coral snake, but the pattern of red, black, and white bands was unmistakable.

"That's a mountain kingsnake!" I blurted out, my jealousy increasing a hundredfold. The man was skeptical at first, swearing he'd seen coral snakes in Texas and that this looked the same. I quickly rattled off a few features, like the lack of yellow and the overall length, that disqualified it from being a Sonoran coral snake (and I later wondered about his Texas "coral snakes"). Eventually the old couple was convinced; my snake hook must have helped my credibility. We all had a good laugh at the extreme caution they had exercised with the harmless kingsnake, though better safe than sorry.

They described to me roughly where they had seen the snake, though it had been a couple of hours ago. I thanked them for the lead and the story, and they headed back up the road. When Taylor returned, I told him he'd missed a good coral snake story and explained the comical tale. We were glad to know that there indeed were mountain kingsnakes active nearby, but we weren't any closer to finding one. We did go check out the spot, but the "coral snake" was long gone.

Though snakes were scarce, we did see plenty of scelops on Chiricahua. "Scelop" (pronounced like "skuh-lop") is slang for any lizard of the spiny lizard genus *Sceloporus*, also known as the blue-bellies. There are currently over a hundred members of this genus, and Arizona was home to many I had never seen before, including several on Chiricahua. My favorite of these was Yarrow's spiny lizard (*Sceloporus jarrovii*). Named after some long-deceased herpetologist, Yarrow's spiny lizards are variable in color, with the brightest individuals sporting blackish-greenish iridescent scales along with a bright blue tail. They are also big enough to deal a painful bite if you aren't careful.

The scelops on Chiricahua hold a special distinction for me because they were the first animals that Taylor and I euthanized. So far the only specimen we'd preserved on the trip was an already-dead diamondback rattlesnake (*Crotalus atrox*). We had collected a blind snake (*Rena humilis*), but it had escaped. We had seen several other DOR (dead-on-road) snakes, but all the ones in salvagable condition were gopher snakes (*Pituophis catenifer*). Gopher snakes are perhaps the most common snakes in the western US, and are the one species I can confidently say that the Bean Museum herpetology collection already has way too many of. This meant that with the multi-week trip just about halfway over, our specimen count was at a grand total of…one. Taylor and I knew it was time to suck it up and start euthanizing—part of the reason the trip was funded was to bolster the collection. All we could catch on Chiricahua were scelops, so those were the first to go. (We saw some whiptails too, but failed to catch any, unsurprisingly.)

There are multiple ways to euthanize reptiles, some better than others. The process we used was humane—first a diluted numbing injection followed by the stronger knockout dose—at least as humane as it could be to end the life of a perfectly healthy animal. We set up our makeshift lab station on the tailgate of the truck. Taylor carefully prepared the proper chemical solutions and I weighed the lizards—stowed securely in cloth bags—to calculate the appropriate dosages. With the solutions prepared, I held the first scelop down and Taylor injected it. The numbing solution caused the lizard to go limp as a ragdoll, a dramatic change from its once-feisty attitude. Taylor then administered the lethal dose, which finished the job without causing excess pain. We repeated the process for several more lizards, the smiles of earlier in the day replaced with grimaces. We both agreed that we hoped to never become desensitized to euthanizing, though we knew that specimen collection is an essential part of herpetology.

While it sounds odd, herpetologists have been preserving their study animals for hundreds of years. For a species to be described, the description has to be based on a holotype specimen, which is often accompanied by several paratypes. Type specimens are immortalized for science as official representatives of their species, but the lives of the individuals are ended. However, specimens are collected not just for describing new species. Museum collections—like the one at the Bean Museum where Taylor and I worked—are full of thousands of specimens caught and euthanized by herpetologists for the sake of science. They provide a repository of biological information on the distributions and physical characteristics of the specimens contained within.

Specimen collecting has been the gold standard for documenting biodiversity for hundreds of years now, though it is not without its contemporary critics. In a 2014 opinion article published in the prominent journal *Science*, Ben Minteer and three other authors argued that in an extreme scenario, a scientist may be consigning a species to extinction by "discovering" it. Imagine the irony if the only individuals of a species ever seen were euthanized by a scientist so that the species could be formally described. High quality photos, extensive measurements, and a nonlethal DNA sample could be a possible substitute for type specimens if the species is on the brink of extinction, they proposed. Minteer and his colleagues weren't calling for the end of all scientific collecting; they were just advocating that in extreme scenarios (such as with rediscovered or likely endangered species) it would be best to not risk extinction.

It turns out that this was an unpopular opinion. Only a month after the initial article was published, the scientific establishment hit back. The rebuttal was written by Rocha *et al.* Normally, "*et al.*," which is a Latin phrase meaning "and others," refers to more than one additional author; usually two or three, but sometimes ten or more. In this case, "*et al.*" refers to a whopping 120 other authors that signed off on the response, including the late legendary biologist E. O. Wilson. They argued that while photographs, audio recordings, and tissue samples can augment voucher specimens, nothing can replace them. Additionally, they dismissed the argument that scientific collecting could ever contribute to the demise of a species—the impact is just too small compared to natural predation and other kinds of human-caused mortality (hunting, habitat destruction, etc.). They closed their article by stating "we believe that responsibly collecting voucher specimens and associated data and openly sharing this knowledge...are more necessary today than ever before."

Minteer and two of the authors of the original paper did write another response, reiterating that they were only arguing against collecting in extreme scenarios. But I think the most important line in any of these papers came from the initial rebuttal by Rocha *et al.*, which says "Scientists have come a long way from the days of indiscriminate collecting."

Before I worked in a museum, I would never have imagined that for some herpetologists of the past, every animal that they could catch ended up dead in a jar. But "indiscriminate collecting" is a good description of what used to be the status quo. For some early naturalists, their collections were an important source of income that made their trips possible. Yet even those who weren't as directly financially dependent on specimens—naturalists like Charles Darwin or even Wilmer Tanner come to mind—still collected prodigiously. I've read a paper from 1934 where the author shot a whopping 2,600 lizards over three years. Biologists weren't necessarily tree-hugging conservationists back then.

Nowadays, many scientists still collect some specimens, but institutional rules and governmental regulations ensure that scientific collecting is done responsibly. There is a high degree of caution and restraint that ensures impacts on wild populations are negligible.

To be fair to the avid collectors of bygone eras, collecting whole physical specimens was the only good way to document biodiversity until relatively recently. If you caught an animal back in 1850, or even 1950, you couldn't just pull out your phone and snap clear photos of all the head scales on a snake. Sketches were excessively time consuming and difficult to draw to scale. A preserved specimen acts as a permanent record and will last basically indefinitely when preserved right. Colors fade but features like size and scale counts remain unchanged. The specimens housed in museums form the very backbone of our scientific knowledge of species, each specimen acting almost like a book within a vast scientific library. Having held specimens that were over a hundred years old—and some collections have even older ones—I can attest that museum specimens create a lasting and valuable record of biodiversity.

But today, other viable options for documenting biodiversity do exist, and it would be old-fashioned to cling to specimen collection as the sole method. Nowadays, research is often focused on molecular data anyway. A harmless throat swab of a frog or tail clip of a lizard is able to capture the strings of nucleotides that have become as important for defining species as scale counts. Whole specimens are not necessary to get quality genetic data. The proliferation of smartphones also makes it easy to capture high quality images and audio recordings. These kinds of records can't perfectly replace preserved specimens but can provide significant value without costing the organism its life.

It should also be noted that scientific collections are not without shortcomings. For example, museum specimens have historically been used to determine the diets of many animals, but recent research has shown this approach to be imperfect. One 2017 study, which took place in South Africa, investigated the feeding habits of puff adders (*Bitis arietans*), a large viper native to Africa.

Puff adders are as girthy as they are venomous, and they hunt by ambush. The scientists used radio trackers implanted in the snakes to find their ambush sites, where they would then set up cameras. Once puff adders have found a good spot, they'll remain motionless—and perfectly camouflaged—until prey comes within reach, making them a perfect subject for this experiment. The researchers were able to capture footage of twenty-four strikes—as well as over 4,500 hours of puff adders chilling in place—which were then compared to eighty-five prey items found in dissected museum specimens.

Turns out, these two methods told very different stories. Eighty-one of the eighty-five identifiable remains recovered from the stomachs of museum specimens were mammals, but only nine of the twenty-four attacks caught on camera were. While the data from living puff adders indicated they ate a relatively equal amount of amphibians and mammals, the museum data made them appear to be almost exclusively mammal eaters. The study authors attribute the difference to the relative speeds that different animals break down in the snake digestive system (amphibians have less keratin, and thus break down faster).

An older 1998 study on gopher snakes (*Pituophis catenifer*) compared the stomach contents of museum specimens to published literature records of predation events, and found a similar, though less severe, mammal bias. Museum specimens can be used to determine some of the things an animal eats, but they shouldn't be viewed as a perfect portrayal. Admittedly, filming dozens of predation events in most species isn't feasible since not every herp will remain perfectly still for hours on end. But nonlethal techniques such as stomach flushing—where water is pumped down the throat of the animal until the stomach contents come up—have been shown to work well in some scenarios. One 2020 study even used photos posted to Facebook to record what herps were eating and being eaten by, with great success (though this method has the potential for biases of its own).

Once again, I don't want to discount the immense value of museum specimens. Some kinds of studies would be impossible without them, and type specimens are especially irreplaceable. I just want to highlight that technological advancements have given us more options to document biodiversity that don't involve killing the animal.

Alright, tangent over. Suffice it to say that euthanizing those scelops on Chiricahua caused me to do a significant amount of self-reflection. Taylor and I knew that we would still need to euthanize additional specimens throughout the remainder of the trip, but even if we collected sparingly, we could still photograph and tail clip with reckless abandon.

After leaving Chiricahua, Taylor and I went further west to Madera Canyon in the Santa Rita Mountains, our last stop before returning to Mount Lemmon. Much like Chiricahua, Madera Canyon is a biodiversity hotspot and a legendary locale among herp hobbyists. Our expectations were tempered by our lack of success on Chiricahua, so we weren't too disappointed when we saw nothing special at a place that was supposed to be a herper's paradise. The coolest thing we saw—by a wide margin—was an elegant trogon, which is a bird. A cool bird, but when the best thing you see is a bird, you know things were disappointing. (Apologies to all the birders I just offended. The elegant trogon was actually amazing.)

After our disappointing day in the Santa Ritas, Taylor and I headed north again towards Tucson and Mount Lemmon, the gap area in the Burbrink study between *L. pyromelana* and *L. knoblochi* where we were hoping to find a mountain kingsnake. My wonderful relatives were once again more than happy to let us stay with them for a few more nights, and being able to shower after another spell in the wilderness felt glorious.

This time around, we explored some spots on Mount Lemmon we hadn't visited previously. At one point, we even ended up forking over the ten-dollar entry fee to visit Rose Canyon "Lake." I say "lake" because, while some body of water may have existed in the past, the current body of water is the result of human intervention. It was here that Taylor and I found the biggest tadpoles either of us had ever seen. We could barely believe our eyes at the golf-ball sized amphibians that were found along the entire shoreline of the small reservoir. Seriously, the bodies of the bigger tadpoles were comparable in size to a large chicken egg.

The green tadpoles were bullfrogs (*Lithobates catesbeianus*), a species that belonged as much as the reservoir itself. Bullfrogs are native to eastern North America, but today are found across all of North America, as well as much of South America, Europe, East Asia, and Indonesia. The International Union for Conservation of Nature (IUCN) named them as one of the hundred worst invasive species on the planet on their Global Invasive Species Database. (The wonderful brown tree snake also made the list, in case you were curious.) Given their status as an invasive species, I had no reservations about collecting one of the monstrous bullfrog tadpoles as a specimen, though I was more than happy to let Taylor be the one to wade barefoot into the lake water.

Another species we encountered on this stint on Mount Lemmon was the short-horned lizard (*Phrynosoma hernandesi*). We saw both adults and juveniles, with each individual round lizard doing its best impersonation of a rock in hopes of being overlooked. They are sometimes erroneously called horny toads, but these scaly critters are reptiles, not amphibians. A few species of horned lizard (genus *Phrynosoma*) are famous for their ability to squirt blood out of their eyes as a defense. But even the horned lizards that lack this blood-squirting superpower are still interesting.

Horned lizards have adopted a totally different evolutionary strategy from the majority of lizards they share their habitats with. They are built sort of like a pancake with legs and spikes, and rely mainly on their excellent camouflage. When spotted by a predator, they inflate their bodies, accentuate their spiky form, and do their best to appear impossible to swallow. Sometimes they'll dash a few feet and freeze in place, hoping their camouflage will save them, but their sprint speed is closer to a tortoise than a whiptail. Compared to most lizards, catching horned lizards is a breeze. Horned lizards also have a knack for looking grumpy in the most adorable way when held in your hand.

After several snake-less days hiking all over Mount Lemmon, Taylor and I took a break to try our luck in the desert for another evening. Retracing our steps from a week prior, we drove to the same nature preserve outside of Tucson. It didn't feel like wilderness, but since it had turned up a blind snake the last time, it was worth revisiting. After wandering towards the large, artificial pond and being swarmed by mosquitoes, Taylor and I ended up walking along the same dirt path we had previously. The park's posted closing time was still an hour away, but it was dark enough to break out our flashlights. At one point, we wandered over to an underpass that cut beneath the nearby paved bike path. The large rocks piled next to the concrete structure looked like ideal reptile shelter, but there was nothing on or under them.

While walking through the small underpass itself though, we spotted something pink wiggling back and forth in the thin layer of sand on the cement floor. It was another blind snake! A quick check of the head scales confirmed it was the same species (*Rena humilis*, the western blind snake) we had encountered a week ago. This individual was slightly smaller and a brighter pink, and we were less weirded out by its bizarre musk this time.

Despite their worm-like appearance, blind snakes above the surface will move with undulations like other snakes. However, blind snakes don't quite move with the same grace as most snakes, and this individual flailed about on the flat concrete as Taylor and I looked on, barely believing our luck. Two blind snakes, virtually in the same spot, a week apart. It was almost like the place knew that our last blind snake had gotten away and we still needed one for the collection. We knew we had to euthanize it that night, lest we risk repeating the escape of the previous week.

In the parking lot, we discovered yet another surprise. In the dark, I noticed a shadow bouncing along the pavement. I shined my flashlight towards the creature, and the beam of light illuminated a green blob. A beautiful, toad-shaped green blob. Our latest herp, and yet another new species for Taylor and me, was a Colorado River toad (*Incilius alvarius*).

Colorado River toads are the largest native toad in the US, with the biggest chonkers reaching seven inches in length, though this individual was much smaller. The green toad was covered in orange warts, and its mediocre jumping ability made it easy to catch. Like all true toads, it had toxin-filled parotoid glands on its back. The oval-shaped bulges, one behind each eye, contain concentrated amounts of toxins intended to deter predators. Consuming toads is a fatal, or at the very least unpleasant, experience for predators that haven't evolved resistance. But adventurous people have realized that these toxins can have some *interesting* effects on humans, to say the least.

Basically, you can get high by licking toads. I imagine there are side effects from licking any species of toxin-toting toad, but the Colorado River toad is especially famous for its chemical concoctions. A guy by the name of Albert Most published a pamphlet in 1983 entitled "Bufo alvarius: The Psychedelic Toad of the Sonoran Desert," which describes how to extract and smoke the hallucinogen 5-MEO-DMT derived from the toad's parotoid glands. The genus has changed (from *Bufo* to *Incilius*) but I imagine that everything else that Albert Most wrote forty years ago is still valid. His pamphlet, complete with diagrams, is available online if you want to read it, but please don't actually go collect toads for this purpose. Many populations of these so-called "psychedelic toads" are in decline largely due to human exploitation; please don't support the small but very real recreational toad drug industry. If you need another reason to not lick toads, know that it can land you in the hospital. These toxins evolved to discourage, not encourage, predation.

While Taylor and I joked about it, neither of us were interested in exploring the wonders of toad toxins. After taking some pictures, we let our psychedelic toad friend hop off into the night; we already had collected one interesting specimen that hour anyway.

Hoping to replicate our night cruising success of the previous week, we left the blind snake haven and headed down the same roads as before. This time, though, there were no diamondback rattlesnakes, no leafnose snakes, and no Gila monsters. Just miles of boring pavement. We eventually made it back to my relatives' place, where we preserved the pink blind snake before heading to bed.

After our latest desert excursion, it was back to Mount Lemmon. Our time in Arizona was running low and the taxonomic controversy was still unresolved. However, after visiting several sky islands, I have to admit that they did *feel* distinctly different from the pyro habitat farther north. Part of the argument of the Burbrink paper was that the two species, *L. pyromelana* and *L. knoblochi*, occupied separate ecological niches in addition to having been reproductively isolated. I felt the difference, but unscientific feelings don't count as additional evidence—I would much rather have a genetic sample from the area to sequence.

Taylor and I spent the next several days hitting trails at different elevations all around Mount Lemmon. The mountain kingsnakes continued to elude us, but we did find one local resident we hadn't seen yet: the Madrean alligator lizard (*Elgaria kingii*). While their thick, elongated body does vaguely resemble a miniature gator, alligator lizards are very smooth and have much more dinky limbs than any true crocodilian. But I probably shouldn't make fun of their tiny arms and legs, because the first alligator lizard got the better of us.

Taylor was hiking in front of me, and he spotted it first. The brown alligator lizard was basking in the late morning sun at the base of a clump of bushes, but quickly dove into the leaf litter. We positioned ourselves on opposite sides of where Taylor had last seen it and started rooting through the leaves with our hands. Over the next several minutes, we both caught a few more glimpses of the streamlined lizard swimming nimbly through the leaves, but neither of us were able to get a hand on it. Eventually it fully gave us the slip—likely disappearing down a hole—and we were left empty-handed. Alligator lizards: 1; humans: 0.

That was not the last alligator lizard we would see on Mount Lemmon though. On another hike close to the end of the day, I spotted a large granite stone that was lit by the setting sun. I lifted the heavy rock with both hands and spotted a beautiful adult Madrean alligator lizard on the dirt underneath. Careful to not smash the lizard, I gently lowered the rock back down. "Taylor, get over here! Alligator lizard!" I called. Tag-teaming the capture, Taylor lifted the rock and I did the honors of securing the lizard. We weren't about to let this one get away.

The alligator lizard was about a foot long, though more than half of that was tail. The smooth scales on her back alternated in bands of light and dark brown. Her face looked almost grumpy, but she didn't squirm much. She did bite, and it was probably the most comical lizard bite I've ever received. Usually, lizards chomp down quickly and with as much viciousness as they can muster. This alligator lizard was much more methodical. Her small brown eyes locked on my finger, intently focused. Then she slowly yet deliberately opened her mouth, twisted her head, and clamped down. The bite was more comical than painful, but it was well deserved.

My initial elation at finding the lizard turned to deflation, knowing that she was destined to end up in a jar of ethanol. It was for a good cause, but that didn't make me feel much better. We took care of the alligator lizard that night, and by now we had gotten the process down pat. I restrained the lizard while Taylor numbed and then euthanized it. After the lizard was dead, it was my job to find the liver for a tissue sample. After doing it enough times, you get good at making the incision right where the liver is.

But I was in for a gut punch of my own when I sliced through the beautiful brown scales of the now-deceased alligator lizard. She was obviously a she because inside her body were half a dozen small white orbs. Eggs. Each one was somewhere between the size of a BB and a mini marshmallow, and each one represented an additional lizard life I had taken. When I found her under that rock, she had been absorbing some of the last of the sun's rays to warm her developing eggs. Taylor and I were crestfallen, but the deed was already done. I told myself that scientific collections were important. My research wouldn't have been possible without museum specimens. I wouldn't have my job or be on this trip if it weren't for scientific collections. But staring at the cold body of the gravid alligator lizard made me feel like a part of my soul was bleeding too.

Eventually, our time in Tucson had to come to a close. Despite countless hours on Mount Lemmon, we had failed to find our mountain kingsnake there. The trip couldn't last forever, and there was no knowing how much more searching it would take before we would finally get lucky. The sampling gap between *L. pyromelana* and *L. knoblochi* would have to be addressed by someone else. (Until then I think it is best to accept the species boundary proposed in the 2011 study.)

The morning that Taylor and I left Tucson, we stopped at another nature area located northwest of Mount Lemmon. It was here that we discovered a magical rock. I'm normally not one to believe in the supernatural, but something was different here. Our hike was an out-and-back hike near a dry wash. The greener slopes of Mount Lemmon loomed in the background, but the dry habitat here was definitely desert.

At one point, the dirt path intersected a small dry streambed. In it, there was a flat, vaguely circular rock a couple of feet in diameter. It was only a couple inches thick and excellent shelter for any reptiles looking for a hidden spot to warm up for the morning. A perfect rock to flip.

Sure enough, when I lifted the rock, there was a lizard. Even better, it was a species we had yet to see. It was a regal horned lizard (*Phrynosoma solare*), and it looked so much like the other rocks underneath that I almost didn't notice it—talk about good camouflage. The short-horned lizards (*Phrynosoma hernandesi*) that we'd encountered on Mount Lemmon have modest, almost nub-like horns. Regal horned lizards, on the other hand, boast an impressive array of large horns fringing their heads. Their spiky heads look like they belong on a dragon or a dinosaur, not a puny lizard that fits in your palm.

The light tan lizard angrily puffed itself up—an adaptation to make the already-spiny body even more difficult to swallow—as we admired and photographed it. We opted to take a tail snip rather than collect it as a specimen; I was still feeling guilty about the gravid alligator lizard. We released the regal horned lizard and continued on our way. I put the rock back precisely as I found it, unaware of its magical properties.

Taylor and I continued on, following another dry wash and watching for more lizards. At one point, we saw the biggest whiptail either of us had ever seen, which promptly dove into a hole, never to be seen again. There were plenty of greater earless lizards (*Cophosaurus texanus*) too—the sassy, tail-wagging ones—and by some incredible miracle I even caught one. The lizard was perched on a small rock alongside the trail. Rather than teleporting away when I got close, it stood still as I leaned in. When I shot my hand out, the lizard's reflexes were just a touch too slow and I was able to pin its slim body to the rock. There would be no tail taunting today!

On our way back to the truck, we stopped at the same large rock I had found the regal horned lizard under earlier. It was nearing midday and I figured that the temperature under the exposed rock would be far too hot for any reptiles to be hiding underneath. But, on the off chance that the horned lizard from earlier had hidden under the stone again, I decided to check. As I lifted the rock, my eyes immediately locked on a beautiful horned lizard. I called Taylor over, surprised at our luck yet again. As Taylor came over, I reached down to pick up the lizard. And suddenly, I realized that the small brownish lump next to it wasn't a rock—it was another horned lizard! Its tan coloration and bumpy skin looked exactly like the sand and stones underneath.

We quickly apprehended both of the horned lizards (which compared to catching earless lizards is a walk in the park). They were both regal horned lizards (*Phrynosoma solare*), with the characteristic ring of horns extending from their heads, but neither was the same individual from earlier. This was easy to confirm because our friend from before was now missing the tip of its tail, and while lizards can grow their tail back, they can't do it in an hour. The only logical conclusion was that the rock was magical. My field guide claims this species lays eggs, but if they simply spring from rocks, that would explain their excellent camouflage. (This also shows why you should always put back any rocks, logs, or trash you flip over as perfectly as possible so that herps will keep hiding under it!)

Heading north from Tucson, Taylor and I spent the last couple days of the trip driving and visiting a few final spots along the way home. Our most interesting finds came near Prescott, Arizona, which was a place we hadn't stopped at on the way down. The pine forests around here were crawling with adorable short-horned lizards (*Phrynosoma hernandesi*), like we had found on Mount Lemmon. We also managed to spot another alligator lizard here, which we happily released after some photographs, and I was appreciative that my last memory of the species wasn't bloody.

We didn't see any snakes near Prescott, save for the tiny fragment of a tail that Taylor found. It's not uncommon to come across shed snake skins, and occasionally you'll find an entire mummified (and often mangled) body of a deceased snake. But this was the first and only time I've found just a tail. The segment was an inch or two long, and the only patterning that was visible was a light band flanked by two dark ones. "No way! Is this a pyro?" Taylor said, showing it to me.

I felt like I was back on Chiricahua again, where the old couple recounted their story of the "coral snake." Nature was teasing us. We'd searched for over two weeks without seeing a single mountain kingsnake, and now we had just found the mummified tail of one? It felt like we were being tortured, though it was really all in our heads. After looking at it again and thinking a little harder, I realized it didn't quite look like the tail of a pyro. Given the pattern and size, it almost certainly belonged to a gopher snake (*Pituophis catenifer*). With pyros on the brain, we'd jumped to conclusions.

Eventually, Taylor and I made it back home to Provo, Utah. Somehow we'd been driving, camping, and hiking for two and a half weeks without finding a single mountain kingsnake. Despite spending a large chunk of that time running around Mount Lemmon, we had failed to find the snake that could have neatly put an end to the only legitimate complaint regarding the pyro species split that had upset so many. Getting the special research permit that increased our allotted limit of mountain kingsnakes from five to sixteen turned out to be completely unnecessary.

The whole endeavor reminded me of the definition of insanity erroneously attributed to Einstein: doing the same thing over and over and expecting different results. It felt true, though we had still managed to see at least forty-five other species of herp. (I say "at least" because I gave up on identifying whiptails towards the end.) Taylor and I didn't bring back nearly as many specimens for the collection as we maybe should have, but at least we had tail clips and pictures aplenty. We also obtained all the necessary photographs of specimens at the two herpetology collections we visited, which would be crucial for our next research endeavor. Overall, what had started with a frozen toe had still turned into a fun and memorable trip, despite the lack of mountain kingsnakes.

EIGHT

Color Me Confused

"Whoa, those are poisonous, aren't they?"

That's a question I often get after showing someone a picture of a pyro, and it takes a lot of self-control to not roll my eyes—especially when the photo is of the snake in my hand. Much of my exasperation comes because people invariably mean venomous, not poisonous. Venom is injected via fangs, spines, or other structures, while poison is ingested, inhaled, or absorbed through the skin. Basically, if you eat it and you die, it was poisonous. If it bites or stings you and you die, it was venomous.

Only a handful of snakes are poisonous, and unless you are planning on having snake for lunch there is no need to worry about poisonous snakes. The potentially dangerous snakes are the venomous ones. Drinking snake venom is theoretically harmless, though the idea does sound risky. There's at least one video on YouTube of someone downing a swig of king cobra venom, proving both that it is safe to swallow and that people on the internet will do anything for views.

Pyros are neither venomous nor poisonous. But it's not a coincidence that a lot of people—like that old couple on Chiricahua—

think they are. In fact, that's exactly what the snakes want you to think. It's all part of an evolutionary deception millions of years in the making, and one that is intimately intertwined with pyros.

Mimicry was first described in 1862 by a British chap named Henry Walter Bates. Bates had just spent eleven years in the naturalist's paradise that is the Amazon rainforest. He wasn't studying snakes, though there is a species of South American boa named after him (*Corallus batesii*). Bates was an entomologist (a bug scientist), and his big breakthrough was with butterflies. He noticed that while butterflies generally were easy targets, there were some varieties that predators avoided. Moreover, closer observation revealed that many of these were toxic. Not toxic enough to kill, but foul-tasting enough that a predator would think twice before chowing down on a similar-patterned butterfly again. Some butterflies were perfectly palatable, yet were avoided nonetheless *because they resembled the distasteful ones*. They were mimics.

I like to imagine that Bates reached this conclusion not merely through observation but rather by tasting a bunch of butterflies himself. What better way to find out which species were unpalatable than to use your own palate? Unfortunately, if Bates did in fact conduct personal taste tests, he left it out of his paper. All he mentions is the "peculiar smell" and the avoidance of the butterflies by animals.

Bates' discovery was trumpeted as proof of Charles Darwin's theory of evolution by natural selection, which had been published to the world just three years earlier in 1859. Darwin, in a letter to Bates, called it "one of the most remarkable and admirable papers I ever read." This type of mimicry, which came to be known as Batesian mimicry, clearly demonstrated how natural selection could evolve.

Here's a simplified version of how it would work. Imagine you have two species of butterfly. Butterfly species A is a solid blue color and tastes like filet mignon (or the butterfly equivalent of filet mignon). Butterfly species B is blue too, but it also has neon orange spots and tastes like rotten eggs. The orange is an eye-catching warning sign that butterfly B's taste terrible, referred to as aposematic coloration. Predators will easily learn to avoid the orange spots of the B's and only prey on the tasty A's.

Now imagine that if, through a random mutation, some offspring of butterfly A have a few orange spots. Predators might avoid them too, mistaking them for the foul-tasting B's, even though they actually aren't toxic. Because they resemble the distasteful species, these butterflies will survive more and make more mutant babies with orange spots (assuming the trait is heritable). Before long, all the butterfly A's have evolved to mimic the toxic species. The mutation in color was random but the proliferation of the trait through natural selection was not.

There is one more main type of mimicry, though it isn't relevant to pyros. In Müllerian mimicry, named after the naturalist Fritz Müller, two species that are both dangerous or distasteful evolve to resemble each other. This lessens the evolutionary time that it takes for predators to recognize and avoid the aposematic signal. Unlike Batesian mimicry, Müllerian mimicry is less deceptive since the warning signals of both species are honest.

Pyros and other tricolor kingsnakes are generally considered to be Batesian mimics of venomous coral snakes. In the Americas, there are two genera of coral snakes, *Micrurus* and *Micruroides*. They are elapids, members of a family of snakes with small, fixed fangs that deliver a potent neurotoxic venom. While snake venom evolved for subduing prey, it also doubles as an excellent defensive weapon (but not a perfect one, because the effects aren't instant—an envenomated predator could still kill the snake). Most, though not all, species of New World coral snake have vivid aposematic colors—bright reds, yellows, and/or oranges—to warn of the consequences of messing with them. Their colorful bands, due to their resemblance to vibrant tropical corals, are also the source of their common name.

Since the cost of tangling with a coral snake can be deadly—

unlike a distasteful butterfly, which can be spit out with no lasting damage—the evolutionary pressure for predators to avoid them is very strong. The animals that avoid the multicolored danger noodles are less likely to end up dead than the ones that keep trying to eat them.

Taking advantage of this, many coral snake copycats have evolved similar coloration and obtained the same protection without having to evolve any venom. Evolutionarily, it is much easier for a snake to change its color pattern than to develop toxins. Changing colors mostly just involves expressing different pigments, whereas venom is a complex mix of proteins and needs modified teeth to deliver it effectively. Neither is a conscious choice—animals can't will themselves to evolve traits—but one is much easier for natural selection to make happen.

This is all straightforward. Predator avoids brightly colored snake. Brightly colored snake lives—whether or not it was actually venomous.

But the confusing thing about pyros is that they are found in places where coral snakes aren't. Pyros are supposed to mimic the Sonoran coral snake (*Micruroides euryxanthus*), a red, black, and yellow banded snake found in Arizona, New Mexico, and Mexico. But pyros are also found in Nevada and Utah, hundreds of miles from coral snakes. Additionally, Sonoran coral snakes are primarily desert-dwellers, while pyros prefer mountains, so even those that are geographically close to each other aren't always sharing the exact same habitat. And pyros are far from the only snakes that don't perfectly overlap with the species they are supposed to be mimicking. For example, western milk snakes (*Lampropeltis gentilis*) range even further away than pyros, and California mountain kingsnakes (*Lampropeltis zonata*) don't overlap with coral snakes at all.

This clearly violates the theoretical expectations of mimicry. Without dangerous snakes in an area (or anywhere close), there should be no reason for predators to avoid the harmless doppelgängers, and their flashy colors should even make them easier to spot. This principle was first articulated by Alfred Russel Wallace—who had spent time in the Amazon with Bates and had developed a theory of evolution before Darwin finally went public with his own idea—in an extensive paper in 1867 titled "Mimicry, and Other Protective Resemblances Among Animals." The paper outlines as many documented instances of mimicry as he could, including Bates' butterfly example, and gives three theoretical laws of mimicry.

The very first principle Wallace lists is that "in an overwhelming majority of cases of mimicry, the animals (or the groups) which resemble each other inhabit the same country, the same district, and in most cases are to be found together on the very same spot." Basically, the mimics and the mimicked will overlap. Wallace had heard about coral snake mimics in the tropics, where the mimics did play by the rules. But he hadn't heard that if you go far enough north, you'll run into territory where there are only mimics.

A fair amount of ink was spilled over the topic of coral snake mimicry in the scientific literature in the decades following Wallace's publication. Throughout the nineteenth century and for most of the twentieth, all the evidence supporting coral snake mimicry was anecdotal—the occasional chance field observation combined with additional descriptions of harmless snakes that resembled venomous ones. At the time, there were a handful of skeptics that argued that coral snake mimics weren't mimics at all, though they didn't have any experimental evidence either. The doubters contended that many potential snake predators were colorblind anyway and hypothesized that the pattern of repeating bands simply served to make a moving snake harder to follow visually.

The first significant piece of evidence came in a 1981 paper by legendary herpetologist Harry Greene. Greene's paper pointed out the lack of empirical testing on the subject, though he and his co-author didn't run any actual experiments either. They did show that the coloration of some mimics in Central America varied to match whatever coral snake was in the area. This wasn't numerically quantified and the paper doesn't mention how many specimens they looked at, but at least it was some sort of evidence (and had a neat map showing the variation in these mimics).

It wasn't until Edmund Brodie III in the 1990s—well over a hundred years after it had been described—that someone finally decided to try empirically testing the effectiveness of coral snake mimicry. (C'mon scientists, you are supposed to love testing hypotheses!) Brodie's methods were relatively simple and have been replicated in many studies since. Using colored clay threaded onto an S-shaped wire, Brodie constructed fake snakes with various patterns—some matching venomous coral snakes—and left the replicas out in the Costa Rican jungle. Based on marks in the clay left by the beaks or talons of birds, he could estimate how frequently different kinds of patterns were attacked.

Brodie published two papers in the 1990s on the subject, and both provided convincing evidence of the effectiveness of mimicry. The predatory birds at his study sites avoided snake models with colored rings like the plague, but had no problem attacking the brown, patternless models. Mimicry worked great in Costa Rica, where there are (at least) five species of coral snake.

But how well would it work where that number was zero? To investigate, several experiments similar to Brodie's were conducted by David Pfennig's lab in the 2000s in different parts of the US. They used a similar experimental design, setting out clay models of snakes of different patterns and recording "attacks" in the clay by predators. The results showed that predators tended to avoid the coral snake look-alikes only in areas with coral snakes. As expected, mimicry wasn't protective without coral snakes around, though this experiment didn't necessarily show that the out-of-place mimics would be preferentially preyed on.

So if mimicry wasn't effective in areas without coral snakes around, wouldn't that mean that there might be evolutionary pressures to start evolving away from it? This has been the other main avenue for analyzing coral snake mimicry in recent decades. It has long been recognized that within a single species of mimic, some individuals look much more like coral snakes than others. In most tricolor kingsnakes specifically, the amount of red and black varies considerably, whereas coral snakes are more consistent in coloration. This means that scientists can compare the accuracy of mimics in different areas to see if those found outside of the range of coral snakes are evolving to look less like them.

It would take forever for one herpetologist to catch enough snakes to do a study like this—you need to measure hundreds of snakes. This is where museum specimens come in handy. Using photographs of preserved specimens, the amount of each color on a snake's back can be digitally measured and quantifiably compared to the average coral snake to see how the accuracy of their mimicry varies.

The first study to use this approach, published in 2007, looked at scarlet kingsnakes (*Lampropeltis elapsoides*). Found in the southeastern US, scarlet kingsnakes have red, black, and yellow bands that resemble those of the eastern coral snake (*Micrurus fulvius*). The authors measured kingsnake specimens from two areas: the middle of Florida, where both species are abundant, and North Carolina, which is at the edge of the range of eastern coral snakes (and where they are much rarer). The study showed that the mimics on the edge were more accurate, which makes sense. The kingsnakes deep in the range of coral snakes didn't need to be as precise; there were enough coral snakes around to keep predators wary. But where coral snakes were few or absent, the mimics had to be more convincing. Since the mimics on the fringe were the most accurate, it seemed reasonable that their range could extend a bit beyond the range of coral snakes.

But other results using the same approach didn't make as much theoretical sense. A 2014 study on the same species—scarlet kingsnakes—showed that their mimicry had improved in the years since coral snakes were eliminated from the study area back in 1960. Yes, rather than get worse without the real deal around, the mimics had evolved to be better; almost like a desperate attempt for their mimicry to keep working. This explanation is plausible in the short term, though if mimicry theory and the previous studies that used clay models were right, eventually the predators would figure things out and start eating the mimics.

A 2017 study that examined the accuracy of four different coral snake mimics was even more puzzling. Two of the four were more accurate mimics where they overlapped with coral snakes, as theoretically expected. But the other two weren't. One mimic got more accurate the further it was from coral snakes, strangely, and the last mimic showed no geographic pattern in accuracy whatsoever. For these two species, the absence or presence of coral snakes didn't have the anticipated effect on their coloration. These results suggested that the evolutionary pressures on the coloration of different mimics in different places are, well, different. Conceptually, mimicry should start to go away without coral snakes around, but this is only the case sometimes.

Despite these confusing results, the general idea of coral snake mimicry was better supported at this time than ever before. Further studies in Central and South America generally confirmed what Brodie's initial experiments had shown: Impersonating coral snakes will deter predators. On top of this, an excellent phylogenetic analysis of all New World snake species, published in 2016, strongly supported mimicry from an evolutionary history perspective. The study indicated that in the New World, mimetic phenotypes were highly correlated with the spatial distribution and temporal evolution of coral snakes. To put it in normal English, mimics tended to evolve when and where there were coral snakes around. But the nonoverlapping mimics still had biologists scratching their heads.

This takes us to a trio of twenty-something year olds with minimal research experience and several hundred pictures of snakes.

Taylor, Jacob, and I wanted to see if pyros that overlapped with coral snakes were better mimics than those that didn't. To replicate what had been done in studies on different species, Taylor and I had photographed all the pyros (and the "pyros" that are considered Chihuahuan mountain kingsnakes, *Lampropeltis knoblochi*) at the three herpetology collections with the most specimens (the University of Arizona, the Museum of Southwestern Biology, and the Bean Museum). We also took pictures of the coral snakes from these museums, and incorporated additional high-quality photos of the two kingsnake species from iNaturalist to increase our sample size.

Getting the pictures turned out to be the easy part, but it took Jacob, Taylor, and I almost six months to complete all the measurements. Each of us spent countless hours hunched over a computer, drawing and measuring digital lines, diligently recording how much of each color was present on every snake's back. All the time I spent staring at a screen for this project made me feel like a real twenty-first-century biologist.

We came into the project predicting that the pyros found near coral snakes would be better mimics than those from further away. For some pyros, many black bands cover up the conspicuous red ones, decreasing the amount of red visible from above. The blackest pyros have almost no red visible at all. These pyros look nothing like a coral snake, but sure stand out a lot less (and are able to warm up faster in the sun too). Given this tradeoff, it would be natural for the pyros found far away from coral snakes to evolve more and more black, making them look less like a coral snake and improving their camouflage. Only those that overlapped with coral snakes would have a good reason to still have lots of flaming red scales. To prevent our expectations from biasing the results, all measurements were made without knowing where each snake came from.

In addition to pyros, we also looked at their closest relative, the Chihuahuan mountain kingsnake (*Lampropeltis knoblochi*). They are basically the same in coloration as pyros (except for those classic *knoblochi*, whose bands don't go all the way to the belly). Unlike pyros, Chihuahuan mountain kings mostly overlap with Sonoran coral snakes. This offered the opportunity for a comparison between these sister species.

After our raw measurements were made, we used some stats wizardry to combine the proportions of red and black into a single score. We could then compare each individual mimic to the average coral snake, which showed how the accuracy of their mimicry changed in relation to proximity to coral snake populations.

Our results showed that, as expected, pyros did become worse mimics the further away they were from coral snakes—though even those that overlapped tended to not be great mimics. The correlation between resemblance and distance wasn't huge, but it was statistically significant (the p-value was roughly 0.003, well below the typical threshold of 0.05, meaning that the pattern was unlikely to be due to random chance). About 9.7 percent of their variation in color could be explained by distance from coral snake populations. 9.7 percent doesn't sound like a huge number, but it was actually greater than the amount in any of the four other mimics examined in the 2017 study. On average, the pyros that were further away from coral snakes tended to swap more of their eye-catching red for inconspicuous black.

But this was only half of our results. The southern cousins of pyros, the Chihuahuan mountain kingsnakes (*Lampropeltis knoblochi*), tended to be slightly more accurate mimics overall than pyros. Yet they showed no correlation between distance from and their resemblance to coral snakes (the p-value was a whopping 0.529). This meant that for Chihuahuan mountain kingsnakes, the degree of resemblance didn't change regardless of if they overlapped with coral snakes. Unlike pyros, they didn't follow the evolutionary expectation of becoming worse mimics.

It is important to note that we only had thirteen samples of this species from outside of the range of coral snakes (whereas we had seventy-one such pyros), so there is a decent chance that with a larger sample size a trend would have emerged. Unfortunately, there just aren't a lot of Chihuahuan mountain kingsnakes from this area of Mexico in museum collections; we basically used all the ones available. But remember, this kind of result wasn't unprecedented; two of the four mimics examined in that 2017 study also didn't follow the expected pattern in color variation.

(I also should mention that there are some people who say the divide between pyros and Chihuahuan mountain kingsnakes is arbitrary and should be disregarded [or that only the rare Chihuahuan mountain kings with their distinctive patterning, of which we only had five samples, should be considered a separate species]. If the two species were lumped together, as they had been until 2011, there was a statistically significant correlation with about 7 percent of the variation in coloration explained by distance. I think that the split is valid, which is why this entire paragraph is in parentheses, but thought this was still worth mentioning.)

To make things even more interesting, in both species there was a correlation between the amount of black coloration and the latitude of the specimen. Having more black instead of red would hypothetically help a snake warm up slightly faster in sunlight, which would be more relevant at higher latitudes where average annual temperatures are colder. However, due to the lack of precise location data, we weren't able to measure elevation—like latitude, elevation strongly influences temperature—and this would have given a clearer picture of how beneficial extra black coloration is. Pyros are rarely found in direct sunlight though, potentially minimizing any thermal benefits of black coloration. And if having more black was super beneficial at higher latitudes, you'd think that the pyros would just ditch their red altogether.

In the end, our results didn't have a clear answer to the main problem: What in the world are these flamboyant mimics doing so far away from coral snakes? Even though some species—like pyros—become less accurate mimics, if their mimicry is totally ineffective without coral snakes around, shouldn't they just fully evolve away from it?

One idea that has been floated in the past is that gene flow has maintained the mimicry (i.e. mimics moving out of the range of coral snakes and taking their genes with them). Snakes are generally poor movers, but one genetic study did support the idea that mimicry in scarlet kingsnakes was maintained by the northward movement of individuals. This explanation is hard to believe with pyros (which have many populations isolated by miles of inhospitable desert) and makes even less sense for species like California mountain kingsnakes that don't overlap with coral snakes at all. But it could explain why Chihuahuan mountain kingsnakes look similar throughout their range, which is less disjunct in the areas of Mexico that don't overlap with coral snakes.

Importantly, there are several reasons why their coloration might not be as disadvantageous in the absence of coral snakes as originally thought. Snakes may not move long distances, but some of their predators do. Raptors such as hawks and eagles often migrate hundreds of miles, seeking warmer temperatures during the cold North American winters. If birds of prey spend several months every year in coral snake territory, they might just avoid all mimics regardless of location.

This explanation is further strengthened by the fact that the stakes of coral snake mimicry are higher than with nonlethal mimics. Think back to the butterfly example. If a predator eats a bad butterfly, it spits it out and learns its lesson. If it tangles with a coral snake, things go one of two ways: Either the predator successfully kills the snake without getting envenomated, or it gets bit and dies. If predators are going to "learn" that coral snakes are venomous, it's going to evolve over many generations. The innate avoidance of coral snake-like patterns has been demonstrated in some birds, so it makes sense for them to err on the side of caution. It's one thing to evolve to avoid colorful ringed snakes; it's trickier to evolve to avoid them for only half of the year (something that would be easier if the avoidance was learned).

Another potential factor is that many other snake predators don't see color very well. Most birds (except owls) have great vision; their eyes even have more color receptors (four) than us humans (three). But mammals like foxes, racoons, or coyotes are basically red-green colorblind (primates are the only mammals with good color vision). They rely on good hearing and an excellent sense of smell to supplement their mediocre eyesight. The last main category of potential predators are other snakes, which also lack full color vision. This means that the bright red that stands out so much to our human eyes isn't so obvious to a large proportion of possible snake predators. And the predators with the best color vision—birds—are also the ones that migrate (potentially spending several months of the year in areas with coral snakes).

Yet another interesting hypothesis is a phenomenon called flicker fusion. The basic idea is that when a pyro, coral snake, or other banded snake moves fast enough, the bands blur together. Flicker fusion has a number of potential benefits. The uniform blur of the snake may make it harder for a predator to distinguish it from the background or tell what direction it is moving in. Alternatively, when the snake stops moving, it may be difficult for the predator to recognize it again, or the shift from a solid color to multicolored bands could even be startling. While still not thoroughly investigated, one study indicated that the size of kingsnake bands and the vision abilities of predatory birds should in fact result in the hypothesized blur when the snake moves at top speed. The effects of flicker fusion have been anecdotally reported from a human point of view too, including by Edmund Brodie III, one of the pioneers in coral snake predation studies.

The fascinating thing about some of these explanations is that they make nonoverlapping mimics seem less like true mimics. Maybe their coloration is fooling migratory raptors. But to the (partially) colorblind mammals, perhaps the point of their banding patterns is not to mimic anything but rather to suddenly cause confusion via flicker fusion. After all, many mimics have their bands in the wrong order and often have a wrong color too. Interestingly, this line of thinking is not unlike what a few scientists used to argue against mimicry in the mid-twentieth century. This idea—of mimics not actually being mimics—is almost heretical in contemporary biology (especially given the preponderance of evidence for coral snake mimicry). But given the number of headaches these nonoverlapping mimics have caused, maybe biologists have been trying to shove them into a box they only partially belong in.

If you're still a little confused, don't worry. I am too. This is a rather complex niche of evolutionary biology. Hopefully in the coming decades, additional research will clear things up. What I've outlined here are just a few hypotheses for why mimicry for nonoverlapping mimics isn't as disadvantageous as once thought. It's likely a combination of some (or all) of these possible explanations, and perhaps additional factors yet to be considered.

This is how scientific knowledge usually accumulates anyway. Breakthroughs are great, but incremental discoveries add up over time, and one day these mystifying mimics might make more sense.

NINE

In Too Deep

After returning from the long trip to Arizona and New Mexico, I took a much-needed break from the wilderness for a few weeks. I didn't come home with any major sunburns miraculously, but my sock tan line was absolutely impeccable. Yet as the itch of my bug bites faded, the itch to get back out to look for pyros only grew stronger.

In mid-June, I was invited on another expedition by Mark Hazel, amateur herper extraordinaire. Unlike our prior milk snake expedition, this time we would be looking for pyros. That weekend our destination was the Deep Creek Mountains, a remote range in western Utah, just across the Nevada border. I hadn't even heard of the Deep Creeks before I met Mark, but he spoke highly of the place. Mark, of course, had been there many times; the man has been to practically every mountain range in western Utah.

There was just one catch: Pyros might not actually be found in the Deep Creek Mountains. No formal documentation of the species in this mountain range exists. No museum specimens, no iNaturalist records, and no firsthand accounts from reptile enthusiasts. Mark and several other mountain kingsnake aficionados had been looking intermittently for the past two decades and had yet to find one. We might be looking for a snake that wasn't even there.

There was reason to hope that pyros were hiding somewhere in the Deep Creeks though. Given how elusive they are even in known localities, it wouldn't be surprising for pyros to have flown under the radar for so long. The mountain range has plenty of suitable upland habitat, with verdant forests and many perennial streams, though its remoteness limits the amount of visitors it sees. Additionally, the Deep Creeks lie only a few miles to the north of Nevada's more visited (and aptly named) Snake Range, where pyros are well known.

Mark was relatively confident that pyros were hiding in the Deep Creeks, but in a way it felt like we were going to look for bigfoot. I've watched a fair amount of the TV show *Finding Bigfoot*, and despite episode after episode of anecdotal accounts, spurious evidence, and seemingly ideal conditions, they never actually find bigfoot. Pyros do exist though (sorry bigfoot!), so there was still a chance.

Our route to the Deep Creeks took Mark and I across the flat desert of western Utah. The wind was strong that day, which caused two disconcerting things. First, we encountered a major dust storm. Visibility dropped to almost nothing for several seconds, with fine dirt enveloping the car on all sides. The dust was so thick that it felt like a scene from a movie—maybe aliens had picked this spot to land a spaceship. The second problem was even more off-putting: The gas gauge of Mark's old Outback started to drop like a rock. You could literally see the needle moving down, which is not something you want to see anywhere, let alone in a place so remote that the aliens could actually land without anyone noticing. The air pressure from the storm must have somehow been messing with the gauge though, because after the storm subsided, it crept back up.

With the initial dangers in our rearview mirror, Mark and I continued on. We encountered the first few reptiles before we even arrived at our destination. Several unlucky desert horned lizards (*Phrynosoma platyrhinos*, or more like "*flat-yrhinos*" given their condition) were smashed flat on the dirt road. Thankfully, we also found one that had yet to be run over, though it darted under the tire of the stopped car. Each species of horned lizard can be identified simply by the shape and number of horns on their head, and I don't think there is a group of lizards that have more dragon-like heads. Desert horned lizards have two main horns that point straight back, flanked by two smaller horns on each side.

While their horns vary, all horned lizards share the same wide, spiky body shape. Since they rely heavily on camouflage, they tend to evolve to match the dirt and rocks of the local area, meaning that a single species can come in a variety of colors. I've seen desert horned lizards from localities with red sandstone rocks that have gorgeous ruby red colors to match. The desert horned lizards Mark and I came across that day were a whitish brown with stylish orange accents.

While many other lizards rely on speed and agility, horned lizards aren't known for being fast. Fascinatingly, these lizards will tailor their defense responses to different predators, and even to different kinds of snake. An excellent 2008 study on Texas horned lizards (*Phrynosoma cornutum*) utilized large outdoor enclosures specially designed for safely observing lizard responses to predators. The snakes were placed on a wire ceiling suspended above the lizards, which were on the ground itself, allowing them to see but not catch the lizards. No lizards were physically harmed in the conducting of the study (though there may have been some psychological trauma).

The first kind of snakes tested in the experiment were western diamondback rattlesnakes (*Crotalus atrox*), a large bodied, ambush predator. Interestingly, the rattlers provoked different reactions than the slender, speedy whipsnakes (the coachwhip, *Masticophis flagellum*, and the Sonoran whipsnake, *Masticophis bilineatus*, were both used). Upon seeing a rattlesnake, the horned lizards in the experiment opted to run away almost every time. But when the predator was a whipsnake, the lizards only ran about 3 percent of the time. Instead, they flattened their already-wide body and tilted towards the snake in order to appear larger and thus harder to swallow. The horned lizards "knew" (evolutionarily speaking) that they could outrun the rattlesnakes but had no chance of outpacing the whipsnakes. Advertising their wide spiky girth showed how hard the lizards would be to swallow, a more effective deterrent to a skinny whipsnake.

Knowing this, I get offended whenever a horned lizard thinks its faster than me and tries to run away, which is what this live desert horned lizard attempted to do. Plenty of other lizards are faster than me, but horned lizards sure aren't. I'm not sure what response a horned lizard would have to a moving car, but judging by the smashed bodies Mark and I saw on that road, it isn't an effective one. After photographing the lone live lizard, we released it safely away from the road.

Unfortunately, the flattened horned lizards weren't the only roadkill reptiles that afternoon. Soon after, we came across a squished long-nosed leopard lizard (*Gambelia wislizenii*). Named for their leopard-like spots, these speedy lizards can run on just their hind legs for maximum speed. They are roughly a million times faster than horned lizards, but unfortunately this leopard lizard still wasn't able to dodge the tires that ran it over.

Before long, we came upon a dead gopher snake (*Pituophis catenifer*) sprawled on the dirt road. Based on the seven lumps in its body, Mark was able to discern it was a gravid female. The limp body was in excellent condition, especially considering it had been run over, but given the ridiculous amount of gopher snakes the Bean Museum herpetology collection already has, we left it for the scavengers (though we did salvage some of the dead lizards to pickle later).

After several hours on the road—slowed down by both the dust storm and the reptiles we had encountered—Mark and I finally arrived at the Deep Creeks. The name of the mountain range sounds generic, though admittedly I haven't seen the namesake creek. (For all I know, it could be some deceptive stream that looks shallow but is actually ten feet deep. Maybe.)

People don't usually refer to the Deep Creeks as a sky island, but the way the range rises out of the surrounding desert reminded me of the Madrean Archipelago I had been so fond of in Arizona. Maybe the Deep Creeks just need a better PR person, because they certainly are an oasis of mountainous forest in the midst of a desolate basin. The arid landscape surrounding the Deep Creeks is less exciting than the Sonoran Desert, featuring hardy shrubs instead of imposing saguaro cacti. But just like any good sky island marooned in an ocean of desert, things get greener the further up you go. A blanket of conifers covers much of the towering mountains, and the clear water of the many streams has carved impressive canyons. These mountains are many miles from anywhere that could be called a city, and the sheer remoteness of the range is impressive.

This remoteness certainly helped the native inhabitants of the area, the Goshute people, successfully fend off violent encroachment efforts from white settlers and the unjust attempts by the federal government to displace them. Today, much of the western and southern portions of the Deep Creeks still belong to the Goshutes, though there are only a few hundred left in the area.

The first day, Mark and I explored a canyon located in the southeast portion of the Deep Creeks. The creek wasn't unusually deep, but its water was clear and had many trout swimming in it. Mark informed me that this was one of the few spots with purely native cutthroat trout in Utah, though neither of us were interested in catching fish. It was late afternoon when we parked at our eventual campsite near the end of the rough dirt road and headed up the canyon on foot. If there were pyros in the Deep Creeks, there was only one way to find out.

We hiked a few miles along the trail, as well as several

additional off-trail miles, wandering around rocky scree and in vegetation between the trail and the creek. We saw two species of scelop (sagebrush and western fence lizards; *Sceloporus graciosus* and *Sceloporus occidentalis*, respectively), though neither were in high abundance. Mark found the desiccated body of a gopher snake (*Pituophis catenifer*) that had likely died the previous year, but that was the only semblance of a snake we saw that day.

The most—or really only—eventful parts of that first hike were the creek crossings. The water level was higher than Mark had ever seen it, high enough that these crossings were quite precarious. Not that the water was so high that it was dangerous—nor enough to call it a truly deep creek. No, it was just high enough that the crossings had no margin for error; one slight blunder and your feet got wet, which happened to both of us.

After the long hike, we returned to our predetermined campsite. The daylight was gone and the temperature was falling, so we settled down for dinner and an early bedtime. On the drive up, Mark had described the spot as the canyon's "one good campsite," and he was worried that someone else might have already claimed the idyllic site. When we parked at it though, I didn't even realize it was a campsite. The spot was just a small clearing near the creek with space for one tent—if we had brought any tents. I later realized that the main reason why Mark thought it was such a perfect spot was because you could sleep right on the edge of the creek bank, so close that if you rolled over at night you'd tumble down the bank into the bone-chilling water. Some people like to play artificial water sounds in their bedroom at night; Mark prefers the real thing.

Both of us overslept a bit, presumably worn out from the long hike the previous day (or perhaps in subconscious preparation for the even longer treks that awaited us). Rather than drive elsewhere, we opted to explore the same canyon again, though this time Mark wanted to first search below our campsite. This area was out of the canyon and more exposed to the sun, so most of the trees were restricted to the immediate vicinity of the creek. Cacti, yucca, sagebrush, and other desert plants dotted the rocky landscape along with the occasional juniper tree. In a way, it was the coastline of the sky island, where the ocean of desert mixes with the upland habitat.

After an hour or two of exploring, I finally sighted the first live serpent of the trip. Out of the corner of my eye, I saw a flash of movement to my left as a black streak shot across the dirt. The striped whipsnake (*Masticophis taeniatus*) quickly clambered up a juniper tree, a wise decision. The snake, sporting the distinctive white stripes running down its dark body, watched me warily with its large eyes. I called Mark over, though he wasn't very interested in such a common snake. This was the guy that had barely gotten excited about a milk snake, after all. I took some pictures of the whipsnake in the tree but didn't bother trying to pull it out of the branches.

Where they occur, whipsnakes are among the most frequently seen snakes. This is partially because they are relatively large and active, diurnal predators—greatly increasing their chances of being happened upon by a human. Being easier to find also means that whipsnakes have been studied much more than pyros, and they are the subject of one of the most entertaining stories I've ever read in a scientific paper. (I know, "entertaining scientific paper" sounds like an oxymoron.) The 1976 paper was a summary of several days of observation of whipsnakes at a single site in the deserts of Tooele County, Utah. The authors had painted the heads and necks of a large number of whipsnakes with unique markings. The colored markings allowed them to identify individuals as they observed their social behaviors from afar using binoculars.

It is a common misconception that snakes are nonsocial animals. Although snakes don't interact in the same ways and to the same degree that humans may, they still have their own social interactions. There is no verbal communication, but body language, touch, and scent do the trick. Snakes will often hibernate with others of their species, as well as those not of their species, in large congregations. Some species lay eggs at communal sites, and the males of some snakes, like striped whipsnakes, will duel for dominance.

Interactions between snakes are normally tricky to document, especially in any large quantity, but thanks to the paint, binoculars, and a large population of unwitting reptilian volunteers, the scientists in the 1976 publication were able to record a large number of social behaviors.

The study showed that male whipsnakes were rarely aggressive towards each other when females weren't present, but as soon as a lady was around, the odds of conflict increased dramatically. The funniest anecdote included in that paper was about a pair of courting whipsnakes who were interrupted by another male. Upon seeing the intruder, the female quickly hightailed it out of there, leaving the two males to duke it out. The males intertwined their long bodies, a common wrestling technique male snakes use to determine dominance. What happened next sounds like it came out of a rom-com. To quote the paper, "The combating males *then rolled ~8 m [26 feet] down a rocky hillside, remaining entwined throughout the entire fall and subsequent landing.* After remaining entwined for about five min[utes] longer, the two snakes separated and the intruder retreated out of sight." (Emphasis added). The paper unfortunately makes no mention of whether the female returned to congratulate her victorious suitor.

Half an hour after sighting the first whipsnake, Mark and I headed back in the direction of our camp. On the way, Mark predicted, "I bet one of us finds another one before we make it back." Not five minutes later, his words came true. This striped whipsnake was much smaller, only a juvenile, and Mark quickly apprehended it. He showed a little more interest in this one—it was his find, after all—taking some photos and recording the surrounding flora in his field notes. This was standard practice for Mark, who could name almost all of the nearby plant species. My plant classification skills weren't much beyond "bush" or "tree," though I could at least recognize the flat spiky paddles of the prickly pear cactus, whose vivid yellow and pink flowers were in full bloom.

While the temperatures had warmed up rapidly in the morning, overcast skies quickly took over. The afternoon and evening were almost chilly, an unusual occurrence for June. After searching below the campsite in the morning, we spent the remainder of the day re-searching the upper reaches of the canyon. Like the previous day, the only herps we saw here were a smattering of the same common lizards. Still no pyros, though they weren't the only possible serpentine residents of the canyon that had eluded us.

On our third and final day in the Deep Creeks, we opted for a change of scenery. In the morning, we drove north to another canyon. This one had a parking area and more extensive campsites—there were actual campsites here—but the place was just as devoid of people as the previous spot. We were now going on three days without seeing any other humans. The overall lack of people was one of the reasons that I think Mark loves the Deep Creeks. Of course, the potential of being the first to document a pyro in the mountain range is a significant draw too. But there is something nice about truly being alone in the wilderness. I've been on some "trails" that are so popular that you might as well be in a city park. Isn't part of the point of getting into nature to get away from other humans? For people like me and Mark, the answer is yes. For anyone hoping to escape the hubbub of modern life, there are plenty of remote mountain ranges to explore in western Utah and eastern Nevada. Just don't plan on having cell service. Sorry, I digress.

We spent the majority of the day on one long, winding hike. Thankfully there were no difficult creek crossings here. The western fence lizards (*Sceloporus occidentalis*), which were few and far between at the previous canyon, were remarkably abundant here. These lizards are a gray color with dark markings on their back and big blue patches below. Covered in coarse, spiny scales, adult western fence lizards grow well over six inches from head to tail. Their relatives, the sagebrush lizards (*Sceloporus graciosus*) are an inch or two smaller, more brown, and less spiky. They were also more plentiful here than at the previous canyon, though not by as much.

I snapped pictures of several to later upload to iNaturalist, but there were enough lizards that I didn't bother photographing them all. Mark periodically pointed out the plants that he felt were noteworthy, often pausing to record the coordinates in his field notes. I repeatedly tried to persuade Mark that he should be uploading his observations to iNaturalist. He'd remarked to me numerous times that he'd photographed organisms, be it snakes or bumblebees or something else, that no one on iNat had observed in a given area—and it's these records that are most valuable.

It would be nigh impossible for a single scientist to survey the entire range of a species. Having a community of thousands or millions of online users is a massive boon to biological research. I've talked about citizen science before, but it's important enough that I want to highlight it again, just in case you are also sitting on a mountain of potentially useful data.

The easiest way to get involved in citizen science is through online platforms such as iNaturalist, eBird, eMammal, HerpMapper, etc. Most of these are available as a website and as an app, and it is relatively easy for users to upload observations. My preference is for iNaturalist because it encompasses all organisms and involves the user community much more than other platforms, though the more taxon-specific efforts have their own advantages. While they lack the same scientific rigor of museum collections, citizen science observations provide important contemporary information on where organisms are found. This data can also be taken a step beyond simply outlining ranges and be used in modeling of present or future suitable habitat for an organism, which can be hugely helpful in informing the conservation of threatened species. Observations of interactions (predation, interspecies fighting, mating, etc.) are extra valuable.

I encourage anyone who spends time outdoors to contribute to iNaturalist, especially if you have documentation of less common organisms or visit less-traveled areas. Please only upload quality pictures though; blurry pictures can be impossible to identify to the species level, even for experts. Taking multiple photos, especially from different angles, can also be important; you never know what characteristics are needed to distinguish between similar looking species. Focus on getting good documentation of a few noteworthy organisms instead of a million out of focus pictures of every squirrel you see.

If you already know a lot about a specific group of organisms, you can also contribute by identifying the observations of other users. Platforms like iNaturalist benefit greatly from an active community of identifiers, which significantly reduces the potential for error. If you disagree with someone on an identification, please always be polite and provide reasons for your opinions—iNaturalist is one of the few places on the internet where disagreements (almost always) stay amicable.

iNaturalist isn't the only form of citizen science. Data from social media can be effective too if curated well. One of my favorite citizen science-related papers comes from Bhutan, a tiny mountainous country between China and India nicknamed "Land of the Thunder Dragon." Herpetologists there used a Facebook group to aggregate sightings, leading to the reporting of forty-eight previously undocumented species of reptiles and amphibians within its borders. (In the acknowledgements section of the paper, the authors even give the king a shout-out for prioritizing conservation, which is awesome.)

Another Facebook group, this time in southern Africa, was used to gather predation records. In the past, to scientifically report one organism eating another, you would have to write a formal note and submit it to an academic journal for peer review. This takes a lot of time, effort, and prior know-how—too much for the vast majority of people to even consider doing. But uploading photos to a Facebook group (or iNaturalist) and tagging an expert is significantly easier. The 2020 study from Africa was able to collect 1,917 feeding observations of herpetofauna from 2015 to 2019, far more than had been recorded from the region in the scientific literature ever, let alone during that short span. Given that most impacts of the technological advancements of society have been negative for the environment, it is good to know that there are some positives.

Citizen scientists can also get involved in more formal efforts, such as surveying for locally threatened species directly in conjunction with researchers. Conservation organizations and state wildlife agencies often have ways for volunteers to help out. As long as the protocols are effective, studies have found that involving citizen scientists leads to increased data without the loss of quality. Mark, who was a veteran of the UDWR kingsnake surveys in the early 2000s, already contributed to citizen science in this way and through his contributions to the Bean Museum herpetology collection, though he has yet to upload any of his important findings to iNaturalist.

I have to tease Mark about this a bit since he teases me about my abysmal lack of plant identification skills. My real point here is to convince you, my dear reader, that you don't need formal training in biology to make meaningful contributions to science.

By early evening, Mark and I made it back to the parking area. We had walked many miles up the canyon, both on and off trail. We hadn't seen any snakes that day, but the abundance of lizards was better than nothing, and the remoteness was refreshing. I didn't feel too disappointed about not seeing a pyro, given that I came in with minimal expectations. I don't know if I will ever be back, but maybe it is only a matter of time before Mark finds a pyro in the Deep Creeks on his own. I just hope he'll upload it to iNaturalist.

TEN

Fire on the Mountain

It was now the middle of the summer, and my count of pyros for the year was still a pitiful one. Though one was infinitely more than the zero of the previous year, I was desperately craving the adrenaline rush of spotting those shiny scarlet scales again. It was time to go back to snake paradise: Kanosh Canyon. Seeing another pyro at Kanosh would be scientifically insignificant—especially compared to the prospect of documenting the first pyro in the Deep Creeks or putting the nail in the coffin of a taxonomic controversy by finding one on Mount Lemmon—but at this point I wasn't interested in chasing scientific significance. I just wanted to see another pyro. And perfect conditions were right around the corner.

Typically, temperatures in July in Utah are hot and dry. The thermometer regularly soars into the triple digits and rain is rare. Some people mistakenly think that because snakes are cold-blooded that they inherently love extremely warm temperatures. In reality, most snake species enjoy baking under the blazing sun in hundred-degree heat about as much as people do. This means that when the rare summer thunderstorm rolls in, bringing both moisture and a break from the heat, the snakes appreciate it as much as the people. Seeing raindrops in the forecast means it's time to get off the couch and head for the mountains.

The afternoon rain was just beginning to peter out as I exited the freeway and drove through the tiny town of Kanosh. On my way south from Provo I'd driven past an electronic sign along the freeway that had referred to a forest fire in the nearby area. I had seen some smoke too, though it was hard to tell what was smoke and what were dark storm clouds looming over the mountains. Before heading into the canyon, I took the chance to do a quick wildfire check while I still had cell service. Based on what I saw online, the fire was far away, and the rest of the forest was now thoroughly soaked. I was too preoccupied with finding another pyro to worry about a literal fire anyway.

The dirt road up Kanosh Canyon held up fine in the rain. Though it's one of those roads where the most common vehicles are ATVs and side-by-sides, the wide road is smooth enough to drive a passenger car up no problem. You can also haul a massive camper up with your lifted truck, which is what most of the other people up the canyon had done. Surprisingly, the place was busier on a Wednesday in July than it had been on the weekend in May when Jacob and I had last visited.

While most of the campsites were occupied, though, the familiar trail up the wide, main fork of Corn Creek was empty. The path was muddy, and droplets of water fell from the leaves with every gust of wind. Maybe this was why everyone else was hunkered down in their RVs.

On the way up the canyon that evening, I saw a handful of spiny lizards (mostly *Sceloporus tristichus* but some *Sceloporus graciosus*), undeterred by the wet conditions and overcast skies. Most of these brownish lizards were splayed out on the rocks, attempting to soak up any heat that the afternoon sun had left. I took a few pictures to upload to iNaturalist later, but didn't bother with the lizards too much.

Before long, I stumbled—almost literally—onto the first snake. It was an adult Great Basin rattlesnake (*Crotalus lutosus*), casually lumbering across the dirt trail. I didn't notice the serpent, which was several feet long, until the unmistakable buzz of the rattle caused my eyes to snap downwards. I was so busy scanning for snakes off of the trail that I missed the well-camouflaged, dull-colored snake smack dab in the middle of it. The snake's tan body, accented by regular dark brown blotches, blended right in.

The snake didn't appear too rattled (pun intended) by my presence. I was still several steps away when it first alerted me. Rather than coil up and assume a defensive posture, the snake merely kept an eye on me and continued on its way. It slithered lazily across the trail, occasionally shaking its rattle, and crawled up the hill as I snapped a few pictures. I assume it was headed to its ambush site for the night, though it wasn't in a hurry.

As if rattlesnakes weren't interesting enough already, their rattles glow. The rattle doesn't produce light but rather absorbs light at high frequencies and emits lower frequencies back out. You might never notice though, because the glow is ultraviolet (UV). UV light has wavelengths much smaller than the visible light that our human eyes are able to detect, but that doesn't mean it isn't there. Many other animals, like birds, can see UV light, but since *Homo sapiens* is the only species to figure out physics, we say what wavelengths are considered "visible." The UV glow of a rattlesnake's trademark adaptation can be seen with our limited vision with the aid of a black light though.

A 2021 paper—with the wonderful title "Glow and Behold: Biofluorescence and New Insights on the Tails of Pitvipers…and Other Snakes"—revealed how surprisingly widespread this trait is in vipers. Their methods were incredibly simple; the authors basically pointed a black light at a bunch of different snakes and wrote down how much of each glowed. Of the twenty-eight species of pit viper tested, twenty-two glowed to some degree. For some snakes it was just a few scales on the tip, and for others it was several inches of tail. For rattlesnakes, the entire rattle glowed, though this was already known.

What is the point of this bizarre trait? The leading hypothesis is that the glowing tails evolved to enhance vermiform caudal luring. Before your eyes glaze over, here are some definitions: *Vermiform* means worm-like, and *caudal* means tail (and hopefully you already know what lure means). Ambushing snakes—usually juveniles—can attract prey by flicking their worm-like tail in the air, almost like an angler will twitch bait on a hook in the water. I've never seen it personally, but vermiform caudal luring has been well-documented in many species of pit viper.

A glowing tail is thought to enhance the display (though this hasn't been explicitly tested yet), making it more likely an unsuspecting animal will wander too close to the ambushing snake. Caudal luring is generally done by young pit vipers, who often have a tail tipped with bright colors that fade as the snake grows older. However, caudal luring isn't common in adult snakes, yet the entire rattle of a rattlesnake glows regardless of age.

Potentially, rattlesnakes use their glowing rattle for a different kind of caudal luring. The "Glow and Behold" paper points out that the rattle is similar in shape to the seeds of grasses which emit a similar UV glow under a black light. Rather than impersonating a worm, rattlesnakes might draw in rodents by having the tail resemble seeds. The glowing rattle also likely accentuates the defensive display of a rattlesnake (which is the rattle's main purpose anyway) for predators, like hawks, that can see in UV. Not only does the relatively small rattle produce a remarkably loud sound, but perhaps the glow adds to the intimidation. These hypotheses have yet to be empirically tested though and represent a fascinating area for further research.

While we're on the topic of caudal luring, there's one other thing I can't help but mention. One species found in the Middle East, called the Iranian spider-tailed viper (*Pseudocerastes urarachnoides*), takes caudal luring to the next level. The tail of this species has thin, leg-like appendages extending from the tip that resemble a spider, especially when the snake expertly shakes it across the ground. When an unsuspecting bird flies in to snatch the "spider," the viper strikes. It may sound like it can't possibly be realistic, but the tail does an absolutely flawless spider impression in all the videos I've seen. No word on if the spider-tail glows too, but it very well might!

Saying goodbye to the rattlesnake, allowing it and its glowing rattle to slink off, I continued up the canyon. It felt odd to be back on this fateful trail again, two months after finding my first pyro. The beautiful orange sandstone of the canyon was unchanged, and the rushing waters of Corn Creek continued to flow. Some things had changed though. Everything was soaking wet for the moment, but overall there was significantly less green thanks to the last two months of summer heat.

One other key difference I noted was that the grasses were also markedly shorter, and it wasn't hard to spot the culprits. Cows. "Public land" is almost synonymous with "cow pastures" in the western US, and I have a strong distaste for the lumbering brutes. Ranchers pay only a ridiculously small amount for the privilege of allowing their bovines to desecrate wild landscapes with green and brown sludge. Their impacts are more than aesthetic too. Cows dramatically alter the plant communities where they graze, and tear up cryptobiotic soil crusts—the cool name for the living "dirt" composed of fungi, lichen, cyanobacteria, bryophytes, and algae—while they're at it.

To top it all off, cows contribute more to climate change than any other animal on the planet (except humans, of course). Via farts and belches, cows release copious amounts of methane, a greenhouse gas that traps heat about twenty-five times more effectively than carbon dioxide, the notorious poster child for greenhouse gasses. Methane doesn't last as long in the atmosphere as other gasses, but when it does break down it turns into water and carbon dioxide, which continues to trap heat. Imagine that earth's atmosphere is a big blanket of gasses around the planet. One of those metaphorical blankets—an extra thick one—comes from cows. Now imagine trying to sleep in the middle of the summer with a bunch of blankets on top of you and you'll have a good idea of how the planet has been feeling lately. Think about that before you order your next cheeseburger.

There had been no cows back in May polluting either the atmosphere or my view. Bemoaning their presence, I quickly moved (moo-ved?) on from where the cows were congregated, though they had left brown, smelly presents for me all throughout the canyon.

As the sun was setting behind the tree-covered mountains, I turned around and headed back down the canyon. The cloudy sky still trapped some of the warmth from the day, with air temperatures just a shade above seventy degrees. A couple of the resident plateau fence lizards (*Sceloporus tristichus*) were still out, trying to soak up leftover heat from the rocks, but most had gone to bed for the night.

Not long after I had turned around, I wandered off the trail towards a rocky outcropping. There was a circular open space ringed by oaks with several large sandstone rocks strewn about. As I walked up, I scanned the area, judging which of the orange rocks might be worth checking under. Suddenly, something made me freeze in my tracks. In the middle of the small clearing, with its body sprawled on a rock and head in the air, was a snake. Despite the distance, the red, black, and white bands were unmistakable. It was a pyro.

We both stood—can a legless creature stand?—absolutely still. My heart began pounding with excitement, but I remained motionless. The pyro must have spotted me a second or two before I spotted it, because it was positioned as though it had been frozen in the middle of crawling down the rock. I could clearly see the head, with its round eyes staring back at me, and most of the body. The snake remained stationary, stiff as a log, probably hoping I would walk in any direction except towards it.

I slowly reached my hand into my pocket and pulled out my phone. I snapped a quick picture, silently gawking in disbelief. The snake still hadn't moved a muscle. Not wanting to risk it bolting down a hole, I started to delicately inch my way forwards.

The pyro must not have realized quite how obviously it stood out, as the snake didn't move for several seconds. When I had crept to within a couple steps, it finally decided I was too close and made a run for it. Rather than moving in the direction it was originally headed though, the snake turned around, as though its preferred hiding spot was behind it. I jumped forward and gently scooped up the snake with my right hand.

I felt the cool scales of the snake in my hand, its colorful bands sliding across my palm. I couldn't believe my luck. I had spent weeks in Arizona without seeing a pyro, but I had found one just hours into this trip—and in the exact same canyon as my first. Unlike that first pyro, this one didn't bite or even attempt to strike. It squirmed in my hands, vainly trying to get back to the ground, but declined to even musk on me.

She was a tad shorter and significantly skinnier than my first pyro, though that one was unusually hefty. Given the time of day and weather conditions, I imagine she was either out looking to get a drink of freshly fallen rain or was hoping to stumble upon a lizard, reflexes slowed by the cool temperatures.

I took some pictures of the snake on my phone, but it was difficult to get a great shot. If I had been more patient, I would have tried setting up some flashlights to make up for the increasingly dark sky, but it was hard enough to balance taking pictures with preventing the snake from getting away. Some people say you should always be with a buddy in the wilderness in case you get hurt. I say you should always bring another person so they can keep the snake from escaping while you take pictures.

Though I was only a mile or two from where I had found my first pyro, the circumstances of the sightings were completely different. Before, I had barely spotted a tiny glimpse of tell-tale scales peeking through the fallen leaves. This time, the snake was climbing on rocks out in the open and I spotted it from a mile away. Even against the reddish sandstone rocks, the brightly colored snake was incredibly obvious.

While finding a pyro at all is unusual, the conditions were ideal and in line with the results from the only full-fledged field study on the species. Published in 2008, the study took place in May of 2006 and 2007 in the Snake Range of eastern Nevada. The goal of the authors—Bryan Hamilton and Polly Conrad—and numerous volunteer surveyors was to document as many pyros throughout the range as they could; before the study, fewer than ten pyros had ever been documented in Nevada. Each survey recorded variables such as habitat, temperature, humidity, cloud cover, distance to water, and more.

In all, their 424 person-hours of searching yielded a total of ten pyros. The snakes were found at an average temperature of seventy-two degrees, typically in high cloud cover and relatively high humidity. Four of the snakes were found in cloudless conditions, but all of these were in the shade. Most snakes were close to permanent water sources, but two were found in areas without perennial water. These conditions—relatively low temperatures, very cloudy, close to water—perfectly matched my latest pyro encounter.

Of the ten pyros the Nevada study found, only one was female. Finding mostly males is relatively unsurprising given the time of year the study was conducted. Male snakes tend to move more in the breeding season, actively searching out females (though the nine-to-one ratio is probably a little extreme and a product of the low sample size).

Although the study is limited by the small sample, having any sort of field study on the species is great. The results generally matched anecdotal reports—a preference for mild weather, and often but not always found near surface water. It also confirmed that pyros are just plain hard to find. Even in good conditions, it takes time and a lot of luck. I was grateful to have gotten lucky for a second time.

Eventually, I gave up trying to get a good picture of the wiggly snake in the dim light. It was time to let the pyro go. I had no intention of taking her out of the wild to be a pet. To take such a precious jewel out of her home seemed downright sacrilegious. You could argue that collecting a snake is "saving" it from a harsh life in the wild and giving it a cushy, idyllic existence in captivity. But transitioning to captive life is often stressful and many wild snakes will refuse to eat and starve to death. At the end of the day, wildlife should be left, well, in the wild.

I let the pyro crawl from my hands onto the rock she was originally situated on. At first, the snake looked unsure if she was truly free or if I would again pull her back once she got too far away. But this time was for real, and she eventually clambered down and slid into a small cavity under an adjacent rock. She coiled herself up, barely visible, and I said my final goodbyes.

It was practically dark by the time I got back on the trail. I almost got hit in the face by a bat, after which I decided it was time to pull a flashlight out. I kept my eyes peeled, but I didn't encounter any other reptiles the rest of the night. Thankfully, one of the few previously vacant campsites was still unoccupied, so I pulled my car in and set up camp.

As I crawled into my sleeping bag, I changed the background screen on my phone—I'm sure you can guess to what—and contemplated the events of the day. Finding another pyro had been an amazing rush, but the feeling of euphoria faded faster this time. Last time I felt on top of the world for hours, and couldn't help but smile about it the whole weekend. This time, the exhilaration and satisfaction had already largely dissipated. Perhaps this was why Mark was so dedicated to finding pyros in unvouchered locations instead of just trying to find as many as possible.

The next day, I woke up with the first rays of the sun and quickly broke camp. That goes fast when "camp" is just a tarp, a sleeping pad, and a sleeping bag. I scarfed down a pair of Pop Tarts (my favorite easy camping breakfast) and hit the trail as soon as I could.

I was itching to see if the pyro was still wedged under the same rock as the previous night. I had arranged a line of rocks in the dirt as a sign in case I didn't remember where I had veered off the trail. The reminder turned out to be unnecessary though, as I immediately recognized the spot. I crossed my fingers as I walked up, but my friend wasn't under the rock I'd left her under, nor any of the nearby ones. I carefully scanned the small clearing, hoping to find her basking in the morning sunlight or hidden at the base of a bush, but she was nowhere to be seen. The pyro was gone, but that was okay. She was off doing whatever nature intended.

After hurrying up the canyon that morning, I took my time on the way down. Plenty of lizards were out basking, soaking up the sunshine. The cows were out too, eating and pooping like only cows can. The herd of bovines had just come into view when I noticed a snake I had seen many times before doing something I had never seen.

Off to the left of the trail, under a clump of rocks, was a snake poking straight up out of the ground. It was a yellow-bellied racer (*Coluber constrictor mormon*) doing its best impression of a submarine periscope. These diurnal snakes have large eyes and good vision, and this one must have been taking a careful look around before deciding if it was time to leave its shelter. I'd seen snakes raise their heads off the ground to look around before, but I'd never seen one do it with the rest of its body still underground.

I stopped in my tracks and the dull green snake froze as well, with ten inches or so of its body still sticking up in the air. It really did look like a periscope, and I couldn't help but laugh at the silly sight. Snakes have bad hearing due to their lack of external ears, so thankfully it wasn't startled by my chuckling. A few of the cows in the meadow glanced over, but they were more interested in pumping methane into the atmosphere than looking at a snake.

Both the racer and I knew we each had seen each other. Every slight movement I made prompted the snake to retract itself into the hole a bit more. It was like a bizarre game of "red light, green light," except the snake wasn't giving me any green lights. Trying to keep my movements limited, I snapped a couple of pictures. By now, the racer was barely sticking out of the hole. Snakes may lack external ears, but I'm sure it could detect my footfalls, even as I tried to step as lightly as possible.

Running out of patience, I lunged towards it. The racer rapidly slid down the cracks between the rocks. I quickly moved as many rocks aside as I could, only to discover—as I had feared—that there was a snake-sized tunnel underneath the pile. The racer was gone, safely underground, but at least it had given me another memorable snake experience in my favorite canyon on the planet.

After taking a break for lunch, I hiked the nearby north fork of Corn Creek. This canyon is narrower and has more trees, but the red sandstone and overall vegetation are the same. The morning had been relatively sunny, but the cloud cover was steadily increasing.

The first snake of the afternoon was yet another yellow-bellied racer (*Coluber constrictor mormon*). It was probably around three feet long, adult size for the species. The snake rapidly slithered away from me, but rather than stick to the ground, it shot directly up one of the gangly Gambel oak trees alongside the path. That was fine by me; usually when I catch a yellow-bellied racer I end up putting it in a tree for pictures anyway. The snake didn't hold perfectly still, but it was much calmer than it would have been in my hands.

From below, I had a nice view of the yellow belly of the snake, which eyed me warily with its large, round pupils. The greenish color of the snake's back blended in nicely with the green leaves; it almost made me wonder if any of the racers that had escaped me in the past had secretly avoided detection by climbing upwards.

I saw one other yellow-bellied racer not long after, but this one immediately disappeared from view into the underbrush.

I gradually became aware that the clouds, which had continued to roll in, were looking increasingly ominous. I had purposely timed my trip to coincide with what was possibly the wettest week of the summer for central Utah, yet I wasn't bright enough to bring a raincoat. In retrospect, I should have turned around from the hike sooner, or at least looked for some more effective shelter.

Soon, the skies opened up and the rain came down. At first it was light, and I moved around trying to find the driest tree possible to shelter under. Before long though, the drizzle turned into a downpour, and even the tree with the densest branches I could find wasn't keeping me very dry.

The circumstances reminded me of a time, almost exactly a year ago in a different part of the Pahvant Mountains, when I had been stuck outside in a thunderstorm by myself. That last time I had found a nifty rock ledge to keep me dry as I waited out the storm. This time I was getting drenched.

Yet now, I couldn't help but smile. Last year I couldn't find a pyro for the life of me. Now I had found two, which felt like a million compared to zero. Before, I had no clue if I was going to be able to get into graduate school. Now, my prospects were looking good. Thanks to pyros, I had two papers, at varying stages, that would make my CV competitive. Over the last couple of months I had been in the process of contacting potential advisors and looking for a good fit in terms of research, finances, and location. I had narrowed things down to just a few programs, though I wasn't in a rush to make a decision.

Eventually, the rain let up. Most Utah summer storms aren't very long, though this one felt longer than most. I was dripping wet by the end of it and was left vainly wishing that the sun would come out to dry me off. Originally, I had planned on staying the rest of the day and possibly through to the next day. But I was now cold, soaked, and—most importantly—had already accomplished my mission. I had found my pyro. I'd also seen several other snakes and had some nice relaxing time in the wilderness by myself. Satisfied, I opted to simply drive home. Sometimes it's best to quit when you're ahead.

ELEVEN

Rattlesnake Roulette

The Border Inn. Part casino, part motel, part gas station, and part restaurant, the Border Inn is located along highway fifty in central Nevada, a stone's throw from the Utah border. Even if you miss the state sign, you always know when you cross into Nevada when you see the telltale casino, even in the middle of nowhere. The Border Inn is miles from anything that remotely resembles a town; it's marooned in the middle of the desert but more akin to a floating trash clump than a sky island. Though its highway sign proudly proclaims otherwise, the Border Inn isn't much of a casino; the place just has a few dozen slot machines smartly situated between the convenience store entrance and the bathrooms. I stopped there with my friends Jacob Searcy and Taylor Probst to top up on gas and use the restrooms (which were about as clean as you'd expect for a place as high class as the Border Inn). I had Jacob take a picture of me in front of the casino sign for fun, but the three of us were not in Nevada to gamble. Not literally anyways.

Jacob, Taylor, and I were headed to the towering mountains

that loomed to the west of the Border Inn: the Snake Range. I wish there was a good backstory behind the name of these mountains—like if they had been the site where a legendary Native American chief had died of snakebite—but unfortunately I have yet to find any explanation for the name. The southern half of the Snake Range is home to Great Basin National Park, though it sees little traffic compared to most of its counterparts. The pinnacle of both the park and the mountain range is Wheeler Peak, which tops thirteen thousand feet and is the twelfth most prominent peak in the contiguous United States. The northern half of the Snake Range is even less traveled, except for those that come looking for the range's namesake animals.

Further to the north of the Snake Range lie the Deep Creek Mountains, which I'd visited with Mark not long ago. There is one big difference between these two ranges though; a certain red, white, and black banded scaly creature that might not even exist in the Deep Creeks is well known from the Snake Range. My friends and I were on a collecting trip for the Bean Life Science Museum, and we'd picked the Snake Range for that very reason. I'd seen two pyros and Jacob had seen one, but Taylor had yet to see any despite running around half of Arizona with me. The fact that it was in Nevada—even if it was only a couple of miles from the Utah border—made the Snake Range a touch more exotic too. And who could say no to visiting mountains with such a great name? And thus we were off to find Taylor's first pyro and collect a few reptiles for the Bean Museum along the way.

After our pit stop at the Border Inn, we headed north on a dirt road for a few miles until we arrived at Hendry's Canyon. This rocky canyon was the site of several past pyro sightings, and we were eager to add to the list. The creek runs above ground intermittently, and the canyon is relatively wide for the first few miles. The high desert landscape is dotted with sagebrush and other hardy shrubs, along with a smattering of juniper and pine trees. If you go high enough in elevation in the Snake Range, there are even bristlecone pines, a famous kind of gnarly pine that can live for several thousand years.

After parking the museum truck near the mouth of Hendrys Canyon, Taylor, Jacob, and I set off, occasionally wandering off the trail to explore rocky patches or shaded areas. The first exciting find of the afternoon wasn't a snake, nor was it a vertebrate. It was a massive tarantula hawk, the largest one I had ever seen. These menacing, dark colored wasps grow huge and possess one of the most painful insect stings on the planet. The main purpose for their incredible venom is to paralyze tarantulas, which they then drag into a burrow. The wasp lays a single egg on the arachnid's paralyzed body, which remains alive until the larvae hatches and feasts on its first meal. Not a pretty way to go, if you ask me. These wasps have to be big enough to carry the paralyzed body of a tarantula across the ground, and thus are several times larger than a run-of-the-mill yellow jacket. I'd seen plenty of tarantula hawks buzzing around before, but this one was an absolute monster.

I was close to the creek, away from Jacob and Taylor, when the hulking wasp appeared and began flying directly towards me. The tarantula hawk wasn't really attacking me—I (presumably) smelled nothing like a tarantula so it had no reason to—but it was unnervingly close. My brain went into panic mode, and rather than shouting something sensible like, "Tarantula hawk!" I yelled something along the lines of, "It's huge!" Jacob and Taylor sprinted over, unsure what kind of giant creature I had stumbled upon. Though they were hoping for a snake, they weren't too disappointed to see the enormous wasp. I was ready to get out of there as fast as possible, but Jacob had other ideas. "That would look great on a pin!" he said with glee. (Unlike reptiles that are preserved in liquid, insects are usually preserved dry on pins.)

Usually when he hikes, Jacob carries a butterfly net with him. While it typically gets used to nab swallowtails, painted ladies, or other delicate butterflies, turns out it works just as good for tarantula hawks. I stood well away from the action as Jacob and Taylor attempted to capture the monstrous insect for Jacob's personal insect collection. Getting it in the net wasn't too hard. The loud buzzing of the wasp's humongous wings vibrating against the net perfectly conveyed its fury. Jacob and Taylor carefully maneuvered a large plastic container under the net, which was being held to the ground to prevent the wasp from escaping. After a few close calls, they were able to coerce the wasp into the container and snap the lid shut.

Up close, the tarantula hawk was even more visually imposing. The wasp's large stinger was extending out of its abdomen, repeatedly, vainly trying to sting its way out of the predicament. Its body color was somewhere between a midnight black and an iridescent, metallic blue, which contrasted nicely with the orange wings extending from its thorax. She was an absolute monster, larger than many of the lizards we would see that trip. Jacob later measured her at two inches long. Two inches sounds wimpy, but when you add six gangly legs and a three-inch wingspan, you've got a wasp that would fill your entire palm. Thinking of it still makes me shudder.

While a tarantula hawk has the strength to drag the body of a paralyzed tarantula over rocky terrain, thankfully they aren't adapted to opening plastic leftover containers. Lid securely fastened, Jacob stowed the angry wasp in his backpack and we carried on. The skies were cloudy and the temperatures mild, making for a comfortable afternoon.

After a couple hours of hiking, we came across the first snake of the trip. I was walking in front along the primitive dirt trail, but all three of us noticed the serpent at the same time. It was a medium-sized Great Basin rattlesnake (*Crotalus lutosus*), stretched out parallel to the trail just a few feet away. The snake hadn't rattled at first, probably hoping we would walk right past it. After realizing its cover was blown, the rattling began in earnest.

Rattlesnakes are quite comical when they are trying to intimidate you and move away at the same time, as this individual was attempting to do. They will lift their head off the ground and cock their neck into an S-shape, ready to strike if necessary. The end of the tail, the vibrating rattle, will be held straight up in the air. And with both the front and back ends held off the ground, the middle part of the snake's body will move. This is especially hilarious when the retreating snake is also trying to keep its head pointed towards you while moving in the opposite direction. Snakes are normally extremely graceful animals, but this rattlesnake was demonstrating the limitations of a limbless body plan.

After a few minutes and plenty of pictures, the three of us moved on. We were on an official trip through the museum—which basically just meant we got to use the museum truck and didn't have to pay for gas—so we knew we would need to bring back at least a few specimens. It's safe to say though that none of us were eager to euthanize a venomous snake for the first time.

Not long after that initial rattlesnake encounter, we turned around to head back down Hendrys Canyon. Our stomachs were starting to rumble, signaling it was time to head back to the truck for dinner. It had been less than half an hour since we'd seen the rattlesnake, so we weren't surprised to see the snake just a few paces away from where we'd left him. The snake rattled its displeasure again, its forked tongue flicking slowly and deliberately in our direction. We laughed at the silly snake and continued down the trail, figuring we had intruded on his personal space enough already.

We encountered one other serpent on the way down. I was a bit behind the other two when I heard Taylor yell "Snake! Whipsnake!" and immediately dash off in pursuit. Jacob and I quickly followed. Like any other striped whipsnake (*Masticophis taeniatus*), this one was blazing fast. Evading Taylor, the snake dove into a large clump of bushes. The three of us surrounded the bushes, trying to catch a glimpse of the snake—and crossing our fingers that it didn't have a burrow underneath.

At first, we thought we lost it. Maybe there was a hole at the base of the bushes, or perhaps it had silently slipped away. But after a few seconds, we spotted the whipsnake again, still in the same large thicket, hoping to find an opening to escape. With some encouragement, the snake eventually got close to Jacob, who quickly seized a portion of its slender body. With Taylor's help, he gently untangled it from the bush and held the beautiful serpent in the air.

The snake's dark body, lined on either side with the classic pearly white stripes of the species, was long, even for a whipsnake. Her big, round eyes stared at us—probably annoyed we had interrupted her afternoon lizard hunt—but she didn't resort to biting. We took a quick snip of the tip of her tail before releasing the snake back into the wide world.

We were almost back to the truck when we came across something on the dirt road I had never seen before: a velvet ant orgy. Okay, maybe orgy isn't the right word. But I had never seen this many velvet ants in one place.

Velvet ants aren't real ants, though they are velvety. They are part of the order Hymenoptera, the massive group of insects that includes ants, bees, wasps, and more. Velvet ants are in fact wasps, more closely related to the giant tarantula hawk from earlier than any true ant. Female velvet ants lack wings but have a stinger capable of dealing an excruciating sting. Conversely, the males have wasp-like wings but no stinger (this is because the stinger is a modified ovipositor, a uniquely female insect part).

Both sexes have patches of colored fuzz on their bodies, which typically comes in red, orange, or yellow. The color of the velvet ant is an advertisement of its painful sting, which has earned them the nickname of "cow killers." A velvet ant couldn't actually kill a cow, but the sting is supposedly orders of magnitude more painful than a bee sting. I'd seen plenty of female velvet ants crawling around before, but this was the first time I'd seen the winged male velvet ants, and there were lots of them at the orgy.

I shouldn't make things sound overly dramatic. There were

maybe ten females and ten males in total, spread out over the distance of a few paces. None of the ants were copulating—I guess we interrupted things—but I assume that was what had brought these normally solitary insects together. Much like earlier, I was content to just observe, but Jacob and Taylor had other ideas. Armed with a butterfly net and forceps, they apprehended as many as they could. The flightless females were much easier to catch than the stingless males, as they nabbed five females and only one male before the rest escaped to safety. Turns out if the predator is a human with forceps, wings are more effective than a painful sting; evolution didn't see that one coming.

Velvet ants are especially interesting because they, like pyros, are mimics. In fact, they qualify as both Batesian and Müllerian mimics. In case you need a quick refresher, Batesian mimics are harmless species that copy a dangerous one, while Müllerian mimics are two or more dangerous species that have evolved to resemble each other (trying to make it easy on the predators to recognize their danger signal). Velvet ants check both boxes. The males—which have no stingers and thus are totally harmless—share the same velvety colors as the females, making them Batesian mimics. And many different species of velvet ant have evolved to look like each other, sharing the same colors and pattern to help potential predators recognize them, meaning they count as Müllerian mimics too. Among the sixty-five species found in North and Central America, each species resembles those it is geographically closest to, even if these species aren't close relatives of each other. I guess insects can be cool sometimes.

After a break at the truck for dinner, we headed back up Hendrys Canyon. The sun had yet to set and there would be several more hours of suitable temperatures after dark, so we packed our flashlights and hoped for the best. We were happy that the Snake Range had lived up to its name so far, but there was one species in particular we were still hoping for.

We had hiked for an hour or two, opportunistically flipping

rocks and exploring off the trail, when we neared the spot we had found the rattlesnake at earlier. It was here that the most hilariously well-timed statement I've ever heard was uttered. Jacob said something along the lines of, "We saw our rattlesnake buddy somewhere up ahead, right?" Taylor was hiking in front of us, and before he could reply he suddenly leapt backwards and let out a surprised "WHOA!" He had almost stepped on—you guessed it—a rattlesnake. The equally terrified snake practically leapt away as well, and the synchronous timing of their panicked jumps was rather comical.

The three of us humans burst into laughter. The snake, which was the exact same rattlesnake from a few hours earlier, was less thrilled. It rapidly crawled a safe distance away from us, who were still cracking up, and coiled into a defensive position. We marveled at Taylor's luck; if the snake had wanted to, it easily could have bitten him instead of flinging its body away. Somehow the gravity of the situation didn't make it less hysterical; I've never laughed so hard at a snake in my life. We dubbed the snake Larry the Lutosus, *lutosus* being the species name for the Great Basin rattlesnake. I don't know if Larry gave us a name too, but if he did, it wasn't a nice one.

We made sure to confirm that it was in fact the same snake, but elected to leave the poor animal alone after we finally stopped laughing. Continuing onward, we hiked well past the point we had turned around at in the afternoon, eventually making it to a small stream crossing. It was completely dark by now and the stream made a good stopping point. Our walk back was quiet and uneventful. We didn't see Larry again—I imagine that he crawled as far away from the trail as he could.

I've spotted rattlesnakes before hearing them rattle before, but this was by far the closest I'd seen someone get before the snake reacted. Interestingly, it has been shown that in areas of high human activity that rattlesnakes tend to be less eager to rattle. Normally, the rattle is a great warning signal, but unfortunately it is often taken by humans as an invitation to harass the snake. Those that elect not to rattle and give away their position would be less likely to be bothered, or worse—get decapitated by a shovel.

Some of the strongest evidence of the influence of humans on rattlesnake behavior comes from a 2022 study that took place in British Columbia, Canada. The researchers compared the rattling tendencies of northern Pacific rattlesnakes (*Crotalus oreganus*, a close relative of *Crotalus lutosus*) between areas heavily frequented by people and nearby places where humans seldom were around. Whenever the scientists found a rattlesnake, they used snake tongs to manipulate it under a plexiglass box with no bottom. They left it alone for five minutes to acclimate to its temporary see-through prison. When the researcher returned, they walked directly towards the snake at a standardized pace and recorded the distance at which the snake first rattled. After doing this with sixty-eight different snakes across multiple study sites, the results were very convincing.

The rattlesnakes in areas of high human activity were six to seven times more likely to not rattle at all, and tended to wait until people were much closer before rattling. Having people around made the snakes significantly less rattle-happy. It is likely that shotgun-wielding humans have also selected against eager rattling behavior in some populations, with snakes that prefer to stay silent more often going unnoticed and thus surviving. However, the authors in this study argued that the differences in behavior at their study sites was more likely due to habituation; essentially that snakes in areas with high foot traffic were just accustomed to seeing humans bumble around and getting harassed whenever they drew attention to themselves.

Larry the Lutosus had likely never seen people before—the Snake Range is about as remote as it gets. But perhaps he figured by the third time we would have gotten used to spotting him. Sorry Larry.

None of us lost any sleep over the potentially dangerous

rattlesnake encounter, and the next morning we were ready to hike up Hendrys Canyon one last time. Larry wasn't there this time. I found a western skink (*Plestiodon skiltonianus*) under a rock early on in the hike, but the only thing I caught was a glimpse as it rapidly disappeared down a nearby hole. We did spot another adult striped whipsnake (*Masticophis taeniatus*) but it vanished immediately as well. It was near the spot we had captured the large female the previous afternoon, but without a good look there was no way to know if it was the same snake.

Towards the end of our morning hike, I spotted a skinny tail diving into some sagebrush. This part of the trail was on a steep section of hillside, and the lack of vegetation meant that it was basically dry dirt—not the most stable substrate. I jumped off the trail and around to the other side of the bush to cut off the reptile's escape.

Jacob soon spotted the snake—another striped whipsnake (*Masticophis taeniatus*)—in the sagebrush, but it soon made a beeline for safety. Darting out of the bush and down the hill, the snake almost got past me, but I was able to leap further down the steep slope and snag its tail, bashing my knee against a rock in the process. In pain and with my footing far from secure, I did my best to hold on until Taylor was able to move down and grab its body. He secured the snake and we climbed back up to the trail to admire it.

The whipsnake wasn't quite full grown but was still several feet long. The snake stared at us with its large, round eyes, opting to release some goopy white musk from its rear end but never attempting to bite.

We enjoyed our time in Hendrys Canyon, but the three of us had gotten bored of hiking up the same creek again and again. Despite its supposedly high concentration of pyros and the excellent weather conditions of the past twenty-four hours, we hadn't gotten lucky. Opting for a change of scenery, we climbed back into the truck and drove north to another nearby canyon in the northern half of the Snake Range. The Deep Creeks were visible a few miles to the north, but I was much more confident in our odds of finding a pyro here.

We parked at the end of the road to Smith Canyon just as the ominous clouds that had been looming finally let loose. The rain was just a drizzle, but there were signs all around the canyon of a torrential downpour that had taken place not too long ago. Logs and other debris were strewn across the dry streambed, evidence of a major flash flood that had torn through. There was no surface water in this canyon that we saw, unlike in Hendrys, and the overall landscape was more arid.

The three of us fanned out, aiming to scour as much ground as possible. We hadn't gone far before Taylor spotted a large lizard we were all hoping to see. It was a Great Basin collared lizard (*Crotaphytus bicinctores*), the king of the local lizard species. Collared lizards, named for the black-white-black "collar" that extends around their neck, have a taste for flesh. While most of the other lizards running around North America only eat bugs, collared lizards will use their powerful jaws and lightning-fast legs to catch and eat other vertebrates. Small lizards, snakes, and rodents are all known to be on the menu for collared lizards, though they still eat plenty of arthropods.

However, *seeing* a collared lizard and *catching* a collared lizard are two totally different things. Knowing that collared lizards routinely chase down and eat other lizards gives you an idea of their speed. Taylor, Jacob, and I chased it back and forth between some large boulders, the lizard never letting any one of us get too close before jetting away. Eventually, the collared lizard made a break for shelter further away and scurried under a large rock. If there had only been one or two of us, that probably would have been the end. But there were three of us and we weren't about to let it get away that easily. Taylor and I positioned ourselves on one side of the boulder while Jacob waited, butterfly net in hand, on the other side. With a coordinated heave, Taylor and I lifted the heavy rock up as much as we could and Jacob miraculously snared the collared lizard.

Celebrating, we extracted the now-angry lizard from the net. What had looked like orange stripes by his collar turned out to be congregations of tiny parasitic mites, feasting on his body. He wasn't quite adult sized yet, but counting the tail he was still probably ten inches long, which is big enough to get a good chomp on a wayward finger if given the chance. The collared lizard opened his mouth in protest, but we maintained a firm grip.

Energized by the collared lizard catch, the three of us continued up Smith Canyon. Though we saw no other collared lizards, there were plenty of other four-legged reptiles, the most abundant of which was the western fence lizard (*Sceloporus occidentalis*). We caught several, keeping one to collect and tail clipping the rest. For getting genetic data, a tiny snip of the tail is all that is necessary. I'm sure the lizards don't enjoy being parted with the end of their tails, but if they understood what the alternative was I don't think they would complain.

We were only able to spend a few hours up Smith Canyon, having seen nothing but lizards. I wish we could have stayed until we found a pyro, but we had to return the museum truck the next morning—and who knows how long it would have taken us to get lucky enough to see one, even in a place with as good of a name as the Snake Range.

Saying goodbye to Nevada, we drove south and then east back into Utah as the sun was starting to set. Our plan was to road cruise along the lonely highway in search of nocturnal snakes basking on the pavement for a few hours, and then camp at a spot near the highway.

With our eyes peeled, we drove across the desert towards our target area: Kings Canyon. This canyon cuts through the Confusion Range, named for the supposedly confusing topography of these mountains. We picked it because it was a few miles of paved highway smack dab in the middle of pyro habitat. The Confusions are dry but I know pyros are found there thanks to Mark Hazel, who has spent many hours exploring this range.

We cruised back and forth along Kings Canyon several times, hoping to catch the glint of shiny red scales on the pavement, turning around at the points where the surrounding habitat began to turn back into low-elevation desert. The first live snake on the road was a Great Basin rattlesnake (*Crotalus lutosus*). I slammed on the brakes and Taylor and Jacob bailed out of the car to check out the snake. It was an adult, though not huge by any means. The snake's dark brown on light brown patterning was typical for Great Basin rattlesnakes. After some pictures, they moved the rattler off into the vegetation alongside the road.

We left the snake and headed back up the canyon, but when we drove by the same spot again, once again there was a rattlesnake crossing the road. This time, it was headed in the other direction, so we shepherded it to the other side. The first time, the snake must have been alarmed by the approaching car and started moving back to the closest shoulder. After we left, it waited a while and then tried crossing again. Or it was two similar-sized rattlesnakes in the exact same spot. Given our experiences the previous day, we were all inclined to believe it was the same snake.

It rained briefly as we drove back and forth in Kings Canyon, but a much bigger watery surprise awaited us. After road cruising for a couple of hours without any additional live snakes, we headed to our campsite in the desert just east of the Confusion Range. At the valley floor, we could barely believe our eyes when we saw a raging river alongside the highway. What had been parched desert when we drove along the same road two days prior was now a flash flood, with water flowing on both sides of the pavement. My heart dropped for a second when I saw the road ahead covered by water spilling from one side to the other, but thankfully it wasn't too deep to drive through. We eventually made it to our camping spot, though the dirt roads in between it and the highway were a bit muddy. Our campsite was high enough off the valley floor that we slept on dry ground, but you didn't have to walk far for the dirt to get moist.

Aside from a brief stop for a very convincing looking rope snake, the drive back to Provo the next morning was uneventful. With heavy hearts, Taylor, Jacob, and I euthanized the handful of specimens we had collected. The small whipsnake and a few of the lizards would be immortalized for science as permanent records of their species and populations.

We hadn't gotten lucky enough to hit the snake jackpot on our Nevada trip, and I felt bad that Taylor had now looked for pyros with me in three states without seeing a single one. But at least we could all be grateful that a rattlesnake bite wasn't in the cards.

TWELVE

Roads Less Traveled

Mark and I stared for a few seconds at the big, muddy puddle. For several car lengths, the dirt road in front of us had been replaced by a shallow pool of brown water. Up until that point, the road had been a tad bumpy but otherwise fine. Unfortunately, the previous day's rain—which is normally a good thing when looking for pyros—had rendered the low point of the road uncrossable in Mark's old Subaru Outback.

It was mid-September, and Mark Hazel and I were trying to get to the Mineral Mountains, a range west of Beaver, Utah, where pyros hadn't been formally documented in decades. We had left in the late afternoon, and after driving south for a couple of hours had finally turned onto the dirt road towards the Minerals. The mountains we wanted to explore were right in front of us, but the massive mud puddle at the bottom of the valley forced us to reconsider.

We made our way back to the pavement, and after a bit of discussion, headed west into the remote wilderness towards a new destination: the Wah Wah Mountains. Mark was ambivalent—he'd already been to the Wah Wahs, of course, and all of our other potential destinations—so I got to choose. We could have backtracked to the Pahvants but I was eager to see some new mountains, even if it was further than we had originally wanted to travel. By now it was almost dark though, and there was a chance of encountering snakes that had come out to bask once we made it back to pavement. After leaving the dirt road to the Mineral Mountains, we drove north and then west on highway twenty-one, which eventually bisects the Wah Wahs, eyes peeled for snakes splayed on the asphalt.

It wasn't long before we came across the first. The lucky snake was a gopher snake (*Pituophis catenifer*), likely born within the last week or two, soaking up the warmth of the pavement. Gopher snakes grow to be some of the largest snakes in Utah, but they start off small enough to fit in your pocket. The cute little snake, about the same diameter as a pencil, was probably hoping to find its first meal of the year that night. The species name of the gopher snake (*catenifer*) means "chain-carrying" in Latin, in reference to the chain-like pattern of dark and light brown on their backs.

As I plucked the slender serpent off the road and moved it safely away, it didn't exhibit any of the angry hissing often displayed by disturbed gopher snakes. Maybe it was appreciative of my act of kindness. Unfortunately, the other snakes we saw were not as lucky. After the first live one, we saw four more neonate (newborn) gopher snakes on the road in quick succession, but each of these had been hit by vehicles.

This is part of the unfortunate reality of road cruising. A warm road at night is a temptation that proves fatal for countless snakes. It is kind of hard to evolve to deal with giant hunks of metal flying down the road. Exact mortality rates are hard to come by, especially since scavengers do a remarkably good job at removing carcasses, but it is clear that roads have a strong negative effect on snakes. One 2016 study called them "a thermally-driven ecological trap," a fitting description. Roads offer short-term benefits (a place to warm up) at the risk of higher mortality (due to death by car), a risk that claims the lives of millions of snakes in the US every year.

Some studies have shown that creating "ecopassages" under roads can limit snake mortality. Low drift fences made of mesh placed along the sides of a road can funnel snakes (and other animals) to small, regularly-spaced tunnels underneath. One neat study on massasaugas (*Sistrurus catenatus*, a type of threatened rattlesnake) even had electronic tag readers placed at the entrances of the tunnels that recorded whenever a tagged snake crawled through, proving both that the snakes would use the passages and that they reduce mortality. It would be impractical to build drift fences along every road in the country, let alone dig a bunch of tunnels. But in areas with high traffic and critical habitat for threatened snakes—or any small animal imperiled by road mortality—it is a strategy that should be considered.

There is an extensive amount of scientific literature about snake mortality on roads, a fact that is somewhat ironic since natural snake deaths are difficult to study. Often the only good way to get information about natural snake mortality is to find the radio transmitter you implanted in a pile of scat. Studying mortality on roads is much easier, though also more deflating.

Mark and I cruised back and forth in the darkness along the highway for a bit longer, but we saw nothing after those initial gopher snakes. Eventually, as the pavement cooled off and the fatigue from our many hours on the road set in, we settled down to camp not far off the pavement.

It's always interesting to wake up the next morning and discover what the campsite you picked in the dark actually looks like. Our makeshift site, which was in view of the highway, was a flat, brushless plain near a small hill. It was quite unlike the idyllic woodland where we would be spending the next twenty-four hours.

Pine Grove Canyon, nestled in the western side of the southern Wah Wah Mountains, is as beautiful as it is perfect for pyros. The canyon has a small creek running throughout, bordered on both sides by vegetated slopes interspersed with rocky patches. Titanic ponderosa pines, presumably the namesake for the place, grace the canyon. The only blemish I saw was the herd of cattle that was grazing in the meadows along the creek. "Wah Wah" means "good, clear water," a name that felt less appropriate given the cows standing in it.

Pine Grove also has an interesting historical connection to pyros. In 1980, a male and female pyro were collected in this canyon and taken back, alive, to a lab at BYU. The female laid five eggs, which were incubated successfully, and two BYU herpetologists, Douglas Cox and Wilmer Tanner, published a paper in 1981 with some data on the incubation and hatchlings. Wilmer Tanner happens to be the herpetologist who published two descriptions of subspecies of *Lampropeltis pyromelana* back in the 1950s. Tanner also was instrumental in founding the Bean Life Science Museum and worked for years as the curator of its herpetology collection—many of which were spent at the same desk that I worked at decades later. Cox died of cancer at the age of 63 and Tanner lived to the ripe age of 101, which should dispel the myth that all herpetologists inevitably die of snake bite at a young age.

What that 1981 paper from Cox and Tanner doesn't mention is that their two pyros from Pine Grove, along with their captive-born progeny, were later confiscated by Utah wildlife officials due to a lack of permits. Further punishments probably could have been pursued, but the decision was made to not further sour relations with the state's top herpetologists.

At first, I wasn't even sure if Mark and I would even make it to Pine Grove though. In the morning, as we drove on the highway away from our improvised campsite and lower into the valley, we saw standing water pooled in the gully adjacent to the road. After being forced to turn around due to flooded roads the previous day, this looked like a bad sign. Thankfully, the dirt road to Pine Grove only had a few muddy patches that we traversed without much difficulty (though there was still one more bad road in store for later).

We parked a couple of miles up the road that winds through the canyon. Rather than sticking to a trail, Mark and I spent the day meandering up, down, and across the hillsides and along the creek, checking under rocks and logs as we went. The distance between the furthest points we searched was probably only two or three miles, but we spent a total of ten hours on foot that day scouring as much ground as we could.

The most abundant reptilian residents of the canyon were, of course, scelops. We saw two species: western fence lizards (*Sceloporus occidentalis*) and sagebrush lizards (*Sceloporus graciosus*). Interestingly, almost all of them were juveniles. Perhaps the adults that had survived and reproduced were ready to call it a year, whereas the juveniles were still looking to put on more weight before winter. Though both species have similar diets and lifestyles, the fence lizards grow slightly larger.

Western fence lizards also have a neat secret superpower: Their blood kills the bacteria that causes Lyme disease. Ticks have a nymph stage at which they feed on a small intermediate host (such as a lizard or mouse) before molting and feeding on a larger host (human, deer, or other large animal). Lyme disease is caused by a bacteria transferred to humans via infected adult ticks. But if the ticks feed on western fence lizards during their nymph stage, specialized proteins in the lizard's blood will rid the tick of the disease-causing bacteria.

The first and second snake sightings of the day came in quick succession. In one of the clearings along the creek in Pine Grove are several old, abandoned log cabins. I wondered if they were occupied when Douglas Cox had visited this canyon to collect pyros more than three decades ago. The dilapidated wooden structures are now overgrown with vegetation, and it was in the thorny brambles around one of the cabins that I spotted a western terrestrial garter snake (*Thamnophis elegans*). The snake was a couple of feet long, with the typical combination of dull brown and black patterning with faint yellow stripes. The snake was unbothered by the sharp thorns, but I wasn't about to tear up my hands to grab a garter snake. (If it had been a pyro, maybe.) I waited for a couple of minutes, hoping the snake would forget about me and wander out of the brambles, but it did not.

It was only a couple of minutes later, near the other run-down cabin, that I saw another western terrestrial garter snake. It was out in the open, and I quickly reached down to seize it before it could get away. I almost wished I hadn't, as the upset snake released a copious amount of smelly musk onto my hand. After quickly releasing it, I rinsed my hands off in the creek. This barely helped the smell, and it felt gross knowing I was downstream of the cows. At least I had hand sanitizer with me.

Towards the end of the day, Mark and I selected our campsite and went on one last walk. Unlike in the middle of summer, when you can search for pyros for hours after sunset, it was late enough in the year that the window of possibility closed shortly after dark. We wandered for another hour or so as the night set in, hoping to happen upon the pyro that had eluded us all day, but to no avail. Walking in the darkness not far from the abandoned cabins, we heard the call of a great horned owl, signaling it was time to head back and get some rest. The temperature had cooled off quickly after sunset, and I was starting to get chilly, even in a sweatshirt.

After eating some dinner, we made camp for the night. The view of the sky was incredible; we were literally sleeping under a blanket of stars. Being miles away from civilization changes your perspective in more ways than one.

The next morning, we arose with the sun—nature's alarm clock. After breaking camp, we got back into Mark's trusty Outback and headed out of Pine Grove and further west to the Indian Peaks. Native Americans allegedly called the area "Quich-u-ant," or "spirit mountain." The white settlers weren't as poetic with names; the spot we were headed to was near Indian Creek and Indian Peak, the tallest mountain in the range.

We could have stayed another day at Pine Grove, but neither

of us were too keen on spending another day searching the exact same spots again. Pine Grove Canyon was nice but the Indian Peaks, which weren't far to the west, were calling our names. Mark had assured me that skinks were easy to find at the Indian Peaks too, and I was much more interested in seeing skinks than scelops.

Even better, pyros had never been documented there. Finding a pyro in the Wah Wahs would be fun, but finding one in the Indian Peaks—which Mark assured me had suitable habitat—would be a first. Having already found my second pyro, I was more eager to spend time searching speculative territory with Mark. We had come up empty at the Deep Creeks, but maybe our luck would be different this time.

The Indian Peaks are separated from the Wah Wahs by only a small valley, and in many ways the two ranges are very similar (aside from the fact that pyros have only been documented in the latter). Both of these isolated mountain ranges run north to south, are roughly the same size, and contain similar habitat. Both were ancestrally occupied by what are known today as the Paiute Indians, but nowadays their inhabitants are almost none. Given their remoteness, few recreationists visit these places either; Mark and I would go the whole weekend without encountering any other hikers.

Though the distance between the Wah Wahs and Indian Peaks is short as the crow (or pinyon jay) flies, it took us over an hour to traverse due to the wonderful quality of the dirt road. All the roads were totally dry now, but past rains had eroded large portions of the road into Indian Creek. Huge dips and large stretches of uneven bare rock made our progress slow. Had we known that the road was as rough as it was, we might have stayed in Pine Grove another day, but it was too late to turn around.

Eventually we arrived. Or at least we got close enough that we could park and just walk, with good habitat on both sides of the road. Though a stream flowed aboveground for stretches, the landscape here felt much drier than Pine Grove. I even saw some cholla cactus, which was the furthest north I had ever seen my least favorite kind of cactus (a status owed to some unpleasant experiences I won't recount but I'm sure you can imagine). We didn't see any cows, but the abundance of cow pies made it clear that we hadn't missed them by much.

The majority of the day at the Indian Peaks was uneventful. As we explored the sparsely forested habitat further up the road and the adjacent valley, Mark saw two striped whipsnakes (*Masticophis taeniatus*), one adult and one juvenile, though we were separated at the time—which was fitting since he hadn't been present for either of the garter snakes I saw the previous day. We both found quite a few lizards, but they were the same typical species we had seen at Pine Grove. The skinks that Mark had promised had yet to materialize, though there was still time before we needed to begin the long journey back home.

After a few hours exploring up the main canyon, we came back to the car and Mark led the way to another side canyon. The habitat along the small creek looked perfect for pyros. Plenty of green vegetation, shade, and rocks. We hiked up the stream, flipping rocks opportunistically and scanning the ground for reptiles.

The first interesting thing we saw was not a reptile but a bizarre cricket. Okay, technically it was an ovate shield-back katydid, not a cricket. But it was a weird looking bug, with a splattering of green, brown, and white patterning that looked like a cross between bird poop and a mossy rock. I later uploaded pictures of the strange insect to iNaturalist (which is how I know what species it was), and this happens to be the northernmost record on iNat for the species. Nearby, Mark also found part of a shed rattlesnake skin, but it was old and its owner long gone.

We continued up the side canyon, flipping rocks as we went. Mark had promised that finding skinks here would be easy. Either we have different definitions of easy or the skinks had decided to not cooperate, because no matter how many rocks either of us looked under we didn't see any. By this point, it was late afternoon, and we knew that we should probably start to head back—we were a long, long way from home.

Still hoping to see a pyro, or a skink at the very least, we split up to cover more ground. Mark was going to hike back the way we came, while I would cut south over the small plateau that separated the two forks of the creek and follow the other half.

After crossing over the plateau, I clambered down the rocky edge into the other canyon. As I was climbing down, I saw a streak of brown shoot across the ground. Skink! Mark was right, there really were skinks here. Skinks are usually found hiding under rocks, leaves, or similar cover. But this one had been out in the open until I had inadvertently startled it.

The legs of the western skink (*Plestiodon skiltonianus*) are comically tiny, almost nub-like. They aren't as good at climbing as lizards with more proportionally-sized limbs, but these skinks can still scurry on the ground extremely fast. I barely got a good enough look to identify it as a skink before it scurried under the rock ledge I had been climbing down. I jumped the rest of the way down and stared into the gap in the rock face that the skink had slid into. The little bugger wasn't visible, and I wasn't going to be able to get into his hole without the aid of some dynamite. Unfortunately, I didn't have any on me.

It was frustrating to have been waiting all day to see a skink and be rewarded only with the briefest of glimpses. I waited near the opening for a couple minutes, hoping the lizard would assume the threat had passed and emerge. I soon ran out of patience and figured Mark was probably almost to the fork where we were supposed to meet up. I flipped a couple of the nearby rocks in hopes that the first skink had been hanging out with another, but no dice.

After meeting back up at the fork, we started hiking back towards the car. It was at this point that the reptiles started coming out of the woodwork—quite literally. I lifted up a fallen log and spotted the unmistakable smooth body of a skink underneath. I immediately replaced the log (without squashing the skink, of course) and called Mark over. I got into position, crouching down next to the log, and Mark quickly flipped it over, exposing the lizard. Before I could reach out and grab it, the skink shot under the now upside-down log. Mark flipped the log back, and the same thing happened—the skink dashed back underneath in the blink of an eye. This process repeated itself several more times before I was finally able to pin the agile lizard down with my hands.

The skink was relatively bland in coloration; mostly a uniform dark brown with lighter stripes running from its head to the start of its tail—it had outgrown its bright blue juvenile tail colors. The tiny legs, wide neck, and almost cylindrical body speak to the lifestyle of these lizards, which spend most of their time rooting around debris on the ground or underneath it.

Other members of the true skink family (Scincidae) have even smaller legs than western skinks, and some have lost their limbs entirely. Those that totally lost their legs have elongate, snake-like bodies to help them move through sand, grass, or leaf litter (though these imitation snakes don't have the same grace as the real thing). It might seem backward for an organism to lose limbs, but evolution doesn't care about direction—it just goes with what works. For skinks, losing limbs must be a viable evolutionary strategy as the loss of one or both pairs of limbs has occurred at least twenty-four separate times in this family! They don't have the sprint speed of other lizards, but they are still quite agile, legs or no legs.

We took a few photographs of the western skink before releasing it and continuing back towards the car. We hadn't gone very far before Mark found a different reptile hiding under another fallen log. It was a desert nightsnake (*Hypsiglena chlorophaea*), a species found across deserts throughout the western US. This individual was less than a foot long, which is adult size for these small serpents—a two-foot desert nightsnake is huge. These secretive snakes are a light brown base color, with darker splotches along the back. Desert nightsnakes prey on small vertebrates such as lizards, frogs, and even other snakes. They subdue their prey with the aid of venom, though their "fangs" are just enlarged, grooved teeth in the back of their mouth and the venom is insignificant to humans.

The pupils of the desert nightsnake are elliptical in shape, though it is a misconception that this is an adaptation to facilitate a purely nocturnal lifestyle. The study that demonstrated this was published in 2010 and was based on an analysis of Australian snakes from five families. Using photographs from field guides and the internet, along with museum specimens, the scientists were able to classify the pupil shape (circular, subcircular, or vertically elliptical) of each snake. They then used already-published information on the activity times (diurnal, nocturnal, or some combination) and foraging techniques (ambush or active hunting) of each species. They did exclude information where the activity time or foraging technique were inferred from the pupil shape (i.e. if the paper said a snake was nocturnal because it had vertical pupils, but there was no other evidence, they didn't use that information).

The data showed that, generally, snakes with vertical pupils tended to be nocturnal ambush hunters, while snakes with circular pupils tended to be diurnal active foragers. However, foraging mode was more strongly correlated with pupil shape than preferred time of activity. Having vertical pupils gives a snake more flexibility in the light intensities that it can see in—an elliptical pupil is slit-like in bright light but expands to be almost circular in dim conditions—which is more important for ambushing snakes that have to be ready to seize prey day or night. Purely nocturnal snakes that are active hunters, rather than ambushers, actually tend to have circular pupils.

Although that study focused only on Australian snakes, as far as I'm aware the pattern holds true for North American ones like the desert nightsnake; these snakes are primarily but not exclusively nocturnal, and hunt (at least some of the time) by ambush. Rattlesnakes, which also have elliptical pupils, are also ambush hunters known to be active day or night. Whipsnakes and racers, which actively pursue prey during the daytime, have round pupils.

The pupils of this nightsnake were a very thin vertical slit since it was broad daylight, but I can attest that their pupils expand greatly in the dark. Another oft-cited misconception about snake pupils is that venomous snakes have elliptical pupils while harmless snakes have round pupils. This is sort of helpful in North America where most of the dangerously venomous snakes are ambush-hunting vipers with elliptical pupils, but keep in mind that in low light an elliptical pupil will expand to look like a round one. And if you are close enough to see a snake's pupil clearly, you might be close enough to find out if it's venomous the hard way.

While Mark was photographing the nightsnake, I flipped over an adjacent log a few feet away and found another snake. At first I thought it was a nightsnake too, given its diminutive size, but upon picking it up I realized it was a western terrestrial garter snake (*Thamnophis elegans*). It was a juvenile, and was further from the creek than I would have expected for a garter snake. Like other garters, which tend to be active daytime foragers, the snake had round pupils. Mark and I released both snakes under the respective logs we had found them under. I wonder if the garter ended up being prey for the nightsnake; that would have been an interesting clash to watch, but we weren't going to force it to happen.

By the time we made it back to the car, it was six o'clock. Later than we would have liked given how far we had to drive to get home, but both Mark and I were happy to stop for the snakes and the skink. Finding a pyro at the Indian Peaks was a long shot anyway, as exciting as it might have been. At least we had seen skinks and some snakes, and there was always the possibility of seeing a few more on the way home.

Sure enough, shortly after getting in the car and starting the long journey back north, we came across a large striped whipsnake (*Masticophis taeniatus*). The snake was laid out on the dirt road in front of us, and I bailed out of the car quickly after Mark slammed on the brakes. I managed to grab the snake before it slithered off into the brush. I don't know if she was the longest, but she was certainly the thickest of this species I have ever held. At least four feet long and thicker than my thumb. That would be skinny for a four-foot rattlesnake, but for a striped whipsnake it was hefty. I took a few photos, though unfortunately I missed the shot of the snake striking at my phone. It also musked on me. Whipsnake musk is a different flavor (if you can call it that) from garter snake musk, but I can't say I enjoy either. That's probably the point, isn't it? We soon released the whipsnake back into the desert and continued on our way.

The terrible dirt road eventually transitioned into a decent dirt road, and we were flying along when Mark almost ran over our next snake. It was an adult gopher snake (*Pituophis catenifer*) stretched out perpendicular to the road, and it took a deft swerve from Mark to avoid flattening it. He pulled over and I hopped out to make sure we hadn't hit it and to help it get off the road to avoid future collisions.

The snake didn't move at first—perhaps it was frozen in fear after having its life flash before its eyes—but sprang to life when I touched it. Gopher snakes can be cranky, and this one wasn't appreciative of my efforts to move it off the road. Launching into a full intimidation display, the snake hissed, puffed up its body, and shook its tail. These snakes will even flatten their head, trying to mimic the triangular head of a viper. The tail shaking isn't as loud as a rattle and the patterning of a gopher snake only loosely resembles that of a rattlesnake, but I'm sure the display has scared many a predator (and fooled many a person). Once the snake was safely out of the road, I got back into the car and Mark and I continued on our way.

After making it back to the pavement, we had a repeat of the events of two nights previous. We found one recently hatched gopher snake that was unscathed, but we came upon four others on the rest of the drive that weren't so lucky. Road cruising may be effective for finding snakes, but seeing squashed baby snakes is a little depressing.

In addition to the reptiles, we also spotted a couple of notable mammals on our dark drive. There was a kit fox, with its unmistakably large ears, standing in a field adjacent to the road. We also encountered a large rabbit which darted out in front of the car and miraculously avoided hitting our tires.

It was an eventful drive to end an eventful weekend, but between the poor dirt roads, the stops for snakes, and the sheer distance, it took six hours from when we got back in the car to the time I arrived at my apartment. I enjoyed seeing the Wah Wahs, especially knowing of the past pyro connections to the place. I liked the Indian Peaks far more though, thanks to the snakes and skinks. And maybe, someday, someone will find a pyro at the Indian Peaks—though I wouldn't be surprised if Native Americans already found them centuries ago.

THIRTEEN

Fall Colors and Rock-Paper-Scissors Lizards

With the summer coming to an end, it was time to turn my attention back to the boring part of herpetology: scientific writing. My first scientific paper—the range mapping one—had finally come out of peer review. It had been over four months since I'd submitted it, which naturally meant I'd forgotten everything I'd written. The time required for peer review is an oft-criticized weakness of the process (though four months is on the longer end of turnaround times). But since the majority of scientific research isn't critically time-sensitive (though exceptions exist, like with infectious diseases), the delay in time to publication is generally worth the improvements that come with critical peer review.

The verdict from *Western North American Naturalist* (the journal I'd submitted to) was that the paper needed major revisions in order to be published. The two peer reviewers had done a thorough job of picking apart my draft. Looking through their comments, I felt like my manuscript had been sent through a paper shredder. To be fair, this is the point of peer review. Only high quality, thorough research should be getting published, and the words should be as precise and accurate as reasonably possible. Papers that need improvement should be improved before being published. Besides, scientific writing, like any kind of writing, is a skill. It takes practice, and I didn't have much. Most of the feedback was valid and extremely helpful, though a few of the suggestions felt nitpicky.

The biggest flaw, pointed out by both reviewers, was that I hadn't obtained data from state wildlife agencies in Arizona, Nevada, and New Mexico. The project had originally started with a focus on just Utah, thus my limited scope, but the reviewers were correct that I ought to obtain all possible data (which did result in a couple of additional minor range extensions on the final map).

As part of this process, one person Dr. Whiting reached out to was Bryan Hamilton, a herpetologist in Nevada and the lead author of that excellent 2008 field study on pyros. As Dr. Whiting suspected, Bryan also turned out to be one of the peer reviewers. He had additional data stemming from his earlier field studies and continued research in the region, which he was happy to share. Bryan was also willing to help with further improvements and revisions, so we added him as an author on the final published version of the paper.

This last part—one of the reviewers becoming an author—isn't conventional; peer review is supposed to be anonymous, for good reasons. But I've included it in an effort to be as open as possible. The average person has no idea how scientific research gets funded, carried out, reviewed, and published. The whole scientific publishing world is generally shrouded in secrecy, confusing language, and fees, all of which make it hard for the public to understand how science works—which is why I've bothered including these boring details. There are good reasons why what is published in reputable, peer-reviewed academic journals should generally be trusted, and those that cast doubts on the results of modern science often don't understand the process.

That autumn, as I was revising my manuscript—and still

slaving away on my mimicry research project—I took the time for one last outing in the mountains. After all, snakes don't exist solely so that herpetologists can research them.

The first weekend of October was still warm, and there were no guarantees against a cold snap and snow by the next one. Knowing it might be my last chance to look for pyros this year—and possibly many more—I decided it was time to revisit my favorite place in the world: Kanosh. Given that I had found two pyros at Kanosh Canyon and a grand total of zero everywhere else in the world, it seemed like the right call.

Joining me for the weekend was my friend and classmate Jake Spencer, a fellow coworker in the Bean Museum herpetology collection. Jake is tall, and has short curly hair and an ever-optimistic attitude. He'd spent his summer looking for another one of Utah's rarely seen serpents: the regal ringneck snake (*Diadophis punctatus regalis*). I'd seen one of these small, fossorial snakes the previous year but none since. Hoping to spot one, we started the trip with a brief detour.

On the way south from Provo to Kanosh, there was an unassuming hill not far from the freeway. The area has several piles of wooden boards to overturn, as well as a TV and some other trash that probably wasn't left as potential snake shelter. A handful of juniper trees dotted the landscape, which was otherwise covered in dry grass.

We turned boards and rocks for about an hour, and though we weren't able to find a ringneck snake, the stop wasn't entirely for naught. Jake found a small tarantula under a rock—the furthest north I'd ever seen a tarantula (though some are found as far north as Canada, yikes). I uncovered a tiny gopher snake (*Pituophis catenifer*) hiding among one of the board piles. The newly born snake was less than a foot long and close to the same size as an adult ringneck snake. Its brown and black pattern was much less exciting than the bright orange belly of a ringneck though.

We also saw what might have been the biggest side-blotched

lizard (*Uta stansburiana*) I have ever seen, though "biggest side-blotched lizard" isn't saying much. Only a few inches long, they are the smallest lizards in Utah. Side-blotched lizards are usually brown or gray on top, sometimes with blue speckling, and can vary in color significantly throughout their range. As the name suggests, many have a circular dark blue blotch on their flanks, just behind the armpit. Side-blotched lizards haven't been mentioned in this book much because they don't often overlap with pyros, but these lizards are ubiquitous in lowland habitats throughout much of the western United States. While they are common, it would be a travesty to completely overlooked side-blotched lizards, as they have one of the most intriguing (or at least the best named) mating systems in the animal kingdom.

Male side-blotched lizards are locked in an evolutionary game of rock-paper-scissors. It looks weird to see the words "rock-paper-scissors" in a scientific paper, but if it makes it into *Nature* (one of the—if not *the*—biggest scientific journals), then it flies. There are three main mating strategies, each exhibited by lizards with a different color under their throat. Orange-throated males are the big hunks—larger, more aggressive lizards that defend territories with many females in them. The yellow-throated males are "sneaker males" who aren't territorial but will infiltrate the territory of an orange male to secretly mate with his females. This dynamic of large territorial males and smaller sneaker males isn't unusual and is found in many other organisms, from birds to cuttlefish.

It's the presence of a third male strategy that makes side-blotched lizards fascinating. The blue-throated males loosely guard a small territory. They are often outmuscled by the brutish oranges but keep a close enough eye on their small domain to prevent the sneaky yellows from swooping in. Orange-beats-blue, blue-beats-yellow, yellow-beats-orange; sounds like rock-paper-scissors, right? This three-way dynamic is further maintained by the females, who seem to prefer whichever color morph is the least common in a given year.

FALL COLORS AND ROCK-PAPER-SCISSORS LIZARDS

The initial 1996 paper that reported on the rock-paper-scissors system utilized data from years of careful observation and some mathematical wizardry to show how the frequencies of each color morph would oscillate over time. It was based on a population from California, though side-blotched lizards are found throughout the western US and Mexico. Some populations have lost one or sometimes two of the throat colors. The yellow morph seems to generally be the first one to go, often leading to increases in lizard size. Without any sneaky males around, there is a stronger evolutionary pressure for males to be able to outmuscle each other.

The unusually large side-blotched lizard I saw with Jake probably had an orange throat, given its size, but I'll never know for sure. My first attempt to grab it by hand failed, and I didn't try again. I wasn't about to waste my time chasing side-blotched lizards when there were pyros to find elsewhere.

Leaving the nameless hillside, we drove the rest of the way south. Driving through the tiny town of Kanosh brought back good memories, and I was glad to once again see the orange sandstone of the canyon. Some of the familiar oaks still had green leaves, but the red and yellow colors of fall were starting to appear. A few maples had even turned pink, and the kaleidoscope of colors was beautiful. The canyon was drier overall than on my previous visits, but it was still lush compared to the parched hillside we had just stopped at.

Jake and I had left Provo late in the afternoon, and by the time we could see Corn Creek the temperature was relatively cool. Shortly after arriving, we headed up the main fork of the creek to take advantage of the last hour of daylight. With temperatures already in the low sixties and dropping, our window was limited.

The air temperatures were falling fast, but the red rocks around us still were warm. Heated by the sun's rays in the afternoon, you could feel the heat radiating from the sandstone in the rockier areas of the canyon. We didn't see any reptiles active on the surface, but we did find a baby sagebrush lizard (*Sceloporus graciosus*) and an adult plateau fence lizard (*Sceloporus tristichus*) hiding under separate rocks. These were our only lizards that night, but there were many more to come.

No reptiles were out, but as the darkness descended, the real creatures of nightmares emerged: wolf spiders, and huge ones to boot. The unnaturally large spiders had a leg span roughly the size of my palm, making them bigger than the small tarantula we had seen a few hours previous. Wolf spiders are darkly colored with long, spindly legs, and the reflective glint of their eyes in a flashlight beam makes them easy to spot. Their presence may have undermined my previous assurances to Jake that he would be "totally fine" sleeping without a tent. I tease here; Jake, much like my friend Jacob, has a much stronger affinity for invertebrates than me.

When we arrived back at the car after the hike, I tried not to think about giant spiders as I rolled out my sleeping bag and pad onto the tarp. I've heard people say they'd be worried about snakes crawling into their sleeping bag at night. That doesn't scare me, but thinking about spiders makes me sympathize with the sentiment.

The night was cold and the chilly air was slow to warm up in the morning. Not unlike the reptiles we would be looking for, we didn't crawl out of our sleeping bags until they were warmed by the golden rays of the morning sun. We ate a quick breakfast and soon were back on the trail. We opted to hike the main fork of the creek again, as the wider canyon would warm up faster in the morning and allow us to hike the shadier north fork in the afternoon.

The lizards were out in full force this time, energized by the morning sunlight. You couldn't walk more than a few steps without seeing another lizard. Most of them were juveniles, only a few inches long, likely having been born in the last few weeks. There were two species present, plateau fence lizards (*Sceloporus tristichus*) and sagebrush lizards (*Sceloporus graciosus*). I have only ever seen these two lizard species up Kanosh Canyon, but what the place lacks in diversity it makes up for with sheer abundance—we saw roughly a hundred individual lizards on that first morning hike alone.

Jake spotted the first snake of the day, a Great Basin rattlesnake (*Crotalus lutosus*), peeking out from underneath a rock. While hidden from above, the snake was intentionally positioned to still soak in the sunshine flowing from the side. The brown rattler was small but not tiny. If it was born this year, it must have already had a decent meal and put on some growth. I usually don't opt to disturb rattlesnakes (unless I need to move one off the road), but I did use my snake hook to gently pull it from its hiding place so Jake could get some better pictures. The snake was slightly annoyed and eventually retreated to a similar position wedged under another rock, but here the shadows weren't as bad. It stared with unblinking eyes—all snakes lack eyelids, so don't think this is special—as Jake and I snapped a few photos before moving on.

Later, we caught a few fleeting glimpses of a western terrestrial garter snake (*Thamnophis elegans*) among some brambles near the creek, but the snake quickly disappeared in the large rocky cracks along the steep bank. We saw a yellow-bellied racer (*Coluber constrictor mormon*) towards the end of the hike too, but it also gave us the slip. This put our count of snake species (four) on the outing so far above our count of lizard species (three). But in terms of sheer numbers, the snakes were far behind. The lizards were everywhere.

Given the absurd density of these four-legged reptiles, Jake was tempted to try out a capture technique that was new for both of us: rubber bands. Herpetologists have devised a lot of methods over the years to catch lizards since doing it by hand doesn't always work well. One of the most common methods is a lizard lasso (sometimes called a lizard noose, but I prefer the more innocuous term, plus I'm a sucker for alliteration). It basically consists of a slip knot tied with fishing wire attached to the end of a pole. It works great for most lizards, though not all. Historically, some herpetologists used .22 rifles, which is only effective if you want to collect your quarry dead. Another possible tool are sticky traps—basically flypaper for lizards. You put a few square inches of the sticky paper in a sunny spot in the forest or another location you know the lizards will pass by. The unwitting reptiles get hopelessly stuck when they step on the trap, but add some vegetable oil and they come right off! Pitfall traps—basically a five gallon bucket dug into the ground—are sometimes used too, as are various forms of netting.

But the lizard capture tool that speaks most to your inner child is the rubber band. These large rubber bands are close to an inch wide and several inches long, unstretched. Pulled back with the right amount of force, the band will strike the lizard hard enough to stun it but not so hard as to injure it. Or at least that's what we'd heard.

Neither of us had caught a lizard using rubber bands before—or even seen it done—but I can now confirm it works. Jake took aim and nailed an adult plateau fence lizard from a few paces away. It was only stunned momentarily, but that was enough for Jake to dash over and seize it. We got some pictures of the metallic blue patches on its underside before releasing it. Rubber bands, like most capture methods, have a small potential to harm the lizard and undoubtedly cause some stress, but just about any technique is more humane than a rifle. Jake and I had a good laugh over the experience, though we were content with simply observing the rest of the lizards scattered throughout the canyon.

On our way back, we ran into some cattle herders on horseback. We hadn't seen any cows this time, but signs of their presence (i.e. cow pies) were everywhere. The ranchers were a friendly bunch. Grinning, Jake and I explained we were looking for snakes and they said they were looking for cows—and I think both parties thought the other sounded crazy. I did not express any of my vehemently anti-cow views to them, and perhaps they declined to voice their anti-snake opinions as well. They sounded like nice people and I'm sure they run cattle to make a living and not because they hate the planet. (This is your reminder that cows tear up natural ecosystems and contribute a disproportionate amount to global greenhouse gas emissions.)

After our eventful hike in the morning, we took a break for lunch and then shifted to the north fork of Corn Creek. This fork also had a high density of lizards, though not quite as many as the main canyon. Interestingly, here the sagebrush lizards (*Sceloporus graciosus*) outnumbered the plateau fence lizards (*Sceloporus tristichus*), whereas the inverse was true in the other canyon. The two species are slightly different in size, with the fence lizards growing an inch or two longer and much bulkier, but they presumably have the same sets of prey and predators. Through some combination of chance and slightly different habitat preferences, the sagebrush lizards came out on top in the north fork.

Sagebrush lizards (*Sceloporus graciosus*) don't play evolutionary rock-paper-scissors like the side-blotched lizards do, but they still have interesting social lives. One meticulous study from 1994 focused on the "push-up" behavior of sagebrush lizards. If you've spent any time watching lizards, you've probably seen them do push-ups. They're not doing it for exercise, but rather as a form of communication.

To study these push-up displays, the author, Emília Martins, attached colored beads to the base of the tail of each lizard, a common technique that is supposed to only minimally affect mortality. She did this with all thirty-five individuals in a small population of sagebrush lizards in southern California. After countless hours of observation across two years, Martins was able to show that these seemingly simple displays contain a lot of nuance.

As her 1994 paper describes, sagebrush lizard displays have three main components: the pose (body flattened, back arched, or neck puffed out), leg extensions (zero, two, or four legs), and head bobs (which vary in duration and frequency). The push-up displays are made of combinations of these three elements, but the lizards don't randomly mix different actions. The push-ups, in a way, have grammar. As Martins writes, "although conventional wisdom might deem it absurd to conclude that lizards have language, the push-up display of [the sagebrush lizard] *S. graciosus* does indeed have a distinct structure with explicit rules governing the combination of elements into displays."

This extremely simplified language is employed in a variety of different scenarios. Staking one's territory or challenging another's can be articulated through displays. Flirting, if you could call it that, happens too. Really, this shouldn't be surprising; when there are hordes of lizards living in close proximity, of course there is going to be communication going on. Scientists don't quite have a Google Translate for lizards yet, but it is only a matter of time before AI figures it out, right?

In addition to all the lizards, Jake and I came across another yellow-bellied racer (*Coluber constrictor mormon*). I was away from the trail when I saw the unmistakable olive-green blur take off. I bounded over, chased it for a few steps, and managed to grab it. I quickly handed the snake to Jake and proceeded to remove the dozens of burs that had attached to my shorts, socks, and legs as I had chased the snake through the plants. I never feel more like a mammal than when I'm pulling burs off of me.

Somewhat miraculously, the racer didn't bite either of us. It was still very wiggly in our hands, but it calmed down quickly when we let it climb up a nearby tree, offering a nice view of its classic yellow belly. The snake stared at us with its big round eyes, probably upset we had interrupted its afternoon hunt.

I had always thought that yellow-bellied racers were primarily lizard eaters. Being fast, diurnal snakes and often found in areas with high lizard abundance, it seemed natural that they eat mainly other reptiles. To my great surprise, neither of the available studies on the diet of yellow-bellied racers (*Coluber constrictor mormon*) recorded them eating lizards. Both studies, one in British Columbia and one in Utah, through a combination of dissections and palpating half-digested bits from live specimens, found them to eat insects along with the occasional small rodent. Despite this, I find it hard to believe that the racers that live up Kanosh Canyon don't occasionally get peckish and wolf down some sagebrush lizards.

The last snake of the trip wouldn't have objected to eating sagebrush lizards, or yellow-bellied racers, or really anything else. It was a gopher snake (*Pituophis catenifer*), a species known to consume everything from lizards to bird eggs to, yes, gophers. There is a fascinating observation published about a gopher snake in a different part of central Utah that was found on an overhanging cliff twenty-five feet in the air, raiding the nests of cliff swallows. These small birds nest communally, constructing mud nests in cliffs and other hard-to-reach places.

The gopher snake in question had scaled the rocky face, reached the overhanging ledge where dozens of nests were located, and was now feasting on eggs and hatchlings. The adult cliff swallows looked on helplessly as they watched their progeny being devoured (or, dare I say, swallowed). The observers watched for close to an hour as the snake entered one nest after another, always keeping its body anchored securely.

The gopher snake that Jake and I saw wasn't hanging from a cliff, but rather was smack dab in the middle of the trail. Likely having noticed our footfalls several seconds earlier, the large snake was frozen in place, hoping it would blend in against the dark soil of the primitive path. Had it been anywhere else, we might have missed it, even though it was the biggest snake of the trip.

The gopher snake didn't protest much when picked up. This individual was probably four feet long from head to tail, a respectable size (though the biggest can get a few feet longer). While massive compared to the newborn gopher snake from the very beginning of the trip, this snake had the same calm temperament. There was no biting, musking, or mock-rattlesnake displaying. Just a calm snake that wasn't bothered by the strange creatures that had gently lifted it off the ground. The brown snake contrasted nicely with the vivid fall colors around us, making for good pictures.

Eventually, Jake and I ended up back at the car. It was time to head back home to Provo; we couldn't be gone forever during the middle of the semester. I originally thought it would have been fitting to find a pyro at Kanosh in the fall after having found one in the spring and in the summer. In retrospect, it was probably more fitting to not see one. After all, that was how most of my trips over the past two years had gone.

In the coming months, the temperatures would continue to drop, and snow would soon blanket the mountains. The pyros and other reptiles would take refuge deep underground and hibernate, sleeping through the long winter until the eventual arrival of spring. I'd be waiting too, though perhaps not as patiently, for a shot at one more pyro.

FOURTEEN

Everything's Coming up Roses (Except the Boas)

My first trip in search of pyros the following year almost started in the worst way possible: with me murdering a beautiful snake. I had just turned off the highway in northeastern Arizona onto a dirt road that led eastward into the Cerbat Mountains. I wasn't paying attention to the road itself, which was wide and in good condition. As I drove, my eyes were busy scanning the sparsely vegetated hillsides, looking for good areas to flip rocks and assessing the habitat of the various canyons. I sighed when I noticed the herd of cows scattered throughout. I barely registered the large stick that was perpendicular to the road until I was only a couple car lengths away. The branch was pretty big.

Suddenly my eyes snapped down to the road and immediately realized my mistake. I jerked the steering wheel, swerving towards the middle, desperately hoping my tires would straddle the large snake that had been stretched out in the dirt.

I slammed on my brakes and quickly parked on the shoulder of the road, terrified that I had just flattened the first snake of the trip. Cursing my carelessness, I grabbed my snake hook—just in case—and jumped out of my car.

What awaited me was not a snake with a pancake for a head, thankfully. Instead, I found a western diamondback rattlesnake (*Crotalus atrox*), unhappy but unharmed. The species name for these snakes, *atrox*, is a Greek word meaning cruel, harsh, or merciless. Though diamondbacks can be feisty, I think it's safe to say that the one in this encounter that was almost merciless was me (or my car tires).

As I walked up, the rattlesnake assumed a defensive position. It rattled angrily, head and neck lifted off the ground and cocked into an S-shape, ready to strike if I got too close. At roughly three feet long, it was certainly an adult, though not a huge one by any means. The diamondback was a light brown, similar in color to the road; perhaps that should be my excuse for not noticing it. The snake flicked its long, jet-black tongue out, slowly and deliberately, in a show of distaste not unlike that of an upset toddler.

The threatening display made for some nice photos, which I happily snapped on my phone. I then turned my attention to the more important task: getting it off the road. After all, the next driver might very well swerve to hit the poor animal instead of the other way around. When a snake is cooperative, it only takes a couple seconds to slide the hook under, lift it barely off the ground, and move it safely off the road. This diamondback, still thoroughly perturbed, refused to comply. It was intent on defending its place in the road, and it crawled off of my hook whenever I tried to slide it under. After a couple of minutes, I was eventually able to coax the snake towards the edge a bit at a time until it was safely out of the way.

It was a heart-pounding start to my trip to the Cerbat Mountains. The Cerbats are a small, north-south running mountain range in the northeastern portion of Arizona. The closest place that could be called a city is Kingman, which is located south of the Cerbats and just north of the taller, more famous Hualapai Mountains. There are a handful of small towns scattered at various points around the Cerbats, most of which got their start as mining towns. While they may have been lively places a century or two ago, today they are quiet relics of the past. The canyon that I had planned on exploring was just north of Chloride, which has the distinction of being the longest continually inhabited mining town in Arizona.

I had just spent the last couple of months in search of another kind of buried treasure: desert tortoises. After graduating with my bachelor's at the end of the year, I had taken a temporary job surveying for Mojave desert tortoises (*Gopherus agassizii*) in southern Nevada for the spring. These iconic desert dwellers—which spend most of their time sheltering in underground burrows—have been declining in population for the last several decades, largely due to anthropogenic factors. I had the pleasure of encountering several dozen of these endangered reptiles thanks to the wet weather (though "wet" for the Mojave Desert, one of the driest places on earth, is relative). The tortoises were happy to have plenty to drink, and were also appreciative of the explosion of colorful wildflowers, a veritable buffet.

But after spending so much time in the desert, I was itching to get back to the mountains. By now it was May, close to two years after I had initially begun searching for pyros, and I was eager to find at least one more before I left the western US. I had picked the Cerbats partially for convenience, as it was the closest range with pyros to where I had been in southern Nevada. This area was also home to another serpent I was itching to see: rosy boas (*Lichanura orcutti*). Sometimes called three-lined boas, their pattern consists of thick alternating gray and reddish stripes running along their round bodies. Though there are only a handful of boas native to the United States, this iconic family is found across the world and is headlined by the heaviest snake on the planet, the green anaconda (*Eunectes murinus*). Rosy boas are much smaller, growing only a couple of feet in length but have the same girthy build characteristic of boas.

I had arrived at the Cerbats at the tail end of a cool afternoon.

After almost running over the western diamondback rattlesnake, I picked a west-facing hillside not far from the road to explore. I set about turning rocks, curious to see what I could find basking underneath. The area was relatively dry, with junipers and scrub oaks being the main trees. Banana yuccas and several species of cacti were scattered around too.

One of the first things I found hiding below the surface was a small scorpion, followed soon by a lizard that sometimes pretends to be a scorpion: the western banded gecko (*Coleonyx variegatus*). These desert-dwellers look like a leopard gecko—one of the most popular pet lizards—with smooth skin that has been shrunk down to half its original size. The resemblance isn't coincidental, as these lizards are both part of the same family (Eublepharidae). Instead of the magically grippy toe pads and lidless eyes that other geckos have, geckos in this family have more standard lizard toes and eyelids. Banded geckos are neither particularly fast nor well camouflaged, instead relying on the cover of night to protect them from predators.

When threatened, banded geckos will in fact do their best scorpion impersonation by curling their chunky tail in the air above their body. Admittedly, scientists are unsure if the geckos are actually trying to convince predators that they're scorpions. Though both share similar habitats and are active at the same times, I find it hard to believe that anything would mistake these geckos for a stinging arachnid. Did I mention they squeak too? Their cute vocalizations further ruin any illusion of these small lizards being tough.

That being said, there is some scientific evidence of the effectiveness of their scorpion display. An interesting 1974 study tested it against spotted night snakes (*Hypsiglena ochrorhynchus*) using a setup that sounds like it was inspired by the Romans. The researchers put a total of eight banded geckos at a time into an enclosed "arena" (their word choice; "mini colosseum" would work too).

They then introduced a single night snake and observed the ensuing carnage. Half of the geckos had already had their tails pulled off, enabling the scientists to compare their survival rates with those still able to use the scorpion display. All the tailless geckos that were attacked died, but a third of the tailed geckos that were attacked were able to escape. For these lucky few, the snake struck the waving tail, which popped right off, allowing the lizard itself to escape.

As if watching reptiles fight to the death repeatedly wasn't already a little cruel, the authors also freeze-dried the lizards afterwards, ground them to pieces, and burned them in a calorimeter. This was done to determine the caloric composition of the regrown tails compared to the rest of the lizards' bodies, allowing the scientists to show that lizards that had lost their tails did put a lot of energy into regrowing new ones.

At least for snakes, the banded gecko's scorpion display seems to be less about mimicking a scorpion and more about giving the predator a less lethal target to strike. Whether it functions the same against mammals and birds is a question that I couldn't find a definitive answer to. Papers on other, unrelated lizards do generally support the idea that some of them really are impersonating scorpions, but this is a research avenue that deserves further investigation.

The banded gecko I found held still for a few seconds, declining to deploy the scorpion tail display. Instead, it opted for the tried-and-true strategy of running away as fast as possible. I replaced the rock that I had found the lizard under and continued on my way.

Not long after, I saw a brown streak shoot off across the dirt. I dashed and managed to grab the tail, but not before the snake was halfway in a clump of yuccas. I didn't get bitten by the snake, which turned out to be a western patchnose (*Salvadora hexalepis*), but my hand was stabbed by the sharp leaves of the yuccas—

circumstances eerily similar to the patchnose that had evaded Taylor and me in Arizona the previous summer. I was determined to even the score though, and kept a firm grip on the tail with one hand while I used the other to work the snake's body free from the yucca.

Patchnose snakes are fast, diurnal reptiles with a distinct "nose," and are found in arid habitats throughout the southwestern US. The rostral scale at the front of their face is enlarged and protrudes slightly on the sides, almost looking like a dented snowplow. This adaptation helps them dig in loose soil, usually in search of reptile eggs to munch on. As is common for speedy snakes, the pattern of western patchnoses consists of stripes running down the length of their back; two main black stripes overlayed on a tan background. This one was about average size, roughly two feet long.

I was glad to have finally caught a patchnose snake, but the feeling was not mutual. The snake kept trying to flee in the direction of the yuccas, and I soon gave up trying to get decent pictures of it. When I released the patchnose, it immediately shot into a small hole near the middle of the yucca clump—and I'd bet it didn't come out again until at least the next morning.

The next snake I found was just as uncooperative, but the similarities ended there. I had lifted up a large rock that was situated a couple of inches deep into the ground. Underneath, wiggling in the dirt, was the small but unmistakable brown body of a snake. Balancing the rock with one hand, I reached down and snagged it.

The pint-sized snake squirmed but neither bit nor musked. It was a new species for me, but I recognized it immediately: a southwestern black-headed snake (*Tantilla hobartsmithi*). They are called black-headed snakes because they secrete a mucus that causes severe acne if it gets on your face. Just kidding. They are named because they have a distinctly black head that stands out against their khaki brown bodies and reddish underbellies. This snake was approximately six inches long, slightly skinnier than a pencil, typical size for the species. Too small to eat vertebrates, southwestern black-headed snakes eat things like centipedes, caterpillars, and insect larvae. They spend most of their time underground and typically only emerge at night.

Across the Pacific Ocean, there is an Australian snake from a totally different family that shares their characteristic trait: the black-headed python (*Aspidites melanocephalus*). Black-headed pythons can grow longer than a person, ten times the length and diameter of the southwestern black-headed snake I held in my palm. The purpose of the unique color scheme is known for the pythons, who will sometimes stick just their head out of their burrow, absorbing extra heat to transfer to the rest of their concealed body. I assume that the dark heads of the black-headed snakes in the Americas evolved for a similar purpose—an example of convergent evolution—though these small, fossorial snakes are poorly studied and I couldn't find anything published that confirmed they share this behavior.

After putting the black-headed snake's rock back into place and shifting the dirt to again cover the edges, I let the small serpent crawl back underneath; putting the rock back before the snake avoids the risk of squishing it. That was the last snake of the day, and the cool evening quickly turned into a cold night.

The next day I ended up finding two of the same species as the previous day under very similar circumstances. There was an even larger western diamondback (*Crotalus atrox*) on the road, though I was paying better attention and didn't come close to running it over. It was a bulky behemoth of a snake, yet was more cooperative than the one the previous day and moved off the road on its own. In another side canyon, I also flipped another, smaller southwestern black-headed snake (*Tantilla hobartsmithi*). It was hiding under a rock similar in size to the previous one, and this little brown snake didn't want to hold still for my pictures either.

I spent my time in the Cerbats wandering in various canyons, none of which have formal names, as far as I know. I stayed between roughly four thousand and five thousand feet in elevation, hoping that I was both low enough to see rosy boas and high enough to see pyros, but not sure if I would see either.

Other than one intermittent stream—and another stream that was unfortunately confined to a pipe—the landscape was devoid of water. One of the advantages of exploring arid environments is that it is easy to wander without a formal trail. I mostly stuck to dry streambeds and the bordering hillsides, eyes always peeled for flippable rocks. I also kept an eye out for cacti. I appreciated the kingcup cacti, which grow in short clumps, with their many-petaled red flowers in full bloom. I was less appreciative of the taller, cylindrical cholla cacti, especially the dried and dead (but still just as poky) bits that littered the ground.

On my third day, I stumbled onto a kind of lizard I was not expecting to see. While walking in the middle of a wash, I saw a small brown blur scurry from the rocks into a short bush. The creature moved with the same S-shaped body undulations of a snake, but had a body that was too thick for its length—a skink!

I used my fingers to comb through the bush, looking for the glint of smooth scales concealed at the base. Whenever I got close to the lizard though, it promptly relocated to another part of the bush. I wasn't about to give up without a fight—I at least needed a good enough look to know what species it was. I had to be careful to not accidentally grab only the skink's tail, knowing it would immediately detach. I feel bad enough inflicting psychological harm by catching lizards; I don't want to inflict physical harm, even if it is a natural defense mechanism.

Eventually, I managed to pin down its slippery body and work the skink free from the bush. I was still as befuddled as before though, even with a good look at it. I knew it was a skink. The smooth scales, undersized limbs, and elongated body made that obvious. It was bigger and bulkier than the western skinks (*Plestiodon skiltonianus*) I was familiar with though. The body was a uniform tan-ish gray color, but the head was orange-red, almost as if the lizard had dunked its head into a bag of Cheetos. It tried to twist and bite with its triangle-shaped mouth, but I kept my fingers away.

With the skink secured in one hand, I used my phone in the other to take a variety of pictures from different angles, not sure what features would be needed to distinguish the various possible skink species. When I eventually released the lizard, it promptly scurried into a crevice beneath some loose rocks.

I consulted my field guide, which had been stowed in my car, later in the afternoon. Turns out I didn't need to be as meticulous as I was, as there is only one species of skink in the Cerbat Mountains: Gilbert's skink (*Plestiodon gilberti*). The juveniles of this species have brightly colored tails—some bright blue, others salmon pink—but the tail colors are usually lost as adults. Unwitting predators will grab the neon target, allowing the skink to escape with its life.

The males of this species will sometimes fight during the breeding season. These sparring bouts are no holds barred, though due to the diminutive size of their hands most of the fighting is done with their mouths. Gilbert's skinks reach a decent size, with their bulky, cylindrical bodies topping four inches in length (not counting the tail, which exceeds the length of the body).

Over the next several days, I saw quite a few more skinks—so many that I was surprised I hadn't seen any during my first two days in the Cerbats. It wasn't hard to recognize them merely by the distinct sound of one rapidly diving into the center of a bush or under rocks. I tried catching a few others, but only succeeded once more after that initial capture.

The skinks weren't the only lizards abundant in this portion of the Cerbats. I saw plenty of side-blotched lizards (*Uta stansburiana*; the rock-paper-scissors ones), quite a few tree lizards (*Urosaurus ornatus*), and two species of scelop (plateau fence lizards, *Sceloporus tristichus*, and yellow-backed spiny lizards, *Sceloporus uniformis*). There were zebra-tailed lizards (*Callisaurus draconoides*) at the lower elevations, and I caught a brief glimpse of an eastern collared lizard (*Crotaphytus collaris*) in one of the dry canyons before it jetted away.

The Cerbats were also home to my old nemesis: whiptail lizards (genus *Aspidoscelis*). Whiptails are streamlined, diurnal lizards with long, whip-like tails. They usually move with a jerky pattern of alternating starts and stops, never pausing long in any one spot—and always staying out of reach when you try to get to close. These lizards have a triangle-shaped head, large ear holes, and a snake-like forked tongue. And did I mention that they never hold still?

I saw two species on this expedition, the more common of which was the western whiptail (*Aspidoscelis tigris*), a species found throughout the western US. Whoever gave them the species name *tigris* must not have seen an actual tiger before, as these lizards have spots, not stripes. Their exact coloration varies, but generally they have irregular black spots on a burnt orange backdrop. Having already caught a western whiptail by hand a month earlier while looking for tortoises in Nevada, I was more than happy to not waste any of my time trying for a second miracle. One whiptail grab a year is plenty for me.

The second species of whiptail I saw was the Sonoran spotted whiptail (*Aspidoscelis sonorae*), a species native to the Sonoran Desert of Arizona and Mexico. They have the same classic whiptail build—cylindrical tails, skinny bodies—but have faint, yellow spots and six yellow stripes running horizontally down their brown backs.

Sonoran spotted whiptails are perhaps some of nature's most hard-core feminists, as this species only consists of females. They reproduce via some biological wizardry called parthenogenesis, where eggs develop into viable offspring without ever being fertilized. Basically, the females clone themselves instead of having sex. This special ability itself isn't that unique—it has been documented in everything from sharks to birds to insects, though not any mammals. However, in most instances there are still two sexes (bisexual), and parthenogenesis is more of a rarely used backup option. There are far fewer species of vertebrate that have just one sex (unisexual) and only reproduce through parthenogenesis.

There are multiple species of whiptail—including the Sonoran spotted—that are unisexual (all female). These species have arisen from hybridization events between two sexually reproducing whiptail species, or even between a sexually reproducing and a clonally reproducing one. Scientists have even created new species of hybrid whiptails in the lab by pairing up different species. For science, y'know? Interestingly, these unisexual whiptail species still exhibit courtship and mating behaviors, referred to as pseudocopulation.

These unisexual whiptail species can start with just a single individual, whose offspring would all be genetically identical—since there is no recombination of genes, as occurs in sexual reproduction. Mutations in the replication process still occur though, so not every single individual is perfectly genetically identical. The lack of gene recombination hampers the ability for these species to evolve further, which is why there aren't many unisexual vertebrates.

The Sonoran spotted whiptails in particular have another intriguing historical wrinkle to them. In 1964, they were actually described as two separate species: the Sonoran spotted whiptail (*Aspidoscelis sonorae*) and the Gila spotted whiptail (*Aspidoscelis flagellicaudus*). These lizards were impossible to differentiate without knowing their geographic location, which meant that when a non-native population was discovered in southern California in the 2010s, it was a huge headache to figure out exactly which species had been introduced. The poor scientists who discovered the California invaders even sequenced a mitochondrial gene on the lizards they caught, only to realize the mitochondrial DNA of the two species was virtually identical. (Mitochondrial genes are part of the mitochondria, an organelle that has a different set of genes from the nucleus of the cell, and traditionally have been easier to sequence.)

A study published just a few years later in 2018 simplified things greatly when the authors used multiple scale counts and various measurements to show that Sonoran spotted and Gila spotted whiptails were likely the same species. Now I'm just waiting for a study to come out that teaches me how to magically catch them by hand.

Many of the local snakes surely appreciated the density and variety of the local lizard menu. One species that is especially fond of lizards is the striped whipsnake (*Masticophis taeniatus*), which turned out to be the most common snake in the area. Here in the Cerbats, their lateral stripes were yellowish, unlike the pearly white stripes of the whipsnakes I was used to catching in Utah. These long, diurnal snakes are active predators. On a track you could outrun a whipsnake, but when it comes to navigating rough terrain, climbing in trees, and catching whiptail lizards, I'd bet my money on the snake.

All four of the striped whipsnakes I saw in the Cerbats were adults of roughly the same size, but each encounter went differently. The first one bolted into a tall stand of scrub oaks, and as I chased after it my foot slipped on a smooth rock, smashing my pinky toe as my foot careened into another stone. Mildly injured and infuriated, I shook my head at the snake, which had climbed branches until it was about eye level with me. After a few attempts, I was eventually able to position myself so I could reach far enough in to grab its slender body. I untangled it from the branches, only for it to musk profusely and for me to angrily release it a few seconds later. The circumstances of the second striped whipsnake were similar, though I decided that catching it wasn't worth the bodily harm or the stink. This time, after the snake had climbed into a small thicket of scrub oaks, I simply stood still, observing. I watched silently for several minutes until it casually crawled out, probably smugly thinking it had given me the slip. It slithered in the open briefly before disappearing under a large boulder.

The third whipsnake was perched with the end of its body

on the woody skeletal remains of a dead cholla cactus, head and neck raised in the air, with its eyes peeled for prey. I moved slowly, trying not to get too close, marveling at its patience as it sat there, frozen. I'd never had a whipsnake hold absolutely still for this long, but this one was a pretty convincing stick. After a couple of minutes, it was me that lost patience and left the whipsnake in peace. The fourth and final whipsnake was more true to form and rapidly fled into some bushes and then a tall pine tree. Its large eyes stared at me warily from above, ready to climb to the top of the tree if necessary.

Knowing that both pyros and rosy boas were fond of riparian areas, I spent a disproportionate amount of time around the only creek in the area. In and along the stream, which flowed above ground only intermittently, I saw a couple of red-spotted toads (*Anaxyrus punctatus*), one of the few local species of amphibian. These small, hardy toads are named for—you guessed it—the red spots that cover their backs, though the feature most useful for identification is the shape of the round parotoid glands behind their eyes. These circular bumps are home to concentrated levels of toxins that are the toad's best defense against predators.

Swimming in the creek itself were hundreds of more toads, though these were still tadpoles. The black pollywogs were less than a half inch in total length, clearly not far removed from being laid as eggs. For toads that lay their eggs in ephemeral pools, the tadpoles are in a race against time to mature into frogs before the water dries up. These tadpoles had a cushier life in the small stream, which wasn't in danger of disappearing as quickly.

It was around this creek, in an area where the water was barely a trickle, that I found my favorite snake of the trip: a beautiful Arizona black rattlesnake (*Crotalus cerberus*). These rattlesnakes are highly variable in coloration. Some are light brown with regularly spaced dark brown patches. Others are almost entirely black and have a sinister vibe. The black rattlesnake I found was an absolutely gorgeous blackish-brown with gold trim. It blended in with the dirt along the small creek well enough that I almost walked past it. It wasn't until I was perpendicular with the snake, which was several paces away, that I happened to glance over and notice it. The large serpent was stretched out, practically in a straight line, with its head dipped into the creek slightly. It was drinking, a behavior I'd never witnessed in a wild snake before.

One interesting experiment conducted in California showed just how important water can be for rattlesnakes. The study looked at the effect of hydration on northern Pacific rattlesnakes (*Crotalus oreganus*) by administering extra water to some individuals and documenting the effects.

They say you can lead a horse to water, but you can't make it drink. The same is true for rattlesnakes. The researchers first used a plastic tube to restrain the snake, a standard practice for handling rattlesnakes. (Once the snake's head is in the long tube, its body can be held, preventing the snake from backing up or crawling out the other end of the tube.) The researchers could then insert a catheter down its mouth and into its stomach, allowing them to give exactly twenty-five mililiters of water each time. When the snakes were initially captured, radio transmitters were surgically inserted so that the water procedure could be repeated twice a month for the duration of the study. I feel bad for the snakes in the control group that had to go through the whole stressful ordeal without the added benefit of extra water.

The study involved twenty-one adult snakes. Those that received water had slightly higher body conditions at the end of the study, though there was no difference in movement between the two groups. The most interesting finding was that all of the four females that received supplemental water gave birth (all rattlesnakes give live birth instead of laying eggs), while none of the three control females did. The sample size was somewhat small, but the effect wasn't. Having water, even for dry-adapted species, is critical.

The black rattlesnake I found that day in Arizona was drinking like a college student at a frat party. I'm not sure if the snake didn't notice me at first, or if it just didn't care as long as I kept my distance, but I was able to watch it continue to guzzle from the small creek. I crept a few steps closer and crouched down, trying to get as good of a view as possible without disturbing the beautiful serpent. I could see the muscles contracting on the sides of its wide head as it pulled more and more water down its throat.

After about ten minutes, the snake pulled its snout out of the water. Either it had finally had its fill or it had just now noticed my presence. Either way, now that the snake's heat sensitive pits were out of the water, it fully registered that there was a large, warm-blooded animal standing a few feet away. Its previously straight and relaxed body tensed up slightly. It gave its rattle a halfhearted shake, as if it was still trying to assess if I was a threat. I held still, waiting. After a pause the snake crawled slowly underneath a thick bush.

I continued to watch the snake for the next half hour as it meandered halfway up the rocky canyon and began moving parallel to the creek. I gave it a wide berth, sacrificing the opportunity for perfectly posed pictures in exchange for witnessing the natural behavior of a completely relaxed snake. The dark, metallic scales of the snake fused with the pockets of shadows as it crept along. I don't know where the rattlesnake was going, but it seemed to have a destination in mind.

That gorgeous black rattlesnake was the cherry on top for yet another amazing excursion to the great state of Arizona. I didn't see any rosy boas, but I had enjoyed finding the surprise skinks and the many other reptilian residents of the area.

By this point in time, I knew my path in life was leading away from the western US. Before completing my bachelor's degree that winter, I had finally made a decision on graduate school. I loved the towering mountains and rugged deserts I had grown so close to, but I also wanted to spread my wings and explore some new places. I strongly considered several programs in the southeast before ultimately deciding on an even more far-flung destination: China. I had been accepted to Nanjing Forestry University and was only waiting for a visa before my next adventure could start.

Back when I first set my heart on researching pyros, if someone had told me that it would be more than a year before I saw one in the wild, I might have just given up there (and probably emailed that professor to see if he still needed someone to measure dead fish). Yet I am infinitely glad that I didn't throw in the towel prematurely. Though the path wasn't smooth, pyros had gotten me into graduate school, the next chapter of my life. And along the way, I'd encountered many other magnificent, mesmerizing, and mysterious creatures.

As I drove away from the Cerbat Mountains, I didn't know when I would be able to return to Arizona again. I wasn't sure if I would ever get to see a wild rosy boa. But I knew a place where I would have a decent shot at one last pyro.

FIFTEEN

The Flame Burns On

The vast majority of this book has been lighthearted, but I'd like to devote a few final pages to slightly more serious matters and explicitly talk about conservation (before ending with one final snake story, of course).

The unfortunate reality is that the earth has entered what many biologists have termed the sixth mass extinction. Earth's biodiversity has seen many declines throughout its long history, including five cataclysmic events in the last five hundred million years that saw more than half of all species at the time disappear. The fifth and most recent mass extinction is probably the best known: that of the dinosaurs, the ruling class of reptiles that dominated the planet for millennia before being wiped out by the titanic impact of an asteroid. That fateful space rock of sixty-six million years ago razed forests, launched toxic chemicals into the atmosphere and oceans, and dramatically altered the climate—a recipe of destruction that should sound eerily familiar to modern ears. (Two quick points for accuracy: first, there was one group of dinosaurs that did survive—looking at you, birds—and second, the asteroid may not have been the only driver of this mass extinction event, though it was undoubtedly a major contributor.)

Compared to that unstoppable asteroid of millions of years ago, the anthropogenic asteroid that is threatening earth's present biodiversity is moving at a slower speed. If the current pace of ecological devastation continues unabated though, we'll give the actual asteroid a serious run for its money in terms of total destructive power. But it isn't too late for us as a species to act.

Admittedly, nobody would pick snakes as an ideal conservation mascot. Most people naturally have sympathy for fuzzy animals, but snakes seem to be a harder sell. Yet I hope in this book I've been able to portray snakes (plus the occasional lizard, amphibian, and invertebrate) in a positive light, showcasing just how fascinating and beautiful they can be. Snakes are worth protecting. As such I'd like to conclude with two broad ways you can help our underappreciated scaly friends.

First, be an advocate.

This can be as simple as helping others know how to identify and be safe around venomous snakes. Remember, opting to leave a venomous snake alone instead of trying to kill it is always the safer option. Educating others, whether formally or informally, about the realities of how (not) dangerous snakes are can go a long way. Humans are always more scared of what they don't understand. Help others see snakes as incredible marvels of biology rather than cold-blooded killers.

Thinking of the bigger picture, it is also key to advocate for government policies and corporate practices that truly protect the environment. Habitat loss is the biggest threat to snakes and most other organisms. Whether it's forests getting chopped down, or native grasslands being replaced by crop monocultures, or the constant expansion of cities, the amount of space for wild creatures is decreasing. Protecting habitats is the single most important thing that can be done to conserve wildlife. Full stop. Other threats—climate change, pollution, invasive species, disease, etc.—deserve significant attention too, but habitat loss is the single most pressing issue.

This doesn't mean that all wild places should immediately be fenced off. Conservation efforts that involve and educate locals are far more successful in the long term, and part of why we should conserve nature is so that we can enjoy it. Red tape is no fun, but there do need to be protections in place. In the absence of strong legal regulations, there will always be people who prioritize profits over the environment, and as such I encourage you to be an advocate for protecting snakes and other wildlife. The best ways to protect or restore habitats will vary immensely by place and species; without getting bogged down in details, my point is that formal regulation is something to be discussed, implemented, and fine-tuned, not shunned.

If you have the financial means, advocate for snakes with your wallet too. There are a whole host of excellent non-profit organizations that work to conserve snakes directly, conduct snake research, and engage in public outreach. The Orianne Society, Save the Snakes, and the Amphibian and Reptile Conservancy are just a few reputable examples in the US, and there are plenty of other conservation NGOs making a difference around the world.

Second, collect pictures and memories, not wild snakes.

I hope that reading this book has inspired you to at least keep an eye out for snakes during your next adventure in the woods. But I sincerely hope your newfound appreciation will not inspire you to abduct snakes.

In 1957, legendary herpetologist Carl Kauffeld published *Snakes and Snake Hunting*, a book about his wild escapades searching for snakes that has become a cult classic in the hobby. Virtually every one of Kauffeld's exciting tales ends with a snake getting stuffed into a bag and sentenced to a life behind glass walls. Kauffeld inspired a generation of snake lovers, and, in a way, his penchant for collecting set the status quo—that collecting was fine, and even encouraged—for the emerging snake hobby.

Most of Kauffeld's catches ended up at the Staten Island Zoo, where he worked for decades, and were used for public education. Back in the 1950s, few people were keeping snakes and even fewer breeding them, making his contributions critical for nascent captive-breeding efforts. For these reasons I'll give Kauffeld a pass, but this cavalier, keep-everything-you-can-catch attitude ought to go extinct. Nowadays, many species are available captive-bred, minimizing the need to collect more from the wild for the pet trade. Not all four thousand species are available, of course, but there are more than enough options. However slight the impact on the ecosystem of taking one snake home for your personal enjoyment is, it is undeniably in the negative direction. There are enough other forces that are acting to wipe snakes off the planet; it feels painfully ironic for those that love snakes the most to knowingly contribute to their destruction.

Honestly, snakes make great pets—it is significantly easier to care for a python than a puppy. But please, if you want a pet snake, get a captive-bred one. Do your background research, both on how to care for the snake and to confirm it was truly captive-bred; don't financially support the sale of wild-caught animals.

This doesn't mean that you can't enjoy finding wild snakes though. By all means, go out and look; just don't bring the snakes home. Be aware of and try to reduce the stress that you may cause the animal when observing or handling it. Additionally, remember to minimize your impact on the habitat, particularly by always neatly replacing any objects you check under. Lastly, be aware of and follow state laws; there are some threatened species that are not legal to even touch.

Should you feel the itch to collect, I highly recommend downloading iNaturalist and "collecting" high quality observations instead. If snakes aren't your thing, figure out what is! Frogs? Fungi? Fireflies? Pick a group of organisms to learn more about and to go looking for. Spending time in nature and getting to know your fellow earthly inhabitants is as wholesome of a pastime as there is.

To recap: be an advocate, and collect pictures and memories instead of snakes. Obviously there are other ways to aid the conservation of snakes beyond these two broad suggestions, but both of these are impactful and doable. The anthropogenic asteroid has already started to hit the planet, but we can reduce the size of the crater it leaves.

Knowing my days of pyro searching were numbered, after leaving northern Arizona I embarked on one last trip to my favorite place in the entire world: Kanosh Canyon. I had originally planned on meeting up with my friend Jacob there, but the cold and rainy forecast prompted him to push his plans back a day. I was already there and had nowhere better to go, so I figured I'd see what I could find in the couple hours of good weather.

Shortly after starting my hike up the main fork of Corn Creek, I was startled by a massive golden eagle—or maybe I startled it—perched at the top of a rock wall. The huge brown bird squawked and flew in my direction, staying below the tops of the trees and passing not far above my head before gliding out of sight. At the time I assumed that the majestic eagle was the only noteworthy reptile I would see that day given the gloomy forecast.

Corn Creek itself was a dirty orange from all the silty sandstone carried by the rushing waters. Thanks to the wet winter and spring, the water level was much higher than at any of my previous visits. The air had a touch of humidity, unusual for anywhere in Utah, and the vegetation was a vibrant green. The ground was even moist enough that I half expected to find salamanders instead of lizards hiding under the logs and rocks. The gray skies made it clear that more moisture was in store.

As I do every time I revisit Kanosh, I checked carefully around the areas where I had seen pyros in the past. The large female I had found with Jacob on that fateful day almost exactly a year ago wasn't hiding in the same leaves. The sandstone rocks I had seen my second pyro splayed out on the previous July were vacant too. I hoped that both of these snakes are still alive and well, happily glutting themselves on the overabundance of local lizards. Even if they weren't the most scientifically significant finds, those pyros—especially the first—had meant the world to me.

The sun came out from behind the clouds intermittently as I hiked, and I saw many of the usual residents of the canyon: sagebrush lizards (*Sceloporus graciosus*), plateau fence lizards (*Sceloporus tristichus*), and yellow-bellied racers (*Coluber constrictor mormon*). I came close to stepping on a Great Basin rattlesnake (*Crotalus lutosus*), but it was courteous enough to give me a warning. The snake was nestled up against a rock, absorbing what thin rays of sunshine penetrated the cloud cover.

Not wanting to get caught in a total downpour, I only hiked a couple of miles up the canyon, keeping a close eye on the surrounding clouds. On my way back, I was walking on the broad, gentle hillside between the trail and the north wall of the canyon. There were some small outcroppings with flat pieces of shale strewn about, interspersing the various annual plants that were in bloom.

Many of the gray rocks were an ideal size; plenty big enough to hide a snake, while still small enough to flip and put back neatly. With the cloud cover and cool weather, the stones were at a Goldilocks temperature too; warmer than the surrounding air but not scorching hot. I'd flipped some of these rocks in the past, never finding anything besides the occasional lizard.

I turned a few of the scattered stones, replacing them carefully. After finding nothing under the first few rocks, I grabbed the side of a large, triangular hunk of shale. As I lifted it, I saw a green centipede, about as long as my index finger, frantically scurrying to find a new place to hide. And then, as I lifted further, my eyes snapped away from the centipede and fixed on the red, white, and black scales glistening underneath. A pyro.

With its once secure shelter suddenly gone, the snake was just as bewildered as the centipede. The pyro's reaction was even more bizarre: it bit itself. The snake opened its mouth and chomped down on its own midsection. The only logical explanation I could come up with was that the frightened snake was looking for movement, trying to identify a potential predator. When it saw its own body move, it struck instinctually, only to immediately realize its mistake. I recovered from my initial shock and reached down with my right hand, scooping up the beautiful snake. I lowered the rock back down with my other hand and marveled at my luck.

It was wonderful to feel those smooth, colorful scales slide through my fingers again. Though it was still bewildered, the snake didn't try to bite. It didn't musk either, or maybe I was too excited to notice. It was similar in size to the pyro I had found in July: somewhere in the neighborhood of two feet in length.

The shiny red, white, and black bands of the snake were just as stunning as the other two pyros I'd found up Kanosh Canyon. This snake also had a slight aberration of the normal bands; the second white band split apart on the left side a few inches down from the head, a unique birthmark that gave its appearance a bit of extra personality. Like other pyros, the bands on its belly weren't uniform, but rather were an irregular tricolor mosaic.

I tried to snap some pictures on my phone, but the pyro refused to cooperate. Rather than pose nicely against the rocks or in the grass, it insisted on crawling in the direction of a rocky outcropping further up the hill. Eventually, I settled for a few photos of the fiery red snake aloft in my hand, held up against the verdant hillside on the other side of the creek.

When I finally granted the pyro its freedom for good, it made a beeline for the large outcropping it had been repeatedly trying to reach. The stubborn snake wedged itself, a couple inches at a time, into a skinny vertical crevice in the gray, lichen-covered rocks. Within a few seconds it was entirely in the crack, head positioned at the bottom. The pyro stared out at me with a single dark, round eye. The rock concealed the shy snake from the outside world, but even the shadows of the crevice could only dim its brilliant colors so much.

SOURCES

A note on sources: I consulted many scientific studies in writing this book. If you are interested in reading any of the scientific papers below without paying ridiculous fees, search the title online for a PDF or email one of the authors to request a copy—they are usually thrilled to send it. There is no reason to ever pay a fee to read any of these papers.

For basic biological information (size, diet, range, etc.) on essentially all of the North American reptiles and amphibians mentioned in this book, my primary source has been Robert Stebbins' excellent 2003 field guide to the herps of western North America. Out of convenience, I have listed it once (under "General") rather than list it for every single species of herp in every chapter.

For current scientific names, I have followed the taxonomy from the Reptile Database (circa 2023; scientific names often change and over time some of the names printed will become outdated). As with the Stebbins' field guide, rather than cite the Reptile Database a million times for every single reptile scientific name, I will list the general database information once. Instances where I have gotten information beyond purely the current name (e.g. on etymology) from the Reptile Database are cited specifically.

The remaining sources are grouped by chapter and listed alphabetically.

General:

Stebbins, Robert C. 2003. *A Field Guide to Western Reptiles and Amphibians*. 3rd ed. Peterson Field Guide Series. Boston: Houghton Mifflin.

Uetz, Peter, P. Freed, R. Aguilar, F. Reyes, and J. Hošek. 2023. "Reptile Database." Reptile Database. 2023. http://reptile-database.org/.

Chapter 1

Cope, Edward. 1867. "On the Reptilia and Batrachia of the Sonoran Province of the Nearctic Region." *Proceedings of the Academy of Natural Sciences of Philadelphia* 18: 300–314.

Davidson, Jane P. 1997. *The Bone Sharp: The Life of Edward Drinker Cope*. Philadelphia: Academy of Natural Sciences of Philadelphia.

Deep Look. 2019. *Jerusalem Crickets Only Date Drummers*. KQED. https://www.youtube.com/watch?v=mHbwC-AIyTE.

"Herpetology." n.d. In *Merriam-Webster Dictionary*. https://www.merriam-webster.com/dictionary/herpetology.

Moeller, Karla. 2012. "Edward Drinker Cope (1840-1897)." Embryo Project Encyclopedia. January 1, 2012. https://embryo.asu.edu/pages/edward-drinker-cope-1840-1897.

O'Donnell, Ryan P., Kevin Staniland, and Robert T. Mason. 2007. "Experimental Evidence That Oral Secretions of Northwestern Ring-Necked Snakes (*Diadophis punctatus occidentalis*) Are Toxic to Their Prey." *Toxicon* 50 (6): 810–15. https://doi.org/10.1016/j.toxicon.2007.06.024.

Rossi, J.V., and R. Rossi. 1994. "*Diadophis punctatus punctatus* (Southern Ringneck Snake): Anti-Ophiophagous Behavior." *Herpetological Review* 25: 123.

Stoffolano, John G., and Barton Wright. 2005. "Sösööpa—Jerusalem Cricket: An Important Insect in the Hopi Katsina Pantheon." *American Entomologist* 51 (3): 174–79. https://doi.org/10.1093/ae/51.3.174.

Uetz, Peter. n.d.-a. "*Lampropeltis getula* (LINNAEUS, 1766)." Reptile Database. Accessed January 19, 2023. https://reptile-database.reptarium.cz/species?genus=Lampropeltis&species=getula#.

———. n.d.-b. "*Lampropeltis pyromelana* (COPE, 1866)." Reptile Database. Accessed January 19, 2023. https://reptile-database.reptarium.cz/species?genus=Lampropeltis&species=pyromelana.

Uetz, Peter, and Alexandrea Stylianou. 2018. "The Original Descriptions of Reptiles and Their Subspecies." *Zootaxa* 4375 (2): 257. https://doi.org/10.11646/zootaxa.4375.2.5.

Wilmer, Tanner. 1983. "*Lampropeltis pyromelana*." *Catalogue of American Reptiles and Amphibians (CAAR)*.

Chapter 2

Gangloff, Eric, David Bertolatus, Christopher Reigel, and Jennifer L. Gagliardi-Seeley. 2014. "Effects of Sex, Environment, and Condition on the Musking Behavior of Sympatric Gartersnakes (*Thamnophis* spp.)." *Journal of North American Herpetology* 2014 (1): 40–46. https://doi.org/10.17161/jnah.vi1.11892.

Hubbs, Brian. 2004. *Mountain Kings: A Collective Natural History of California, Sonoran, Durango and Queretaro Mountain Kingsnakes.* 1st ed. Tempe, AZ: Tricolor Books.

Kohler, Dallin B., Bryan T. Hamilton, Drew E. Dittmer, and Alison S. Whiting. 2023. "Citizen Science in Action: An Updated Distribution for *Lampropeltis pyromelana*." *Western North American Naturalist* 83 (2): 2.

Pope, Clifford H. 1958. "Fatal Bite of Captive African Rear-Fanged Snake (*Dispholidus*)." *Copeia* 1958 (4): 280. https://doi.org/10.2307/1439959.

"Utah's Reptiles and Amphibians Online Guidebook." 2021. Utah

Division of Wildlife Resources. December 9, 2021. https://wildlife.utah.gov/hunting/main-hunting-page/reptiles-amphibians.html.

Van Cott, John W. 1990. *Utah Place Names: A Comprehensive Guide to the Origins of Geographic Names: A Compilation*. Salt Lake City, Utah: University of Utah Press.

Chapter 3

Morris, Hal, T. 1979. "General Geology and Mines of the East Tintic Mining District." Professional Paper. Utah Geological Association.

Van Cott, John W. 1990. *Utah Place Names: A Comprehensive Guide to the Origins of Geographic Names: A Compilation*. Salt Lake City, Utah: University of Utah Press.

Walter, Frank G., Uwe Stolz, Farshad Shirazi, and Jude McNally. 2009. "Epidemiology of Severe and Fatal Rattlesnake Bites Published in the American Association of Poison Control Centers' Annual Reports." *Clinical Toxicology* 47 (7): 663–69. https://doi.org/10.1080/15563650903113701.

Chapter 4

Baynes-Rock, Marcus. 2017. "Human Perceptual and Phobic Biases for Snakes: A Review of the Experimental Evidence." *Anthrozoös* 30 (1): 5–18. https://doi.org/10.1080/08927936.2017.1270584.

Boback, Scott M., Melia G. Nafus, Amy A. Yackel Adams, and Robert N. Reed. 2020. "Use of Visual Surveys and Radiotelemetry Reveals Sources of Detection Bias for a Cryptic Snake at Low Densities." *Ecosphere* 11 (1). https://doi.org/10.1002/ecs2.3000.

Chester, Stephen G. B., Jonathan I. Bloch, Doug M. Boyer, and William A. Clemens. 2015. "Oldest Known Euarchontan Tarsals and Affinities of Paleocene *Purgatorius* to Primates." *Proceedings of the National Academy of Sciences* 112 (5): 1487–92.

https://doi.org/10.1073/pnas.1421707112.

Darshani, Avi. 2021. "Releasing Life or Releasing Death: The Practice of and Discourse on Buddhist Animal Liberation Rituals in Contemporary Xiamen." *Journal of Chinese Religions* 49 (1): 109–43. https://doi.org/10.1353/jcr.2021.0004.

Durso, Andrew M., and Richard A. Seigel. 2015. "A Snake in the Hand Is Worth 10,000 in the Bush." *Journal of Herpetology* 49 (4): 503–6. https://doi.org/10.1670/15-49-04.1.

"Explore Current Mammal Taxonomy." n.d. Mammal Diversity Database. https://www.mammaldiversity.org/taxa.html.

Head, Jason J., Jonathan I. Bloch, Alexander K. Hastings, Jason R. Bourque, Edwin A. Cadena, Fabiany A. Herrera, P. David Polly, and Carlos A. Jaramillo. 2009. "Giant Boid Snake from the Palaeocene Neotropics Reveals Hotter Past Equatorial Temperatures." *Nature* 457 (7230): 715–17. https://doi.org/10.1038/nature07671.

Isbell, Lynne A. 2006. "Snakes as Agents of Evolutionary Change in Primate Brains." *Journal of Human Evolution* 51 (1): 1–35. https://doi.org/10.1016/j.jhevol.2005.12.012.

Jensen, Cody. 2019. "Examining Snake Detection Theory: Conscious and Unconscious Responses to Snakes." Master's thesis, California State University San Marcos.

Kawai, Nobuyuki, and Hongshen He. 2016. "Breaking Snake Camouflage: Humans Detect Snakes More Accurately than Other Animals under Less Discernible Visual Conditions." *PLOS ONE* 11 (10): e0164342. https://doi.org/10.1371/journal.pone.0164342.

Malgasto. 2005. "Vandalism of Chalk Creek." *Ancient Lost Treasures*. https://www.tapatalk.com/groups/ancientlosttreasures/vandalism-of-chalk-creek-t3939.html.

Mineka, Susan, Mark Davidson, Michael Cook, and Richard Keir. 1984. "Observational Conditioning of Snake Fear in Rhesus Monkeys." *Journal of Abnormal Psychology* 93 (4): 355–72. https://doi.org/10.1037/0021-843X.93.4.355.

Penning, David A., Baxter Sawvel, and Brad R. Moon. 2016. "Debunking the Viper's Strike: Harmless Snakes Kill a Common Assumption." *Biology Letters* 12 (3): 20160011. https://doi.org/10.1098/rsbl.2016.0011.

Rodda, Gordon H., Thomas H. Fritts, and Paul J. Conry. 1992. "Origin and Population Growth of the Brown Tree Snake, *Boiga irregularis*, on Guam." *Pacific Science* 46 (1): 46–57.

Weiss, Lucie, Pavel Brandl, and Daniel Frynta. 2015. "Fear Reactions to Snakes in Naïve Mouse Lemurs and Pig-Tailed Macaques." *Primates* 56 (3): 279–84. https://doi.org/10.1007/s10329-015-0473-3.

Chapter 5

bobbyfingers. 2020. "iNaturalist Observation 39031825." *iNaturalist*. https://www.inaturalist.org/observations/39031825.

Burbrink, Frank T., Helen Yao, Matthew Ingrasci, Robert W. Bryson, Timothy J Guiher, and Sara Ruane. 2011. "Speciation at the Mogollon Rim in the Arizona Mountain Kingsnake (*Lampropeltis pyromelana*)." *Molecular Phylogenetics and Evolution* 60 (3): 445–54. https://doi.org/10.1016/j.ympev.2011.05.009.

Tanner, Wilmer W. 1953. "A Study of Taxonomy and Phylogeny of *Lampropeltis pyromelana* Cope." *Great Basin Naturalist* 13 (1/2): 47–66.

Taylor, Edward H. 1940. "A New *Lampropeltis* from Western Mexico." *Copeia* 1940 (4): 253. https://doi.org/10.2307/1438582.

"The Sky Islands." n.d. Sky Island Alliance. Accessed January 22, 2023. https://skyislandalliance.org/the-sky-islands/.

Uetz, Peter. n.d. "*Crotalus molossus* Baird & Girard, 1853." Reptile Database. Accessed January 19, 2023. https://reptile-database.reptarium.cz/species?genus=Crotalus&species=molossus.

Chapter 6

Allf, Bradley C., Paul A. P. Durst, and David W. Pfennig. 2016.

"Behavioral Plasticity and the Origins of Novelty: The Evolution of the Rattlesnake Rattle." *The American Naturalist.* https://doi.org/10.5061/DRYAD.C36K6.

Cope, Edward. 1869. "Protocol of the 9 March, 1869 Meeting." *Proceedings of the Academy of Natural Sciences of Philadelphia* 21: 5.

Gienger, C. M., C. Richard Tracy, and Kenneth A. Nagy. 2014. "Life in the Lizard Slow Lane: Gila Monsters Have Low Rates of Energy Use and Water Flux." *Copeia* 2014 (2): 279–87. https://doi.org/10.1643/CP-13-086.

Krochmal, Aaron R., and George S. Bakken. 2003. "Thermoregulation Is the Pits: Use of Thermal Radiation for Retreat Site Selection by Rattlesnakes." *Journal of Experimental Biology* 206 (15): 2539–45. https://doi.org/10.1242/jeb.00471.

Miralles, Aurélien, Julie Marin, Damien Markus, Anthony Herrel, S. Blair Hedges, and Nicolas Vidal. 2018. "Molecular Evidence for the Paraphyly of Scolecophidia and Its Evolutionary Implications." *Journal of Evolutionary Biology* 31 (12): 1782–93. https://doi.org/10.1111/jeb.13373.

Mizuno, T., and Y. Kojima. 2015. "A Blindsnake That Decapitates Its Termite Prey." *Journal of Zoology* 297 (3): 220–24. https://doi.org/10.1111/jzo.12268.

Reid, Jack R., and Thomas E. Lott. 1963. "Feeding of *Leptotyphlops dulcis dulcis* (Baird and Girard)." *Herpetologica* 19 (2): 141–42.

Rhoads, Dusty. 2008. *The Complete Suboc, A Comprehensive Guide to the Natural History, Care, and Breeding of the Trans-Pecos Ratsnake.* Lansing, Michigan: ECO Herpetological Publishing & Distribution.

Uetz, Peter. n.d. "*Phyllorhynchus browni* Stejneger, 1890." Reptile Database. Accessed January 19, 2023. https://reptile-database.reptarium.cz/species?genus=Phyllorhynchus&species=browni.

Chapter 7

"100 of the World's Worst Invasive Alien Species." 2013. Global

Invasive Species Database. 2013. http://www.iucngisd.org/gisd/100_worst.php.

Barreto, Lima, André Felipe. 2009. "Gastric Suction as an Alternative Method in Studies of Lizard Diets: Tests in Two Species of *Enyalius* (Squamata)." *Studies on Neotropical Fauna and Environment* 44 (1): 23–29. https://doi.org/10.1080/01650520902834397.

Gilbert, Anthony L., Olivia L. Brooks, and Matthew S. Lattanzio. 2020. "Multiple Behavioral Contexts of a Melanized Tail Display in a Desert Lizard." Edited by Luis Ebensperger. *Ethology* 126 (3): 333–43. https://doi.org/10.1111/eth.12975.

Glaudas, Xavier, Teresa C. Kearney, and Graham J. Alexander. 2017. "Museum Specimens Bias Measures of Snake Diet: A Case Study Using the Ambush-Foraging Puff Adder (*Bitis arietans*)." *Herpetologica* 73 (2): 121–28. https://doi.org/10.1655/HERPETOLOGICA-D-16-00055.

Knowlton, George F., and Melvin J. Janes. 1934. "Distributional and Food Habits Notes on Utah Lizards." *Copeia* 1934 (1): 10–14. https://doi.org/10.2307/1436426.

Maritz, Robin A., and Bryan Maritz. 2020. "Sharing for Science: High-Resolution Trophic Interactions Revealed Rapidly by Social Media." *PeerJ* 8 (July): e9485. https://doi.org/10.7717/peerj.9485.

Minteer, Ben A., James P. Collins, Karen E. Love, and Robert Puschendorf. 2014. "Avoiding (Re)Extinction." *Science* 344 (6181): 260–61. https://doi.org/10.1126/science.1250953.

Minteer, Ben A., James P. Collins, and Robert Puschendorf. 2014. "Specimen Collection: An Essential Tool—Response." *Science* 344 (6186): 816–816. https://doi.org/10.1126/science.344.6186.816-a.

Most, Albert. 1983. *Bufo Alvarius: The Psychedelic Toad of the Sonoran Desert*. https://erowid.org/archive/sonoran_desert_toad/almost.htm.

Rocha, L. A., A. Aleixo, G. Allen, F. Almeda, C. C. Baldwin, M. V. L. Barclay, J. M. Bates, et al. 2014. "Specimen Collection:

An Essential Tool." *Science* 344 (6186): 814–15. https://doi.org/10.1126/science.344.6186.814.

Rodríguez-Robles, Javier A. 1998. "Alternative Perspectives on the Diet of Gopher Snakes (*Pituophis catenifer*, Colubridae): Literature Records versus Stomach Contents of Wild and Museum Specimens." *Copeia* 1998 (2): 463–66. https://doi.org/10.2307/1447442.

Uetz, Peter. n.d. "*Sceloporus jarrovii* Cope, 1875." Reptile Database. Accessed January 19, 2023. https://reptile-database.reptarium.cz/species?genus=Sceloporus&species=jarrovii.

Chapter 8

Akcali, Christopher K., and David W. Pfennig. 2014. "Rapid Evolution of Mimicry Following Local Model Extinction." *Biology Letters* 10 (6): 20140304. https://doi.org/10.1098/rsbl.2014.0304.

———. 2017. "Geographic Variation in Mimetic Precision among Different Species of Coral Snake Mimics." *Journal of Evolutionary Biology* 30 (7): 1420–28. https://doi.org/10.1111/jeb.13094.

Bates, Henry Walter. 1862. "Contributions to an Insect Fauna of the Amazon Valley (Lepidoptera: Heliconidae)." *Transactions of the Linnean Society of London* 23: 495–566.

Brodie III, Edmund D. 1993. "Differential Avoidance of Coral Snake Banded Patterns by Free-Ranging Avian Predators in Costa Rica." *Evolution* 47 (1): 227–35. https://doi.org/10.1111/j.1558-5646.1993.tb01212.x.

———. 2010. "Dazzled and Deceived: Mimicry and Camouflage." *BioScience* 60 (10): 850–51. https://doi.org/10.1525/bio.2010.60.10.12.

Brodie III, Edmund D., and F. J. Janzen. 1995. "Experimental Studies of Coral Snake Mimicry: Generalized Avoidance of Ringed Snake Patterns by Free-Ranging Avian Predators." *Functional Ecology* 9 (2): 186–90. https://doi.org/10.2307/2390563.

Burkhardt, Frederick, Alison M. Pearn, and Samantha Evans, eds.

2008. "1862." In *Evolution: Selected Letters of Charles Darwin 1860-1870*, 1st ed., 40–65. Cambridge: Cambridge University Press. https://doi.org/10.1017/CBO9780511542596.007.

Carvalho, Livia S., Daniel M. A. Pessoa, Jessica K. Mountford, Wayne I. L. Davies, and David M. Hunt. 2017. "The Genetic and Evolutionary Drives behind Primate Color Vision." *Frontiers in Ecology and Evolution* 5 (April): 34. https://doi.org/10.3389/fevo.2017.00034.

Chandler's Wild Life. 2022. "Can You Drink Snake Venom?" YouTube. January 20, 2022. https://www.youtube.com/watch?v=h92uX7dqDWI.

Davis Rabosky, Alison R., Christian L. Cox, Daniel L. Rabosky, Pascal O. Title, Iris A. Holmes, Anat Feldman, and Jimmy A. McGuire. 2016. "Coral Snakes Predict the Evolution of Mimicry across New World Snakes." *Nature Communications* 7 (1): 11484. https://doi.org/10.1038/ncomms11484.

Greene, Harry W., and Roy W. McDiarmid. 1981. "Coral Snake Mimicry: Does It Occur?" *Science* 213 (4513): 1207–12. https://doi.org/10.1126/science.213.4513.1207.

Harper, George R., and David W. Pfennig. 2007. "Mimicry on the Edge: Why Do Mimics Vary in Resemblance to Their Model in Different Parts of Their Geographical Range?" *Proceedings of the Royal Society B: Biological Sciences* 274 (1621): 1955–61. https://doi.org/10.1098/rspb.2007.0558.

Harper Jr, George R., and David W. Pfennig. 2008. "Selection Overrides Gene Flow to Break down Maladaptive Mimicry." *Nature* 451 (7182): 1103–6. https://doi.org/10.1038/nature06532.

Hart, Nathan S. 2001. "The Visual Ecology of Avian Photoreceptors." *Progress in Retinal and Eye Research* 20 (5): 675–703. https://doi.org/10.1016/S1350-9462(01)00009-X.

Kohler, Dallin B., Taylor S. Probst, Jacob A. Search, and Alison S. Whiting. 2024. "Mystifying Mountain Mimics: Two Sister Species of Kingsnake Show Different Trends in

Mimetic Accuracy in Allopatry with Coral Snakes." *Western North American Naturalist* 84 (2): 200–209. http://dx.doi.org/10.3398/064.084.0204.

Pfennig, David W., William R. Harcombe, and Karin S. Pfennig. 2001. "Frequency-Dependent Batesian Mimicry." *Nature* 410 (6826): 323. https://doi.org/10.1038/35066628.

Pfennig, David W., George R. Harper, Abel F. Brumo, William R. Harcombe, and Karin S. Pfennig. 2007. "Population Differences in Predation on Batesian Mimics in Allopatry with Their Model: Selection against Mimics Is Strongest When They Are Common." *Behavioral Ecology and Sociobiology* 61 (4): 505–11. https://doi.org/10.1007/s00265-006-0278-x.

Pfennig, David W., and Sean P. Mullen. 2010. "Mimics without Models: Causes and Consequences of Allopatry in Batesian Mimicry Complexes." *Proceedings of the Royal Society B: Biological Sciences* 277 (1694): 2577–85. https://doi.org/10.1098/rspb.2010.0586.

Sena, Anthony Thomas, and Sara Ruane. 2022. "Concepts and Contentions of Coral Snake Resemblance: Batesian Mimicry and Its Alternatives." *Biological Journal of the Linnean Society* 135 (4): 631–44. https://doi.org/10.1093/biolinnean/blab171.

Simões, Bruno F., Filipa L. Sampaio, Ronald H. Douglas, Ullasa Kodandaramaiah, Nicholas R. Casewell, Robert A. Harrison, Nathan S. Hart, Julian C. Partridge, David M. Hunt, and David J. Gower. 2016. "Visual Pigments, Ocular Filters and the Evolution of Snake Vision." *Molecular Biology and Evolution* 33 (10): 2483–95. https://doi.org/10.1093/molbev/msw148.

Smith, Susan M. 1975. "Innate Recognition of Coral Snake Pattern by a Possible Avian Predator." *Science* 187 (4178): 759–60. https://doi.org/10.1126/science.187.4178.759.

Titcomb, Georgia C., David W. Kikuchi, and David W. Pfennig. 2014. "More than Mimicry? Evaluating Scope for Flicker-Fusion as a Defensive Strategy in Coral Snake Mimics." *Current Zoology* 60 (1): 123–30. https://doi.org/10.1093/

czoolo/60.1.123.
Umeton, Diana, Jenny C. A. Read, and Candy Rowe. 2017. "Unravelling the Illusion of Flicker Fusion." *Biology Letters* 13 (2): 20160831. https://doi.org/10.1098/rsbl.2016.0831.
Wallace, Alfred Russel. 2010 [1867]. "Mimicry, and Other Protective Resemblances Among Animals (1867)." *Alfred Russel Wallace Classic Writings* 8: 1–27.

Chapter 9

Barrows, Cameron W., Josh Hoines, Michael S. Vamstad, Michelle Murphy-Mariscal, Kristen Lalumiere, and James Heintz. 2016. "Using Citizen Scientists to Assess Climate Change Shifts in Desert Reptile Communities." *Biological Conservation* 195 (March): 82–88. https://doi.org/10.1016/j.biocon.2015.12.027.
Bennion, Robert S., and William S. Parker. 1976. "Field Observations on Courtship and Aggressive Behavior in Desert Striped Whipsnakes, *Masticophis t. taeniatus*." *Herpetologica* 32 (1): 30–35.
Borzée, Amaël, Hae Jun Baek, Chang Hoon Lee, Dong Yoon Kim, Jae-Young Song, Jae-Hwa Suh, Yikweon Jang, and Mi-Sook Min. 2019. "Scientific Publication of Georeferenced Molecular Data as an Adequate Guide to Delimit the Range of Korean *Hynobius* Salamanders through Citizen Science." *Acta Herpetologica* 14 (1): 27–33. https://doi.org/10.13128/ACTA_HERPETOL-24102.
"History: The Goshutes." 2008. Utah American Indian Digital Archive. 2008. https://utahindians.org/archives/goshute/history.html.
Maritz, Robin A., and Bryan Maritz. 2020. "Sharing for Science: High-Resolution Trophic Interactions Revealed Rapidly by Social Media." *PeerJ* 8 (July): e9485. https://doi.org/10.7717/peerj.9485.
Sherbrooke, Wade C. 2008. "Antipredator Responses by Texas Horned Lizards to Two Snake Taxa with Different Foraging

and Subjugation Strategies." *Journal of Herpetology* 42 (1): 145–52. https://doi.org/10.1670/07-072R1.1.

Todd, Brian D., A. Justin Nowakowski, Jonathan P. Rose, and Steven J. Price. 2017. "Species Traits Explaining Sensitivity of Snakes to Human Land Use Estimated from Citizen Science Data." *Biological Conservation* 206 (February): 31–36. https://doi.org/10.1016/j.biocon.2016.12.013.

Wangyal, Jigme Tshelthrim, Deborah S. Bower, Sherub, Sangay Tshewang, Dorji Wangdi, Kado Rinchen, Sonam Phuntsho, et al. 2020. "New Herpetofaunal Records from the Kingdom of Bhutan Obtained through Citizen Science." *Herpetological Review* 54 (4): 790–98.

Chapter 10

Fathinia, Behzad, Nasrullah Rastegar-Pouyani, Eskandar Rastegar-Pouyani, Fatemeh Todehdehghan, and Fathollah Amiri. 2015. "Avian Deception Using an Elaborate Caudal Lure in *Pseudocerastes urarachnoides* (Serpentes: Viperidae)." *Amphibia-Reptilia* 36 (3): 223–31. https://doi.org/10.1163/15685381-00002997.

Hamilton, Bryan, and Polly Conrad. 2008. "The Sonoran Mountain Kingsnake (*Lampropeltis pyromelana*) in the Great Basin." *Iguana* 15 (2): 86–91.

Kurzgesagt. 2021. "Sources - Does Eating Less Meat ACTUALLY Make a Difference?" Kurzgesagt - In a Nutshell. Accessed January 23, 2023. https://sites.google.com/view/sources-climate-meat/?pli=1.

Paul, Laurence, and Robert W. Mendyk. 2021. "Glow and Behold: Biofluorescence and New Insights on the Tails of Pitvipers (Viperidae: Crotalinae) and Other Snakes." *Herpetological Review* 52 (2): 221–37.

Chapter 11

Atkins, Marcus C. P., Chloe R. Howarth, Michael A. Russello, Jabed

H. Tomal, and Karl W. Larsen. 2022. "Evidence of Intrapopulation Differences in Rattlesnake Defensive Behavior across Neighboring Habitats." *Behavioral Ecology and Sociobiology* 76 (1): 3. https://doi.org/10.1007/s00265-021-03100-6.

Schmidt, Justin O. 2016. *The Sting of the Wild*. Baltimore: Johns Hopkins University Press.

Van Cott, John W. 1990. *Utah Place Names: A Comprehensive Guide to the Origins of Geographic Names: A Compilation*. Salt Lake City, Utah: University of Utah Press.

"Wheeler Peak, Nevada." n.d. Peakbagger.com. Accessed January 23, 2023. https://www.peakbagger.com/peak.aspx?pid=3572.

Wilson, Joseph S., Kevin A. Williams, Matthew L. Forister, Carol D. von Dohlen, and James P. Pitts. 2012. "Repeated Evolution in Overlapping Mimicry Rings among North American Velvet Ants." *Nature Communications* 3 (1): 1272. https://doi.org/10.1038/ncomms2275.

Chapter 12

Brischoux, F., L. Pizzatto, and R. Shine. 2010. "Insights into the Adaptive Significance of Vertical Pupil Shape in Snakes: Vertical Pupils and Ambush Foraging." *Journal of Evolutionary Biology* 23 (9): 1878–85. https://doi.org/10.1111/j.1420-9101.2010.02046.x.

Camaiti, Marco, Alistair R. Evans, Christy A. Hipsley, Mark N. Hutchinson, Shai Meiri, Rodolfo O. Anderson, Alex Slavenko, and David G. Chapple. 2022. "A Database of the Morphology, Ecology and Literature of the World's Limb-reduced Skinks." *Journal of Biogeography* 49 (7): 1397–1406. https://doi.org/10.1111/jbi.14392.

Colley, Michael, Stephen C. Lougheed, Kenton Otterbein, and Jacqueline D. Litzgus. 2017. "Mitigation Reduces Road Mortality of a Threatened Rattlesnake." *Wildlife Research* 44 (1): 48–59. https://doi.org/10.1071/WR16130.

Degregorio, Brett A., Thomas E. Hancock, David J. Kurz, and Sam Yue. 2011. "How Quickly Are Road-Killed Snakes Scavenged? Implications for Underestimates of Road Mortality." *Journal of North Carolina Academy of Science* 127 (2): 184–88. https://doi.org/10.7572/2167-5880-127.2.184.

Gangloff, Eric, David Bertolatus, Christopher Reigel, and Jennifer L. Gagliardi-Seeley. 2014. "Effects of Sex, Environment, and Condition on the Musking Behavior of Sympatric Gartersnakes (*Thamnophis* spp.)." *Journal of North American Herpetology* 2014 (1): 40–46. https://doi.org/10.17161/jnah.vi1.11892.

Lane, R. S., and G. B. Quistad. 1998. "Borreliacidal Factor in the Blood of the Western Fence Lizard (*Sceloporus occidentalis*)." *The Journal of Parasitology* 84 (1): 29–34. https://doi.org/10.2307/3284524.

Mccardle, Logan D., and Clifford L. Fontenot. 2016. "The Influence of Thermal Biology on Road Mortality Risk in Snakes." *Journal of Thermal Biology* 56 (February): 39–49. https://doi.org/10.1016/j.jtherbio.2015.12.004.

Rodríguez-Robles, Javier A., Daniel G. Mulcahy, and Harry W. Greene. 1999. "Feeding Ecology of the Desert Nightsnake, *Hypsiglena torquata* (Colubridae)." *Copeia* 1999 (1): 93–100.

Rose, Barbara R. 1976. "Habitat and Prey Selection of *Sceloporus occidentalis* and *Sceloporus graciosus*." *Ecology* 57 (3): 531–41. https://doi.org/10.2307/1936437.

Sites, Jack W., and Margaret M. Stewart. 2001. "Historical Perspective: Wilmer W. Tanner." *Copeia* 2001 (2): 571–75. https://doi.org/10.1643/0045-8511(2001)001[0571:HPWWT]2.0.CO;2.

Tanner, Wilmer W., and Douglas C. Cox. 1981. "Reproduction in the Snake *Lampropeltis pyromelana*." *Great Basin Naturalist* 41 (3): 314–16.

Van Cott, John W. 1990. *Utah Place Names: A Comprehensive Guide to the Origins of Geographic Names: A Compilation.* Salt Lake City, Utah: University of Utah Press.

Weaver, Robert W. 2010. "Activity Patterns of the Desert

Nightsnake (*Hypsiglena chlorophaea*)." *The Southwestern Naturalist* 55 (2): 172–78.

Chapter 13

Brown, William S. 1973. "Ecology of the Racer, *Columber constrictor mormon* (Serpentes, Colubridae), in a Cold Termperatate Desert in Northern Utah." PhD Dissertation, Salt Lake City, Utah: University of Utah.

Corl, Ammon, Alison R. Davis, Shawn R. Kuchta, and Barry Sinervo. 2010. "Selective Loss of Polymorphic Mating Types Is Associated with Rapid Phenotypic Evolution during Morphic Speciation." *Proceedings of the National Academy of Sciences* 107 (9): 4254–59. https://doi.org/10.1073/pnas.0909480107.

Czaplewski, Nicholas J., Kent S. Smith, John Johnson, Crystal Dockery, Brandon Mason, and Ian D. Browne. 2012. "Gopher Snake Searching Cliff Swallow Nests in East Central Utah." *Western North American Naturalist* 72 (1): 96–99. https://doi.org/10.3398/064.072.0112.

Hamilton, Alison M., Elaine R. Klein, Mallory E. Eckstut, and Emily E. Hartfield. 2007. "A Simple, Inexpensive Method to Capture Arboreal Lizards." *Herpetological Conservation and Biology* 2 (2): 164–67.

Kohler, Dallin B., Bryan T. Hamilton, Drew E. Dittmer, and Alison S. Whiting. 2023. "Citizen Science in Action: An Updated Distribution for *Lampropeltis pyromelana*." *Western North American Naturalist* 83 (2): 2.

Martins, Emília P. 1994. "Structural Complexity in a Lizard Communication System: The *Sceloporus graciosus* 'Push-Up' Display." *Copeia* 1994 (4): 944–55. https://doi.org/10.2307/1446717.

Shewchuk, Christopher H., and James D. Austin. 2001. "Food Habits of the Racer (*Columber constrictor mormon*) in the Northern Part of its Range." *Herpetological Journal* 11: 151–55.

Sinervo, B., and C. M. Lively. 1996. "The Rock–Paper–Scissors Game and the Evolution of Alternative Male Strategies." *Nature*

380 (6571): 240–43. https://doi.org/10.1038/380240a0.

Chapter 14

Capehart, Griffin D., Camilo Escallón, Ben J. Vernasco, Ignacio T. Moore, and Emily N. Taylor. 2016. "No Drought about It: Effects of Supplemental Hydration on the Ecology, Behavior, and Physiology of Free-Ranging Rattlesnakes." *Journal of Arid Environments* 134 (November): 79–86. https://doi.org/10.1016/j.jaridenv.2016.06.018.

Cole, Charles J., Laurence M. Hardy, Herbert C. Dessauer, Harry L. Taylor, and Carol R. Townsend. 2010. "Laboratory Hybridization Among North American Whiptail Lizards, Including *Aspidoscelis inornata arizonae* × *A. tigris marmorata* (Squamata: Teiidae), Ancestors of Unisexual Clones in Nature." *American Museum Novitates* 3698 (October): 1–43. https://doi.org/10.1206/3698.2.

Congdon, J. D., L. J. Vitt, and W. W. King. 1974. "Geckos: Adaptive Significance and Energetics of Tail Autotomy." *Science* 184 (4144): 1379–80. https://doi.org/10.1126/science.184.4144.1379.

Lowe, Charles H., and John W. Wright. 1964. "Species of the *Cnemidophorus exsanguis* Subgroup of Whiptail Lizards." *Journal of the Arizona Academy of Science* 3 (2): 78. https://doi.org/10.2307/40022362.

Taylor, Harry L., Charles J. Cole, and Carol R. Townsend. 2018. "Relegation of *Aspidoscelis flagellicaudus* to the Synonymy of the Parthenogenetic Teiid Lizard *A. sonorae* Based on Morphological Evidence and a Review of Relevant Genetic Data." *Herpetological Review* 49 (4): 636–53.

Uetz, Peter. n.d. "*Crotalus atrox* Baird & Girard, 1853." Reptile Database. https://reptile-database.reptarium.cz/species?genus=Crotalus&species=atrox.

Winkleman, Ryan S., and Adam R. Backlin. 2016. "Geographic Distribution: *Aspidoscelis flagellicauda/sonorae* Complex (Spotted

Whiptail)." *Herpetological Review* 47 (2): 256–57.

Chapter 15

Gibbons, J. Whitfield, David E. Scott, Travis J. Ryan, Kurt A. Buhlmann, Tracey D. Tuberville, Brian S. Metts, Judith L. Greene, et al. 2000. "The Global Decline of Reptiles, Déjà Vu Amphibians." *BioScience* 50 (8): 653–66. https://doi.org/10.1641/0006-3568(2000)050[0653:TGDORD]2.0.CO;2.

Hierink, Fleur, Isabelle Bolon, Andrew M. Durso, Rafael Ruiz de Castañeda, Carlos Zambrana-Torrelio, Evan A. Eskew, and Nicolas Ray. 2020. "Forty-Four Years of Global Trade in CITES-Listed Snakes: Trends and Implications for Conservation and Public Health." *Biological Conservation* 248 (August): 108601. https://doi.org/10.1016/j.biocon.2020.108601.

Kauffeld, Carl. 1957. *Snakes and Snake Hunting*. Hanover House.

Kolbert, Elizabeth. 2015. *The Sixth Extinction: An Unnatural History*. First Picador edition. New York: Picador.

ACKNOWLEDGEMENTS

I am immensely glad that my parents and siblings did not laugh when, many years ago, I announced my goal of writing a book before the age of twenty-five. I have to thank my mom and dad for instilling in me a love of both reading and the outdoors, and for always being supportive of a son who never grew out of his childhood snake obsession.

I'm grateful to Jacob Searcy, Taylor Probst, and Jake Spencer for joining me on various herping trips, and not just the ones that made it into the book. Thank you to Mark Hazel for being willing to share your time and expertise on kingsnakes in Utah. And I can't thank Dr. Alison Whiting enough for all her guidance and mentorship during my time as an undergrad.

A huge thanks go to everyone at Torrey House Press for all the incredible effort that went into making this a reality and for being willing to take a shot with this strange book in the first place. Additional thanks go to Quinn from the BYU Writing Center and Jed Rogers of the University of Utah Press for giving me essential guidance and feedback on early versions of the book. I also am very appreciative of my wonderful Aunt Jen for telling me not to give up on it at a time when I was ready to.

Lastly, I would be remiss not to acknowledge those who truly made this book possible. Snakes, you slithery marvels of evolution, thank you for existing.U.S.U

ABOUT THE AUTHOR

Dallin Kohler is a herpetologist native to the western US who has researched Arizona mountain kingsnakes, Mojave desert tortoises, and Japanese giant salamanders, and is currently chasing amphibians as a graduate student in China. Besides slimy and scaly vertebrates, Dallin also enjoys the NBA, classical piano, and bad puns. *Pyro* is his first book.

ABOUT THE COVER ARTIST

Joseph Toney creates art inspired by the vastness of the American West, often reflecting his strong connection to environmental issues. His work reinterprets these landscapes with meticulous detail, turning them into abstract memoryscapes.

ABOUT TORREY HOUSE PRESS

Torrey House Press publishes books at the intersection of the literary arts and environmental advocacy. THP authors explore the diversity of human experiences and relationships with place. THP books create conversations about issues that concern the American West, landscape, literature, and the future of our ever-changing planet, inspiring action toward a more just world.

We believe that lively, contemporary literature is at the cutting edge of social change. We seek to inform, expand, and reshape the dialogue on environmental justice and stewardship for the natural world by elevating literary excellence from diverse voices.

Visit www.torreyhouse.org for reading group discussion guides, author interviews, and more.

As a 501(c)(3) nonprofit publisher, our work is made possible by generous donations from readers like you.

Torrey House Press is supported by Back of Beyond Books, Bright Side Bookshop, The King's English Bookshop, Maria's Bookshop, the Ballantine Family Fund, the Jeffrey S. & Helen H. Cardon Foundation, the Lawrence T. Dee & Janet T. Dee Foundation, the McMullan/O'Connor Family Fund, the Stewart Family Foundation, the Barker Foundation, Kif Augustine & Stirling Adams, Diana Allison, Richard Baker, Karey Barker, Patti Baynham & Owen Baynham, Matt Bean, Klaus Bielefeldt, Joe Breddan, Karen Buchi & Kenneth Buchi, Betty Clark & Gary Clark, Rose Chilcoat & Mark Franklin, Linc Cornell & Lois Cornell, Susan Cushman & Charlie Quimby, Lynn de Freitas & Patrick de Freitas, Pert Eilers, Ed Erwin, Laurie Hilyer, Phyllis Hockett, Kirtly Parker Jones, Emily Klass, Rick Klass, Jen Lawton & John Thomas, Susan Markley, Leigh Meigs & Stephen Meigs, Mark Meloy, Kathleen Metcalf, Donaree Neville & Douglas Neville, Laura Paskus, Katie Pearce, Marion S. Robinson, Molly Swonger, Shelby Tisdale, Rachel White, the National Endowment for the Humanities, the National Endowment for the Arts, the Utah Division of Arts & Museums, Utah Humanities, the Salt Lake City Arts Council, and Salt Lake County Zoo, Arts & Parks. Our thanks to individual donors, members, and the Torrey House Press board of directors for their valued support.

Join the Torrey House Press family and give today at www.torreyhouse.org/give.

www.ingramcontent.com/pod-product-compliance
Lightning Source LLC
Jackson TN
JSHW010057250525
84873JS00003B/3